Sex, Lies & Love

Also by Sandra Sedgbeer

Sexual Power

Sex, Lies & Love

How to Understand the Opposite Sex

SANDRA SEDGBEER

SIMON & SCHUSTER

LONDON·SYDNEY·NEW YORK·TOKYO·SINGAPORE·TORONTO

First published in Great Britain by
Simon & Schuster Ltd in 1992
A Paramount Communications Company

Copyright © Sandra Sedgbeer, 1992

Simon & Schuster Ltd
West Garden Place
Kendal Street
London W2 2AQ

Simon & Schuster of Australia Pty Ltd
Sydney

A CIP catalogue for this book is
available from the British Library
ISBN 0-671-71092-3

Photoset in North Wales by
Derek Doyle & Associates, Mold, Clwyd
Printed and bound in Great Britain by
Billing & Sons Ltd, Worcester

For Pauline Fleming

For 23 years of friendship. And for having spent countless hilarious – as well as innumerable serious – hours over the years stimulating my brain, my curiosity, my sense of humour, and my intellect with her witty observations, pithy arguments, and abiding fascination with our favourite topic of conversation: *them and us*, every one of which was prefaced by the question: 'But why ...?'

Though I doubt it will stop the questions, perhaps this will at least provide *some* of the answers.

Acknowledgements

No work that even attempts to investigate such a complex subject as human relationships can ever solely be a result of the efforts of one person. Therefore, and as always, I would like to acknowledge the important and valuable work of all those psychologists, sociologists, and other professional experts who spend their lives studying, researching, compiling and analysing the data that helps writers such as myself produce books such as this.

However, what knowledge we now have of men, women, sex, love and human relationships is only partly the result of these people's investigations; the rest, of course, has been – and, hopefully, will continue to be – contributed by you, me, and every other man and woman who, despite the many disappointments experienced in the pursuit of love and happiness, still continue to strive towards a better understanding of the opposite sex.

I would particularly like to express my gratitude and appreciation to my good friend and mentor, Dr Robert M Young, PhD, as well as to my female psychotherapist friend who prefers to remain nameless, for their advice, comments, perceptive insights and also the loan of their own precious research material. And also to Dr Glenn Wilson of the Institute of Psychiatry for the invaluable gift of his time and assistance in helping me compile the psychological self-evaluation tests which appear at the end of this book. To Anji Swann, my thanks for selflessly flying to the rescue at the eleventh hour and sacrificing many hours of sleep.

And last, but certainly by no means least, to Sue Waterman for her brilliant first performance as a dedicated research assistant, and for her continuous support and friendship during the 'darker moments'; mere words are not enough ...

Introduction

RELATIONSHIPS BETWEEN MEN and women are founded upon three things: sex, lies and love.

Of course, being optimistic, if we *really* believed that *lies* are an integral component of sex and love, few of us would even bother trying to form successful relationships at all.

Sadly, fewer and fewer of us are.

One only has to look at the soaring divorce rate, the number of second and even third marriages that do not survive, to recognize that something between the sexes has gone awry. And yet, finding a partner with whom to share one's life always has, and always will be, every man and woman's fundamental driving force.

Could the problem be that despite centuries of living and loving together, men and women *still* do not understand how the opposite sex thinks, behaves and relates when it comes to love, sex and relationships?

Ever since Alfred Kinsey first published his twin exposés on sexual behaviour in the human male and female, there has been an avalanche of books and manuals devoted to attracting the opposite sex, improving relationships with the opposite sex, and even how to make love successfully to the opposite sex. But few have yet managed to provide us with the ultimate answer: **how to *understand* the opposite sex.**

Is understanding so important, then? You might be tempted to ask. The answer is: it's more than important, it's *vital*. And the reason it's vital is because for the first time in our collective history, relationships between men

1

and women are in crisis. Our needs today are different and more complex than they've ever been before and because of this, we're finding it so much harder – some say even impossible – to fulfil them. But I don't believe it's impossible, and I suspect that millions of others don't want to believe it either.

For a long time now there has been a common theme underlying men's frustration with and complaints about women. Translated into one sentence that theme has been: *Why can't a woman be more like a man?* Women too have been echoing their own dissatisfaction with relationships, but in their case the lament is a little more specific: *Why can't men be more sensitive, like women?*

The great emotional divide that lies between men and women has become a twentieth-century preoccupation. The enormous conflict we are now experiencing between our intellectual attitude towards modern-day relationships and our emotional and instinctive responses to them is unique to our generation.

At the risk of upsetting the more radical and vehement feminists, I have to say my sympathies do not solely lie with my own sex. I mean, just think of it from the male point of view; once they knew what they were supposed to be, how they were meant to act, the attitudes they'd traditionally been taught to hold and, for them at least, there was no problem. Then, wham! Suddenly everything changed. Now they're being told that women not only have a right to pursue careers but they can also, and often do, have it all; marriage, motherhood, *and* (and this is what many men *really* find upsetting) the right to reject any or all of the traditional female roles if they so desire. The result? Women now take responsibility for their own independence, their own money, their own status, their own happiness, and their own sexuality. And they have no intention of giving up any of the advantages they have gained. Rather, they say, it's time for men to change.

It's hardly surprising that many men are now confused, for if they can no longer fix their identity in the previously undisputed role of breadwinner, provider, all-wise-and-powerful decision-maker, then *who are they*? And if women no longer need men to fulfil these traditional roles, what do they need them for? Is it any wonder men are now asking: where do we fit in?

Whenever an old order changes, confusion reigns and, as every army knows, when in doubt – retreat. Though I dare say few men would acknowledge the fact, substantial numbers of them have retreated behind a barricade built upon myth and fortified by misconceptions and lies. But so too have women. The paradox is that women still seek heroes to make their lives complete, only now their definition of a 'hero' has become altogether more complex than nature could have foreseen.

Men, on the other hand, merely want a return to the *status quo*. And who can blame them? For if to be a hero today means having to dispense blithely with one half of the characteristics that male society, and, indeed, nature itself, have instilled into them over millennia, and immediately replace these with a radically new, wholly foreign set of behavioural attitudes, wouldn't you find yourself more than a little confused? And it's not that men don't *want* to change, so much as they genuinely don't know *how*.

No man willingly sets out to confound, confuse or disappoint a woman, any more than women choose wilfully to impede, frustrate or burden men. It's neither logical, nor practical, that either of us deliberately would set out to alienate those with whom we share many of our most pleasurable hours. But, sadly, and despite our best intentions, it's now more apparent than ever that we invariably and inevitably do exactly that.

Clearly we cannot go back, nor would we want to. What was right for the couples and families of yesterday would not be workable in this post-feminist age. Yet because nature has ensured that men and women will never stop needing, wanting and being attracted to each other, it's inconceivable that we should ever reach a stage of not wanting to share our lives with one another. How, on the other hand, are we to accomplish successful relationships if we truly don't *know* what each other really thinks, feels, needs and expects? And, more importantly, why?

That's what this book aims to reveal.

Prologue

In the Beginning

WHEN A MALE frog feels the urge to mate he simply leaps on to the nearest object of appropriate size and clings on for dear life. Human beings, I'm relieved to say, wouldn't dream of indicating their interest in such a crude or aggressive manner. Of course, different cultures each have differing customs for courtship, and though some of them, it's true, have nothing to do with love, unlike frogs they at least offer their females an element of choice in the matter.

Amongst the Crow Indians of North America, for example, the traditional method of courtship entailed the man putting his hands inside a tent at night in the hope of finding a female whose genitals he could stimulate. If successful in his search, he stood a good chance of persuading the woman to mate with him. (Which might explain how Indians came to be known as 'braves'.)

With the South African Hottentot race, however, a slightly more elaborate though no less curious process used to apply: having decided which of his cross-cousins he wanted to marry, a man was first obliged to seek permission from her parents, knowing full well that this would be denied. The second step of the courting process was accomplished when, after correctly identifying which hut his prospective bride slept in, the love-struck suitor would creep in one night and lie down beside her, whereupon the female would promptly get up and move away. Undeterred, he would repeat this ritual night after night until the girl either signalled refusal, by failing to be there, or acceptance, by staying put and letting him make love to her.

In many eastern cultures arranged marriages are still the norm, even today. Although the rest of us might deplore the idea of being forced to marry a person we do not love, if success can be measured purely in terms of survival, then clearly arranged marriages are a darn sight more successful than the western kind.

In the western world we too have our own elaborate ritual for the selection of a mate. However, being so committed to the twin concepts of absolute 'freedom of choice' and 'love', we've evolved a far more sophisticated and protracted process (commonly known as the dating game) which, on the face of it, not only fits in nicely with our more civilized notions of democracy, but also promises to be much more fun.

The reality, however, is somewhat different. Dating today is somewhat akin to playing a game of snakes and ladders; it looks simple enough, but you never know when a slippery snake is going to catch you off guard or cause your downfall. And what makes it even more complicated is that *the rules of play keep changing all the time*.

Obviously society needs rules as a guideline for appropriate behaviour but, as each successive generation strives to create its own identity, these boundaries are inclined to get pushed back further and further all the time. Thus, what was considered appropriate behaviour by one generation often seems archaic to the next.

So here we are in the progressive 90s, not merely with more and more players in the game at any given time, but with up to three entirely different generations, many of whom are participating for the second, third and even fourth time. To confuse matters even further, each gender in each generation not only has a completely different perception of the game they're playing, but also not one single set of rules now exists to define how the game should be played.

Having observed the manner in which this masochistic ritual has evolved over the last 20 years or so – and seen enough evidence of the walking wounded to convince me there are rarely any winners in our modern version of the age-old dating and mating game – I've often wondered whether the ways in which frogs and Indians mate might not have something going for them after all. (Well, side-stepping the dating and getting straight down to the mating must, at the very least, save a lot of potential confusion, not to mention broken hearts!)

However, if it's true that you have to kiss a thousand frogs to find a prince, then I dare say there's many a romantic-minded woman (particularly those who've suffered at the hands of a loathsome toad or two) who would disagree with such a cold-blooded point of view. On the other hand, I wouldn't be at all surprised to learn that there's an equal number of men out there who sneakingly feel that, given the opportunity, they would choose the marvellously direct sexual approach frogs go in for, in preference to the complications that arise out of dating any time. Which is understandable when you consider that, if women today are experiencing difficulty with their relationships, men (who are never comfortable with emotions at the best of times) appear to be going through a perfectly ghastly time.

So how did we allow such a simple routine as dating and mating to become such a complex and confusing process?

Men and women have similar needs, but different attitudes and expectations

At the root of every man and woman lies an identical driving force: we all need to feel special, and we all want desperately to love and be loved. That, psychologists will attest, is an irrefutable fact. Why then, if men and women have such similar needs, do we experience such difficulty in fulfilling these needs for each other? The answer is, because that's where the similarity ends. Whilst our ultimate goal may appear to be the same, our experiences on the way to attaining it can't help but influence our attitudes and beliefs about the opposite sex. Moreover, the very fact that there are so many cultural differences between male and female society ensures that we grow up with not only a completely different set of expectations about relationships, but also entirely different perceptions of what each sex wants from them.

Nature versus nurture?

For many years sociologists have argued that the behavioural differences between men and women are merely a result of social conditioning, i.e., that from the moment we are born we learn to assimilate stereotypical patterns of male and female behaviour from the expectations our parents have of the different roles boys and girls should play. This conditioning process then shapes our thoughts, feelings and attitudes to everything that is going on in the world around us. Moreover, because everyone else is being subjected to the same conditioning process, our attitudes and beliefs are continually being reflected back at us, both by society as a whole, and by every other individual with whom we come into contact. Thus, they are destined to become more and more reinforced as time goes on.

Recently, however, scientific research has confirmed that social conditioning is very much a *secondary* process, with the primary influence on male and female behaviour being the undeniable differences in the biological blueprints of our brains. Moreover, these fundamental biological and biochemical differences govern virtually everything from the way we first *perceive*, and then relate and respond to things, right through to the forces that drive men and women at different stages of their lives.

For example, that girls mature earlier than boys is an accepted fact. Girls reach puberty earlier and display a need to form relationships with the opposite sex much earlier than boys do. Thus, by the time a girl has reached 15 or 16 she's actively seeking a steady boyfriend. And though boys of the same age do go out with girls, it's far more likely to stem from a desire to flex their fledgling sexual muscles than any real wish to become emotionally involved.

Girls, once they have reached puberty, have always gained their emotional security from their relationships with the opposite sex, whereas boys first find theirs in their own status within their peer group. Consequently, during the early dating and mating years, women will *always* invest more emotional currency in their relationships with the opposite sex than men do – which means that women will *always* be prone to more disillusionment and disappointment in the opposite sex than men will.

Moreover, because these first tentative – and usually unsuccessful – steps towards forming relationships with the opposite sex occur at such a vulnerable and impressionable age, not only do they reinforce all the myths and misconceptions that have been instilled in us virtually from birth, but more importantly, they're likely to influence our relationships for the rest of our lives.

Of course we only have to look at the way society's attitudes towards certain things like dating and sex have changed over the years to realize that the behavioural guidelines one generation grows up with aren't necessarily applicable to the next. But, whether we realize it or not, they do have an influence on a subconscious level that no amount of intellectualizing can alter.

Attitudes change – emotions don't

When I was at school in the 60s, just prior to the sexual revolution that supposedly set us all free, my friends and I never dreamt of questioning the sexual double standard that applied, inasmuch as boys were expected to have sex, but girls who did earned the sobriquet 'slag'. The irony – and the injustice – was that the 'bad' girls were rewarded with the dates, the boys *and* all the fun, while all we 'good' girls got was to stay home. And there we sat many a long night twiddling our thumbs and weaving our virginal fantasies around frogs who could be miraculously transformed into princes by a virtuous maiden's kisses; *not* because we were any better than the 'bad' girls, but because we were more cowardly. The fact was, the conditioning we had been subjected to by the attitude of our parents, the media and society towards pre-marital sex was so pervasive and thorough, we were simply too damn scared to surrender our grim hold on virginity and respectability.

By the end of that decade, everything had changed. Not only had a whole generation of teenagers managed to use their combined talents, energy and new ideas to establish the first ever youth-dominated culture, but also the invention of the Pill had given us the freedom to discover sex. What we hadn't reckoned with, however, was that a mere overnight change in attitude was simply no match for all those years of conditioning and their legacy of guilt. For whilst intellectually we accepted that girls could now have as much sexual freedom as boys, the only way many of us could cope with the emotional conflict was to justify our behaviour by calling it love.

Love, or so we believe, gives us permission to do all sorts of things that are normally taboo. And because sex, or rather, lust, has been taboo for women for so long, we're far more likely to confuse it with love than men are. This is one of the reasons – thought not the *only* one, to be sure – why there is so much misunderstanding between men and women. Nowhere is this more apparent than in the early stages of the dating and mating game, as we shall discover in chapter 1.

1

Dating and Mating

IT'S NATURAL TO assume that when two people arrange a date, each has a common aim. Not when they're teenagers, they don't.

For in reality what happens is this: boy meets girl, mutual attraction is signalled, they agree to a date. So far, so good; she's now aware he likes her, he's confident she feels the same about him. But from here on their mental paths diverge, as the following scenario will illustrate.

As the girl gets ready for her date, some or all of the following thoughts are likely to pass through her mind:

> What shall I wear …? Should I go for the sexy look … or should I wear something more demure? Wonder where he'll take me? Hope we don't get stuck for conversation … what was the advice that magazine article gave …? Oh, I remember … men love talking about themselves … that's it … I'll get him talking about his hobbies and interests … God, he's got real come-to-bed-eyes … so penetrating and soulful … you can tell he's really sweet and sensitive beneath that macho exterior … the way he looked at me made my knees go weak … he's so different from the rest … really *interested* in me … makes a change from all those sex-mad gropers. … Wonder whether I should invite him back for coffee? Better not, wouldn't want him to jump to

11

the wrong conclusion ... on the other hand, it *would* provide the perfect opportunity to get to know him better in more relaxed surroundings. Hope he's a good kisser ... kissing's so romantic with the right guy ... could *he* be *the one* ...?

Meanwhile, the object of the girl's fantasy is busy sprucing himself up to an accompanying mental monologue which goes something like this:

You've really cracked it there, mate ... she's a stunner all right! Terrific body, great tits, fabulous legs ... what more could a fella ask for? Wonder whether she's got a brain to go with all that ...? Not that it matters ... if I play my cards right this could be my lucky night ... hers too ... better go prepared ... just in case. Perhaps we'll stop off at the pub first ... I'd like to see the guys' faces when they see what I've pulled ... hope she's not one of those girls who rabbits on about herself all night ... come to that, hope she's not one of those slushy, romantic types, either ...

Of course the language will differ with each individual, but, generally speaking, the structure and direction of the thought processes will, I'm afraid, be very similar to those outlined above. However, when viewed from a purely biological perspective, it becomes evident that all that's *really* going on here is nothing more sinister than each of our players responding to two totally different sets of needs which, sadly but inevitably, are driving them in diametrically opposing directions, at this stage of their lives.

No matter how far we progress intellectually, or even how much society's attitudes towards male and female roles change, the female will always instinctively – albeit unconsciously – obey the ancient, biologically programmed precept that dictates she endow each man with heroic potential. But, where women once dreamed only of a strong, protective man who would provide food, shelter and a safe haven in which to raise their children, today's list of essential qualifications now runs to several pages.

Nowadays it's not sufficient that men be strong, protective and good providers; they also have to be self-confident (without being brash), sensitive (but not wimpish), protective (but not *overly* possessive), indulgent (but not *too* easily manipulated) understanding, interested, tolerant, respectful, romantic, tender, etc, etc, ad infinitum.

Women, you see, are fundamentally concerned with the emotionally based need to know a man better in order to measure his real or imagined – and during adolescence they're *definitely imagined* – attributes against their Richter-scale of requirements. Younger women in particular are immensely prone to sketching mentally full-blown Mills & Boon-style storylines in rosy-hued ink. Young men's thoughts (which aren't the least concerned with analysing any female's potential as a permanent partner simply because they're tuned to respond – at this stage of the game, remember – to their *physical* needs) are conjuring up explicitly sexual fantasies which owe nothing to romance and everything to raunch.

Me Tarzan – You Jane

At the risk of upsetting all those who believe they have evidence of the existence of the mythical creature known as 'new man', I have to say that, after years of research during which I've interviewed literally hundreds of men and women, I've yet to discover any 'new men'; or even anything startlingly new *about* men. Men are men.

That's why women love them some of the time and find them irritating, exasperating, and woefully obtuse the rest of it.

That's not to say, however, that men can't be recycled and reshaped by experience into 'different', more sensitive kind of men, because clearly they can. For, contrary to what everything in our society encourages us to believe, men are every bit as sensitive, as easily wounded, and as emotional as women. But whereas women have *always* been encouraged to express their tender impulses and their nurturing abilities (as these are quintessentially representative of all that is feminine), everything in male culture conspires to suppress these very same qualities (often to the point of total denial) purely on the basis of gender polarity.

If women truly want to learn to understand men, they must realize that men need *time* to shrug off all the social pressures and role-defining, conditioning processes that dictate the way males think, relate and behave during their adolescent years. (Some men, it appears, need more time than others, and *some*, it has to be said, need an entire lifetime!)

Moreover, because of the biological and biochemical patterns that programme men to spend most of their adolescence and early adulthood chasing fantasies of the love 'em and leave 'em kind, one cannot realistically expect them to develop a more sensitive, caring approach to women (or indeed, even a *need* for exclusive, committed, loving relationships) until time, experience and maturity influence a major shift in gear from their groin to their emotions. (And even when men are receptive to the *idea* of commitment, their concept of it bears no relation to that of women – as we'll discover in a later chapter.)

Unfortunately, nature has ensured that each gender's fundamental biological programming processes *are* quite different. And the fact that our individual maturing processes don't synchronize either doesn't help matters one bit, particularly when one considers that the age at which our attitudes and opinions are most likely to be reinforced coincides with the very period when our emotional and mental paths are at their most divergent. But that doesn't necessarily mean that the situation is entirely impossible, only that we each must work harder at understanding *why* men and women are the way they are, and, more specifically, why they are the way they are *at different stages of their lives.*

The first thing we can do to help us achieve a better understanding is to look at *how* and *why* some of our most cherished myths and misconceptions might have originated. The second thing we can do is to examine these objectively, not only to ascertain how much substance they *really* do contain, but also to discover whether they're still relevant in the light of what's happening *now.*

The strongest – and the most pervasive – myth that threatens women's attitudes to, and relationships with, men is the one that society drums into females virtually from the moment they are born:

All men want is sex

As we have seen in the scenario outlined earlier, the needs and expectations of boys and girls during their teenage years are so vastly different, they're bound to result in disappointment and confusion. Because teenage girl is ahead of teenage boy in that she's biologically ready for some form of *emotional* experience with the opposite sex before he is, every time she meets a boy who shows interest she's inclined to fantasize a big romance. He, on the other hand, is merely inclined to fantasize – period.

This is why the notion 'all men want is sex' has passed way beyond myth to become a universally accepted 'fact'. However, if we're going to be fair to both sexes, we must understand that whilst this 'fact' certainly can be substantiated *biologically*, there are other factors in the equation that have been largely overlooked.

Yes, it *is* true that the male of the species was constructed, built *and biochemically* programmed in such a way that he could impregnate females (with the emphasis on the plural) as often as he desired. And in order to ensure he experienced no difficulty complying with mother nature's decree, man was given a little extra something to help kickstart his desire. The male hormone testosterone governs both the male and female sex drive, but the levels present in the average woman's body are around just one twentieth of that present in the average male.

Moreover, recent scientific findings have proven that as testosterone is the key factor in completing the transformation of the foetus into a male, men's brains are naturally more 'finely-tuned' to the effects this hormone has on them.

[Without going into too much technical detail, scientists have now confirmed that all foetuses are predisposed to be female, and that it is not until around the sixth or seventh week of gestation that the critical deciding factor of the intervention of hormones comes into play. Thus, even when a foetus carries the XY (male) combination of chromosomes, if it fails to follow the normal developmental pattern of formulating the male hormone-producing cells responsible for issuing the genetically correct instructions to stimulate the development of male reproductive equipment, when the baby is born it will look exactly like any genetically normal girl.]

And the higher the testosterone levels in our bodies, the more pronounced our sexual urges will be. A woman's testosterone levels appear to reach a peak when she reaches mid-cycle – or maximum fertility – phase (another of nature's little tricks to ensure we continue to procreate). Men, on the other hand, have a completely different and altogether more rapid cycle of peaks and troughs, and their testosterone levels have a tendency to peak on average seven times a day.

Furthermore, though sex is generally assumed to be a night-time activity, men's testosterone levels usually reach their *highest* peak in the morning (which would account for all those early morning erections which prod women awake) and drop as much as 25 per cent lower in the evening. So those who find it hard to stay hard at the end of the day might benefit from switching their moonlight seduction scenarios to dawn – which could give a whole new meaning to the phrase, 'getting up with the lark'!

And if any further evidence of the differences in men's and women's sex drives is required, take note of the following:

- Men not only become sexually aware at an earlier age than girls, their interest in sex remains stronger, for longer.

- Men can reach orgasm through mere fantasy alone (without *any* form of touching at all), women rarely do.

- Men not only have far more erotic dreams than women, (on average three times more) they can have *wet dreams*! Once again, very few women are fortunate enough to experience orgasm in their sleep.

- Men not only masturbate more frequently than women, their appetite for sexual gratification is stronger, *and* though they mature later than girls, they have sex earlier than them.

- Men are far more likely to be turned on by visual images than women are – which explains why men get more out of pornography than women do.

- And finally, when deprived of a sexual outlet, men are far more inclined to moodiness and irritability than women, who are more likely to miss the *companionship* of sex than the sex itself.

So at last we do have some scientific evidence to support what women have always been told: men are, indeed, largely motivated by sex. On the other hand, for women to say that 'all men's brains are ruled by their balls' is just as inaccurate as the many sweeping generalizations men tend to make about women. For only a fool (or a woman who's had unspeakably bad luck with the men in her life) would believe the fallacy that *all* men function on the level of a sex machine, *all of the time*. And many men, quite rightly, wholeheartedly resent this notion, too.

Men have feelings too

Mick Cooper is part of a collective group which publishes a radical magazine aimed at 'new men' called *Achilles Heel*. Though the magazine's circulation, which currently stands at 3000, is small by commercial publishing standards, Mick believes that there is a growing army of young men who *are* keenly aware of the need to challenge traditional male stereotypes, and are also actively seeking different approaches to expressing their masculinity:

> There's no doubt that men do have more power over women. But in my opinion, the sexist society we live in has been created by men. And in order to maintain the powerful position we ourselves decreed men should play, we've been forced to deny certain of our emotional needs simply because we've been conditioned to regard these as weaknesses.
>
> What's interesting is that when we started running a problem page in the magazine, it was the first page all our readers turned to. The fact that many then wrote in to complain about it only proves that there is a deep conflict in men's psyches about *admitting* that such problems exist. At the same time, however, we know our readers positively welcome an opportunity to read about relationships, to learn more about things like 'how to make love to a woman' or 'what women expect from men'. And this isn't out of a need to boost their egos by being better performers in bed, it's

because they're genuinely concerned about their relationships as a whole.

Clearly, then, when women complain that all men want from them is sex, they're not only doing men a grave injustice, they're actively aiding and abetting our society's continuing presentation of a grossly distorted point of view. For there is another – and altogether more interesting – dimension to men which few women are permitted access to, and that's the one which is fundamentally far more concerned with the organ beating behind a man's ribcage than the one beating behind his zipper – as we shall discover in chapter six, when we delve into *Men's Secret Fears*.

Boys will be boys, but women will be 'slags'

This is the second largest myth that causes so much heartache, resentment, misunderstanding and sheer bad feeling between the sexes.

'The more the pattern of modern-day relationships changes, the more it stays the same,' said Joan Collins in a recent magazine interview. And she's absolutely right, because despite the progress we *appear* to have made on the sexual front, this old double standard still hasn't quite died. While 30-something women may take comfort in the heartening knowledge that it's less evident *now* amongst men of their own age than it's ever been, sadly, their much younger sisters (and their daughters) are still being upset by its existence. Or, to echo an old adage: when it comes to teenage sex, girls are still damned if they 'do', and still damned if they 'don't'. The only difference is that a new set of rules now seems to apply to the appella-tion 'slag'.

After conducting a whole series of group discussions amongst young men, I discovered that the derogatory term 'slag' no longer appears to encompass *all* girls who sleep around, or even *all* girls who sleep with a guy on their first date; merely those who are known (how?) to do it on *every* first date, or those who've had 'several' partners. Interestingly enough, the definition of 'several' seems to be a movable feast; to some boys it represents more than five sexual partners, whilst to others it simply means 'more than them'!

[In a recent nationwide sex survey conducted by the *Mail on Sunday* newspaper it was reported that 57 per cent of teenage boys had lost their virginity illegally before they were 16, against 38 per cent of teenage girls. Moreover, one third of teenage boys confessed to having had sex with five or more partners, with only four per cent of girls saying the same. A similar poll undertaken by *Mori* on behalf of the *Daily Express* newspaper in early 1992 revealed that of all those surveyed between 18 and 50, 81 per cent had lost their virginity by the age of 20, with the figure for women lagging only slightly behind at 75 per cent.]

Luke, an 18-year-old A level student, confessed that while he wouldn't dream of making a pass at a girl on their first date, he certainly wouldn't refuse if she made a pass at him:

> I wouldn't automatically feel she was cheap, but if it became apparent she had no further interest in me, like some of the girls I've been with who've obviously thought, 'Oh, well, had him, move on', *then* I'd think she was.

Ricky, who is also 18, has a slightly different interpretation of the word 'slag':

> If a girl makes it obvious she wants to sleep with you on a first date, fine. But if you do, and it's no good, or she's disappointed in you and then 'blabs' about it, *then* she's definitely a 'slag'.

Chris, a 19-year-old undergraduate, differs from both Luke and Ricky inasmuch as he believes girls should be just as free from all moral censure as boys:

> I wouldn't make a pass at a girl the first time. But then if I liked her enough to ask her out, I'd be more concerned with getting to know her better and wanting her to gain a good impression of me. But if she made a pass at me, I'd be flattered, and I might even go for it. But on the whole, I really don't like the feeling of using a person.

On the other hand Mike, a rather macho 21-year-old finance clerk, echoes the more extreme view still held by quite a few of his less tolerant peers:

> I've probably had sex with about 15 different girls since I was 13 years old. As far as I'm concerned, they were all nice girls while I fancied them, but once I'd had them they were all tarts. I mean, my first thought on meeting a girl I fancy is: 'she's tasty, I wouldn't mind jumping her bones'. But usually I only make a date if I can't pull her straightaway. The thing is, when you do that, girls usually think they're in for a relationship with you. That's too heavy for me. Maybe one day I'll want one, but right now I'm too scared of commitment. Plus, I get bored very, very quickly. It's a bit like the old joke: 'What's the definition of boredom? The time between you coming and her going.'

Clearly there is still a large element of macho posturing about girls and sex amongst young men. What did surprise me, though, was the existence of several boys in their late teens who were honest enough to admit they were still virgins through *choice*. What's more, they insisted they had every intention of remaining so until 'the girl, the relationship *and* the time is right'.

Even more surprising was the fact that not only did

these boys make their admissions in front of their more experienced friends, but not one of their friends scoffed.

If nothing else then, at least two attitudes have changed amongst young men: first, that regardless of which sex makes the initial running, girls with whom they have one-night-stands are in a separate category to those with whom first-date-sex evolves into on-going relationships. And second, they've become a little more tolerant about their friends' failures to conform. Obviously there's still a long way to go, but at least *some* progress appears to have been made.

And as for the girls? Well, some of them still believe nothing's changed at all. At 17, Sarah, who's just started her first job in publishing, has slept with six boys in 18 months; three were one-night-stands, the other three she saw regularly for at least two months. Already Sarah is so hurt and disillusioned by her experiences that she condemns all men with the words: 'You can't win with them no matter what you do. All of the boys I've been with acted as if they really cared about me, but either they never called me again after we'd had sex, or they broke things off soon afterwards.' What worries Sarah even more is that, because she lives in a small town, word about her activities soon spread. 'Even my own brother called me a Flora last week. He can talk! He's had just about every girl I know. But then it's all right for them, 'cause they're just admired as studs.'

[For the uninitiated, 'Flora' (borrowed from the margarine substitute) is one of the current euphemisms for 'slag' – the connection being, 'spreads easy'!]

Unfortunately, Sarah's story typifies the classic situation many young girls find themselves in when they mistake sexual interest for love. But then it's a simple error to make when you're young and inexperienced, as Joan Collins recently confirmed when she said: 'It's easy to confuse sex with love, and younger women often do this. A man can make a woman feel absolutely irresistible and she will then assume he's fallen in love; whereas he might simply want sex.'

And even age and experience don't necessarily protect women from making this mistake, as Madonna confirmed when she said: 'You imbue men with the characteristics you want them to have, then they're not what you expect at all. But it's your own fault for not doing your homework. I'm more cautious now. But I'm still a hopeless romantic.'

Perhaps Sarah – and maybe Madonna too – should take Joan Collins' advice: 'My mother advised us to wait until we knew a man before having sex with him. I may not understand everything about what makes men tick, but I do know this – that men respect a woman more if she doesn't go to bed on the first or second date. It's old-fashioned but true.'

So what's the best relationship advice Joan can give?

'I do think that, early on in a relationship, a certain amount of game-playing is necessary. If you throw yourself all over a man, you can forget it. The best way to get rid of a man is to tell him right away that you adore him, that you want to move in with him and have his baby. But if you play hard to get and tell him you're unsure of commitment, he'll probably start beating on your door.'

Well, they do say there's nothing so appealing to the male hunting instinct as 'the lure of the chase'! On the other hand, I found that for every 'Sarah' I interviewed, there also appear to be two other distinctly different types of teenage women emerging, and neither of these two seem to be the least bit interested in playing games.

(Some) Girls just want to have fun

Apparently, quite a few of today's young girls believe absolutely that they have every right to be as sexually active as boys. First, there are the ones who revel in their self-appointed nickname, the Martini Girls – so-called because their motto is, 'Anytime, anyplace, anywhere – and with anyone'. And second, there are those who, whilst subscribing wholeheartedly to the *theory* of total equality at all levels, simply prefer the intimacy of sex within a relationship as opposed to the casual variety which offers none. Neither appears to suffer any of the guilt that attended my generation's early sexual forays. Clearly there's a strange kind of dichotomy at work here. Whilst on the surface a lot appears to have changed for both sexes, once you scratch away the gloss and glitz of teenage bravado, things have possibly changed far more for girls than they have for boys.

[In one recent survey conducted by *Company* magazine, 20 per cent of the female readers who responded actually admitted sex was better on a one-night-stand. In response to the magazine's question: Who usually makes, or should make, the first move? 60 per cent thought it didn't matter, with individual comments ranging from, 'I don't think I'd ever make the first move, but I'd certainly drop hints that I wanted him to', to 'I always ask – it's my choice, he can always say no.'

When *Cosmopolitan* magazine ran a similar survey, they found that whilst 56 per cent of their readers admitted to having had sex on a first date, women over 30 are more likely to do so. Generally, however, the majority of their readers said that normally they wouldn't go to bed with a new boyfriend until somewhere between the fourth and eighth dates.]

Poet and novelist Fiona Pitt-Kethley describes herself as a female Casanova. But far from being applauded for her frankness, 37-year-old Fiona's honesty has often resulted in denigration (in fact, more than one reviewer has misused his column to publicly castigate her sexual mores in print). And yet the men with whom Fiona chooses to sleep usually have nothing but admiration for her. Fiona, whose discovery of the joys of sex coincided with her renunciation of religion at the age of 18, says:

They find it refreshing that I'm not afraid to speak my mind, or invite them to bed. Life without sex isn't viable. I'd rather be dead. I'm a very chatty person, so I can discover a lot about a man at first meeting. If I like him, I don't see anything wrong with sleeping with him straight away. For me, sex is on a par with a nice night out at the theatre. Sometimes my relationships last a while, sometimes they're just for one night. But more often than not we usually stay in touch and become good friends. It's not a problem for me. Why should it be? I certainly don't consider I'm being used, because I'm using too, so fair's fair. I also believe that there are many women who feel exactly the way I do about it, they just don't express it, that's all.

And I don't doubt Fiona's right. For when *Company* magazine ran a survey on their readers' holiday habits, almost half of those polled admitted to having shed their sexual inhibitions on holiday as quickly as they shed their clothes, with 40 per cent confessing they'd had sex within two days!

Whilst it's true that statistics and surveys can never be representative of the population as a whole, one only has to look at today's most popular women's magazines, such as *New Woman*, *Company* and *Cosmo*, to recognize the incredible impact the feminist movement has had on female culture over the last 30 years or so. And as these magazines' healthy circulations are wholly dependent on their ability both to target their readers effectively *and* to reflect their readers' interests by publishing features on the topics which concern women the most, they're a pretty accurate barometer of what's happening in women's lives today.

Furthermore, as women have always been more concerned with the dynamics of male-female relationships than men, the help they have needed to facilitate any changes has been more readily available to them.

Similarly, one only has to flick through any issue of the magazines mentioned above to realize that today's women place great emphasis on learning how to understand themselves, their relationships, and, of course, men.

Men, on the other hand, have only very recently started showing an inclination to seek the same kind of psychological knowledge, insight or advice. And whilst a new crop of men's lifestyle magazines are now beginning to surface in response to this need, it's still far too early for these to have had much influence on men's perceptions either about themselves or their behaviour.

Not surprisingly, therefore, the issue which preoccupies most single women today isn't so much one of, 'Should I sleep with him?' as:

How soon is too soon?

When a national newspaper asked this question of the film director Michael Winner, he had this to say:

> This is a question all young ladies face, usually under pressure from a man who's attempting to get them to have sex. As a bachelor for nearly 56 years, I hear all the usual concerns expressed. The most common is, 'I don't know you well enough.' But it's not true to say the most successful relationships are those where people wait longest. I don't think you can say that a girl who waits five weeks is a finer human being than one who has sex the first night. Other more weighty matters go into the make-up of a person than that.
>
> I always remember a very beautiful girl who wandered around my apartment, opened the fridge door and said: 'Oh good, there's orange juice for the morning.'

Writer Norman Mailer also expressed a similar point of view when *Cosmopolitan* magazine asked him what his views were on this thorny question:

No woman has ever slept with me too soon. I don't pretend I'm typical but I've always found promiscuous women interesting. I suspect I would have been promiscuous if I'd been a woman. I certainly have been as a man, so I don't make judgements. The faster a woman would sleep with me, the more I liked her.

Ah, but would he marry her? asked *Cosmo*: 'Of course. Did I …? Well, yes.'

Granted, these are two decidedly liberal points of view. But in reality, how valid can they be? Particularly when you consider that, first, it's long been assumed that those who tread the celebrity circuit are somehow exempt from the sexual morality code that governs the behaviour of other more ordinary mortals. And second, one can hardly ignore the fact that age and maturity must inevitably alter a man's perspective – by which I mean that once a man's passed life's half-way mark, he would be far less inclined to put off till tomorrow what he's lusting after today, for no other reason than that time and opportunity inevitably become a diminishing return.

Leaving these two aside then, what do the younger, single men have to say on this score?

'After you've got over the ego-trip phase, when all you want to do is screw as many women as possible just to prove you're as good as your mates, you can't help but realize that there's more to relationships with women than sex,' said Martin, 28. 'And that's when you learn that sometimes you can spoil things by sleeping with someone too soon.'

'First dates are always nerve-wracking,' said Phil, a 30-year-old plumber. 'It doesn't matter how old you are, or how many girls you've taken out before, you never get over that feeling of nervousness, of desperately wanting to make a good impression on the girl. And as for sex, forget it; I wouldn't feel at all comfortable about making love with someone I hardly know.'

Michael, 35, a recent born-again-single who has a high-profile job in advertising sales: 'I don't remember ever feeling nervous when I dated girls the first time round. But frankly, they petrify me now. Most of the girls I meet are in their 30s, have good jobs in the media, own their own homes and cars etc., and they're so self-sufficient, I can't help wondering whether they need men at all. I certainly couldn't sleep with them straight away, I'd be far too intimidated.'

Today's men blame the feminist movement for launching the first offensive in the latest round of the battle of the sexes. Equally, today's women are laying the blame for our present break-down in relationships fairly and squarely at the feet of male chauvinism. And meanwhile, both are conveniently ignoring one immutable natural law: the fact is, whilst Miss Average woman does indeed feel duty bound to espouse allegiance to the feminist point of view, and Mr Average man feels equally duty bound to shout her down, at heart what every ordinary man and woman really wants is a permanent, fulfilling relationship. Why? Because the one incontrovertible truth we all appear either to have lost or be losing touch with is that over and above and beyond everything else we think or feel or say we want, love is the most fundamental and the most enduring of all human needs.

The tragedy is, many of today's singles now feel that love and a fulfilling relationship is one of the most difficult achievements of all. Which is why more and more of them are turning to introduction agencies, singles' clubs and computer dating services to help them find partners. It's not merely the fact that there are so many more singles around now than there were 40 years ago that drives people towards seeking outside help, so much as a need to cut through the confusion by at least attempting to define a prospective partner's expectations and intentions *before* the process begins.

Sue Plumtree, a personnel training specialist, and her partner, Simone Klass, who has a background in marketing, communications and training, both became so concerned about the very real problems facing today's singles that they founded 'Entre Nous', a company which organizes and runs a series of inspiring one-day seminars and workshops aimed specifically at people who want more friendship and romance in their lives.

Although it's difficult to accept that anyone could need training in personal relationships, Sue and Simone have both found that this is indeed the case. 'Whilst there are all sorts of training programmes available to teach employees new career skills,' explained Simone, 'there's an odd stigma attached to the idea of needing help with social skills. Yet Sue and I have both come across so many people who are literally floundering in a sea of confusion when it comes to developing social relationships. Much of the problem is that they just don't know any more what the opposite sex wants, needs and expects.'

One of the 'Entre Nous' seminars, 'What To Do When Someone Takes Your Fancy', covers such areas as: how to break the ice; how to make conversation flow; how to increase your confidence and enhance your self-esteem; how to develop personal awareness; how to conquer fear of rejection, and even how to project yourself and ensure your invitations are accepted. Whilst these topics might sound excruciatingly basic to those who don't have problems in these areas, as Sue says: 'Our clients really do worry about understanding the basics and getting them right. And why not? Because if you can't get the preliminaries right, you won't ever get beyond them.'

The very fact that dating agencies, singles' clubs and seminars such as those run by 'Entre Nous' attract such a large clientele is clear evidence that, despite all the inescapable pressures, the problems, the misunderstandings, and the many, many confusions that are currently preventing us from forming the relationships we want, none of us has yet become so disillusioned that we're ready to give up entirely on the opposite sex. This leaves us with only one option: understanding.

What men want from women

Every man yearns for his fantasy woman: the sublimely erotic goddess who embodies all the physical characteristics of every star of music, stage and screen who's ever turned him on. Of course it goes without saying that this paragon will possess:

• Iridescent beauty (that's wholly natural and *totally* eternal)

• A figure of exquisitely perfect formation (which will be impervious to the ravages of time)

• An infinite capacity for tolerance, benevolence and forgiveness (which means, in effect, that no matter how badly he treats her, how often he betrays her, or how much he ignores her, she'll always be there to stroke his brow and murmur lovingly, 'It's all right, my darling, I understand, truly I do … ')

• An ability to make love like a perpetual motion machine (a hi-tech version that comes with the added facility of an On/Off button as well as a volume control)

• As well, of course, as being that rarest of all creatures – a totally selfless, utterly devoted, *wholly unreal* woman who needs, wants and *expects* nothing – oh, yes, I *do* mean *nothing* – from him in return.

And believe me, I exaggerate not one tiny little bit. Well, not about the physical attributes, anyway. For when *New Woman* asked 100 men which women possessed the various parts that turned them on the most, the resulting Barbie-doll composite looked like this:

Kim Basinger's hair
Rosanna Arquette's eyes
Greta Scacchi's nose

Julia Roberts' smile (failing that, Kim Basinger's would do)

Brigitte Nielsen's silicone implants

Atop Yasmin Le Bon's perfect body.

Ah well, so much for the fantasy. Now, as to the kind of woman most men will settle for? Well, that's not such a difficult order to fulfil. Naturally she will be beautiful (but don't let that worry you because this word possesses both *enormously* elastic properties *and* an endless variety of very odd definitions); sexy (which isn't necessarily defined by big breasts, an endless length of shapely leg and the sex drive of a nymphomaniac bunny, because every man will define a woman as sexy if she finds *him* sexy); reasonably tolerant, not too argumentative, fairly intelligent, but most of all, warm, humorous and understanding.

On the whole, I have to say that most of the men I spoke to are not only realistic enough to rate character above looks but also genuinely do want a caring, sharing kind of relationship. Of course that doesn't mean to say that there aren't equally a good many self-centred and wholly unsavoury rats out there, too. But at least it shows that there *are* some basically good guys around. So if you keep on kissing those frogs, sooner or later you're bound to discover that one of them is – or at the very least has the potential to be – your prince. And in the meantime, remember, most rats are often really nothing more sinister than wary, frightened, timid, overgrown mice.

What women want from men

Every woman shares the common fantasy that she's secretly a princess in disguise, which means that all she's waiting for is Mr Fantasy Prince. And who is he? Why, he's Superman, of course! Moreover, when he puts in his long-awaited appearance she'll have no trouble recognizing him because he'll be:

• Rich (not just comfortably off, you understand, it's

serious, billionaire-megabuck-style rich we're talking here)

- Generous to a fault (to all her demands he'll sweetly respond: 'Just ask, my angel/my treasure/my jewel, and it shall be yours)

- Handsome (with the kind of knock-'em-dead, matinee idol looks that only inch-thick stage make-up or extensive cosmetic surgery could provide)

- Superbly built (definitely *not* Schwarzenneger-style, more a sort of Patrick Swayze-type physique)

- Healthy (because princesses do *not* relish the idea of ending up nursing a broken-down, incontinent old crock – unless, of course, he should happen to be a rich old crock whose condition is terminal)

- A *supremely* sensual lover who always synchronizes his sexual rhythm to hers (no 'juggernauts', 'steam trains' or 'instant bingo' men need apply)

- And, of course, he'll possess the wisdom of Solomon, the tolerance of Job, the patience of a saint, and just enough of Rhett Butler's 'Damn-it-all-Scarlett-I-*am*-a-man' style of masculinity to sweep her passionately off her feet before putting her gently (but firmly) in her place (which probably means underneath him.) But *only* when *she*'s in the mood to play Miss submissive Southern belle.

And according to the 100 women *New Woman* polled, he'll either have:
The bottom of Kevin Costner, Dennis Quaid, or Prince at a pinch (see how flexible women are?)
Legs like Kevin Costner, Liam Neeson, or Sam Shepard
Hair like ... you guessed it ... Kevin Costner, Sam Shepard or Al Pacino

Paul Newman's eyes
Dennis Quaid or Mickey Rourke's smile
Nicholas Cage's body
And, for 42 per cent at least, the nose of Gerard
Depardieu. Yes, I know it's hard to understand, but
remember: perversity thy name is (supposed to be)
woman! Besides, you know what they say about the
relationship between men's noses and ... other parts of
their anatomy!

And what will women settle for in a real man? Well, he
certainly doesn't have to be good-looking (that's because
other, more enduring qualities will always outweigh looks
with women every time). But he must be sensitive (to her
moods, her cycles and her diverse emotional needs); have
a witty mind and a well-developed sense of humour (*all
women find humour incredibly sexy*); and, most important of
all, he must be genuinely caring, a good listener (don't *ever*
underestimate this one because there's nothing guaranteed to make a woman more blazingly, furiously,
'I-could-throttle-him' angry than a man who *doesn't listen
to her*); and above all, he must be constitutionally incapable
of treating her as an intellectual inferior, or of using the
word 'trivia' in conjunction with *anything* she says, does,
or is involved with.

Oh, and it would earn him lots of brownie points if he
could manage the odd romantic gesture now and then.
You know, like tossing a diamond bracelet or two
across the breakfast table, having a dozen red roses
delivered to her office, whisking her off for a romantic
weekend in the Seychelles, any of which – or all of which –
will do very nicely, thank you. But if neither his pocket nor
his imagination can stretch to that, I can assure you she
will be equally thrilled by the unexpected appearance of a
walnut whip, a bag of aniseed balls, a lollipop or any other
peculiar sweetie she has a penchant for munching (I never
said women weren't strange at times! But just don't make
it a gobstopper because that would *definitely* be

misconstrued), a bunch of daffs or a potted plant (for obvious reasons you'd be wise to avoid the plant whose latin name escapes me but is commonly known as a mother-in-law's tongue!), and the occasional bed-and-breakfast weekend in Cleethorpes.

All of which proves that no man need ever fear or worry about what women want from him, because women's needs and expectations are so disarmingly modest that only a complete klutz – or a total boor – could possibly fail to fulfil them. At least that's how women look at it.

So, now we're clear about the things men and women want, all we have to understand is why they do the things they do.

2

The Importance of Orgasm

U P UNTIL A few years ago I dare say that most men
would have sworn that though they'd *heard* about
women who fake orgasms, none of the women *they'd* slept
with had ever needed to.

Then along came the hilarious hit film, *When Harry Met
Sally*, to make them think again. For when actress Meg
Ryan demonstrated, for the benefit of her screen pal,
Harry, the breathless groans, shudders and long
drawn-out sighs of a woman driven beyond all control,
she did it so convincingly, and with such exquisite
attention to detail, that women everywhere were
compelled to smother wry smirks of recognition as their
men shifted uncomfortably in their seats.

If ever proof was needed that women think men have
fragile egos, Meg Ryan's brilliant performance – and the
torrent of magazine articles, newspaper features and
hastily put-together surveys that followed it – surely
brought it forth.

According to the latest research, over 90 per cent of
women admit to having faked an orgasm at some time or
another in their lives. Why? Because, as Dee, a 32-year-old
divorced mother of three, said: 'Men seem to *need* it more
than we do ourselves.'

Moreover, Dee wasn't the only woman who admitted
faking orgasms in the name of love. 'I don't fake it all of

the time,' explained Jean, a part-time secretary and mother of two. 'Most of the time I don't need to. But if I'm tired or distracted for any reason and I know it's not going to happen, I'll pretend for his sake simply because he gets so upset and I love him too much to want to see him hurt.'

In fact, lying about orgasm or their partner's sexual performance is just about the worst thing women can do. And yet, if there's one thing that's guaranteed to be even more damaging than a sexual lie, it's a sexual lie compounded by the truth.

Suzie is a 25-year-old beautician. Three months ago she was looking forward to getting married in the spring. Now the wedding's been called off and she's living on her own.

> Sex with Mark was always pretty good, but I rarely ever have orgasms. Sometimes that bothers me, but mostly it doesn't. But I thought it bothered Mark, so I started pretending that I did. It just seemed like the easiest thing to do at the time. I only wanted to make him feel good, and to keep things loving and peaceful between us. What's so awful about that?

Then Suzie did the unforgivable; she lost her temper during an argument about something else, and out popped the truth:

> He went bananas. I don't think I've ever seen him quite so furious or cold. He told me to get out, and he called the wedding off. I was devastated. I couldn't believe it was so important that he'd actually let us split up over it. But he says there's no point in staying together because he could never trust me again.

Some women, like Jean, use love as an excuse for faking orgasms. Others, like Suzie, just do it to keep the peace. But Jenny, *and* every one of her nine friends who took part in a group discussion with me, all said the real reason women tell sexual lies is because 'men's egos are far more fragile than ours'. Or, as Stella phrased it: 'They simply can't handle the idea that they might not be as good in bed as they think they are.'

The fact is, no matter how valid your reason or how justifiable your excuse, no man will ever again feel secure with a woman who once lied about his prowess in bed.

'Sure we've got fragile egos', said 32-year-old Max. 'But then who hasn't? And of course we find it difficult to accept that we haven't pleased a woman in bed, particularly if it's someone we care about. But that's the whole point, if you *do* care about each other you should both be honest and prepared to work at improving things. If I discovered my girl had been faking it with me, I'd be gutted. It would make me feel like a right prat.'

One female psychologist friend with whom I discussed this subject has a theory that faking orgasms has nothing to do with love and everything to do with insecurity ... the faker's:

> Women who are comfortable with their own sexuality, and confident within themselves, have no need to fake orgasms. Those who do, however, obviously have a greater need for approval and acceptance. In other words they fear their mate will not love them or desire them as much. In effect, what they're doing is contriving to manufacture a demonstration of what *they believe* excites men. But they need to learn that men can become even more excited by a woman with low-orgasmic potential who realizes her potential through *his help*.
>
> Women shouldn't feel ashamed of saying, 'I need extra stimulation', or a different kind of stimulation, because good relationships are built upon honest communication. If a woman feels she has to lie, sooner or later she will become resentful, and that's when the relationship is likely to start falling apart, because she won't be able to prevent

herself from projecting her resentment and dissatisfaction on to him.

But what about the issue of men's 'fragile egos'? Is this a
myth or a fact? According to my psychologist friend, it's
partly both:

> Society has taught women that men have fragile
> egos. Most of today's women grew up in
> households in which mother waited upon father,
> and did her damndest to ensure all his needs were
> met. That's a very powerful kind of conditioning.
> Certainly I think men's egos have *become* more
> fragile in recent years, simply because they
> perceive women's new self-sufficiency and
> independence as a threat to their own traditionally
> dominant role.
>
> But, on the other hand, it's equally true that
> women have fragile egos, too. After all, the first
> thing women say when they discover a partner's
> infidelity is 'I can't accept that *I* wasn't enough for
> him'. So you see, both men's and women's egos
> are just as prone to sensitivity, particularly when it
> comes to the realization that they might not be able
> to fulfil all their partner's sexual needs.

What would you say, I asked Jenny and Stella's group, if
I told you that men sometimes fake orgasms too?

'Impossible,' said Stella. 'Ridiculous,' scoffed Jenny. 'It's
just not feasible,' asserted Lauren. 'Why not?' I asked.
'Well,' explained Jenny to a chorus of nodding heads,
'Men don't have any need to, do they? Besides, they just
couldn't get away with pretending they'd come because of
… er … well, you know.'

On the contrary, as the following interviews will
confirm, men not only *can* fake orgasms, they *do*.

Men fake it too

Why would a man want to fake an orgasm? 'Because
sometimes we just want to get it over with, too,' said Nick,

a single photographer who is 33 years old. 'It's not that hard to do, particularly when you're making it with a woman who doesn't know you very well.' (And if you're tempted to enquire about the evidence – or rather the absence of any – remember, though it can often *feel* like a man has ejaculated enough semen to float the Ark, the total volume of the average emission would barely fill a teaspoon.)

Phil, a 29-year-old computer programmer, also admits to having faked an orgasm now and then, but only when he felt that he was being pressurized to perform:

> It's a point of pride. I'm usually so nervous the first time that I find it really difficult to come. And if I'm wearing a condom – which I usually do all the time now because of Aids – it can take me even longer. It never even occurred to me before, but then I was with this girl one night and we'd been going for so long it was getting embarrassing. I didn't want to admit defeat, so I just thought to myself, well, there's no way she's going to be able to tell, so I just pretended I'd come. Now I reckon I've got it down to a fine art.

Perhaps my psychologist friend's theory that faking orgasms is a sign of insecurity is nearer to being a truth after all. Why else would so many men and women be prepared to settle for less than they really want from their partner in bed if it weren't for a fear of one kind or another?

Why can't women say what they want in bed?

One of the commonest complaints men make about women is that we're ridiculously shy about expressing our wants and needs in bed.

'Why can't women open up?' said Neil, a married artist of 42. 'I've been married for 15 years and my wife still finds it difficult to talk to me when we're making love. But how can I get it right if she won't tell me what I'm doing wrong?'

Do Neil, and all the other men who frequently voice this complaint, have a valid point? According to the *Mail on Sunday* newspaper's sex survey of 1991, they certainly do. In response to the question: do you hold things back from your man about what you want? over a third of the 15 to 19-year-olds, almost half of those between 20 and 29, and nearly 60 per cent of those aged between 30 and 40, said yes.

But why do women find it so hard to talk about sex? Paula is 30. She's been married to Clive for three years having lived with him for two years previously. When she gave birth to their first child last Christmas, Clive helped the midwife throughout the delivery. And yet, despite the years of intimacy she and Clive have shared, Paula *still* can't bring herself to tell him what she wants him to do in bed:

> I do have orgasms, but they're not very often. Clive's really good, he'll try just about everything in the book, from oral sex to using a vibrator. Sometimes it works, but most times it doesn't. The thing is, I know exactly what will do it for me, but I just can't bring myself to say the words. He can't understand it. 'Tell me', he begs, 'it's nothing to be ashamed of, or embarrassed about', but no matter how much I want to, the words just won't come out.

Bev, a 30-year-old housewife and mother of two, says she enjoys sex immensely. Yet her inhibitions go even deeper than Paula's, for whenever she has an orgasm she feels such a deep sense of shame that she *can't even look her husband in the face the following day!* 'I know it sounds stupid,' she said, blushing furiously, 'but I just feel like a whore or something. Isn't it crazy? I even go red when my mother walks into my bedroom because the double bed is proof of our sex life.'

And what does Bev's husband, Gary, think about his wife's maidenly modesty? 'He just laughs,' she says. 'Well, at least he knows I'm not likely ever to sleep with anyone else. I mean, if I can't even look him in the eye and he's my husband, imagine what I'd be like with another man!'

[When *Cosmopolitan* magazine surveyed their readers on this one, 28 per cent of women said they found it difficult and embarrassing to tell their partner what they wanted, with 23 per cent of these saying they just couldn't discuss this delicate topic at all. On the other hand, 39 per cent of their less shy sisters love talking dirty and swearing whenever they're in the 'brazen hussy' mood.]

Chasing the elusive Big 'O'

A good sex life depends on two things: being able to communicate your needs, and realizing that the responsibility for your own pleasure ultimately lies with you. Neither sex should regard the sexual act as something men 'do' to women, or as something women 'allow' men to do to them because they feel they should. But it's amazing how many women still feel compelled to suffer in silence.

Tessa, who's 43, suffered her ex-husband's premature ejaculation in angry silence for ten years before she left him for another man:

> In retrospect I realize it was my own fault. Instead of saying nothing and allowing him to think I was happy with our sex life, I should have discussed it with him. But I didn't have the courage. I ended up hating him. Then I met Ray in the pub where I work. He's eight years younger than me, but boy does he know how to make me happy in bed. But it

took a lot of encouragement for me to open up and
tell Ray what I liked.

Sally, a teacher, lost her virginity at the age of 14. Ten
years and 25 lovers later, she's still searching for Mr Right.
Her definition of Mr Right? 'The one who can give me an
orgasm.' Not that she can't give them to herself, you
understand, because she can and does, frequently, with
the aid of her trusty aide. But: 'I need to know what it's
like with a man,' she says. 'If other women can experience
orgasm during sex, why can't I?' And when each likely lad
fails to perform this amazing feat for Sally, what then?
'Two months is my limit. If they haven't found the magic
button by then, there's not much point in continuing, is
there? Why should I settle for second best?' Which begs
the question: who's more deserving of our sympathy?
Sally, who hasn't yet worked out that if she can have
orgasms on her own what's stopping her from having
them with men? Or her 25 hapless guinea-pigs who never
knew they were being compared with a battery-driven
machine?

Out of the 50 or so women I interviewed, more than two
thirds of them said that the main reason they got little
satisfaction out of sex was because their men were far too
mechanical in bed. Yet, ironically, when I asked them
about other methods of sexual satisfaction, most of them
said mechanical devices – namely their vibrators – were
best!

'But then there are all sorts of different reasons why you
have sex,' explained Sue. 'Sometimes you do it because he
wants to, and you don't really feel you can refuse. And
sometimes you do it because you're in the mood for a
really good screw. When I'm feeling really horny, I just
want an orgasm, so if it doesn't happen then I'll use my
vibrator. But if I'm in a romantic mood I want the works –
lots of kissing, cuddling, foreplay, etc. Vibrators are fine if
all you want is sexual relief, but they're no substitute for
love.'

Unfortunately, to hear women talk, some husbands often aren't much of a substitute for love either. But then as author and agony aunt Irma Kurtz says in her book *Malespeak*, by and large men are indeed lousy lovers: 'Plain, unadulterated fucking is maleish,' says Kurtz, 'and quite a few men manage to pull the deed off; very few men, however, in feminine estimations are better than boring lovers.'

'Because possible failure haunts men and because their erections are vulnerable to the racket of consciousness as well as to the whimpers of the subconscious, they can be grimly determined in bed, and determination is not voluptuous.' Moreover, Kurtz goes on to say that, because men are essentially competitive, their 'moments of climax and dominance are often achieved without tact or sensuousness'.

When it comes to sex, men and women's prime motivations are diametrically opposed. For men, the main factor will always be lust. If lust is combined with love and passion, so much the better, but they can cope without it because the key word is *lust*. For women, however, love and passion are the forerunners of lust; even more so now that pregnancy need no longer figure in the equation. Or, to quote Irma Kurtz: 'Intercourse is a female relating passionately to the man in her arms; he, however, at moments of greatest intensity is relating passionately to himself.'

And that's probably the main reason why sex will, not always, but certainly more often than we care to admit, be one of the greatest causes of misunderstanding and contention between the sexes.

The best description I've ever heard of the difference in the ways men and women relate to sex came from one of the very few people who has ever made love as both a man and a woman – the famous transsexual, Stephanie Anne Lloyd. 'For most men,' said Stephanie, 'all the affection and tenderness seems to come *before* their orgasm – or, to put it another way, for men orgasm is a full stop, whereas for women it's merely a comma, a prelude to a feeling that can become something much, much more.'

However, although orgasm obviously does rank as being fairly important to women, it's by no means mandatory for a good love life. As Fiona Pitt-Kethley says: 'Orgasms are something you can give to yourself. I don't have to need an orgasm to want to make love, and I don't necessarily have to achieve one in order to enjoy the experience.' On the whole I'd say most women would probably echo that sentiment, too.

Men, on the other hand, rarely find satisfaction in sex which doesn't culminate in orgasm for them. Cynthia Payne (the ex-Madame who, after making a lifetime study of the species at play, is reckoned to know a thing or 22 about men) once put forward the hypothesis: 'Men need to be regularly de-spunked.'

That women have just as great a capacity for sexual enjoyment as men is unarguable. Yet men still persist in believing that it's the woman's responsibility to turn *them* on, not vice versa. Which is rather odd considering that sex ranks right alongside cars and sport as the top three male hobbies. On the other hand, I imagine we only have to study men in relation to the latter interests to find our answer. After all, most men don't actively participate in any sport, and of those that do few would actually be classed as any good. Yet amazingly all of them feel qualified to discourse at great length on virtually every sport imaginable – and even on a few that aren't. The same goes for cars: they all lust after the sleekest and most powerful model, and they all feel they could drive any car with ease, but few are so fanatical that they'd invest time in learning how to build one from scratch. Unfortunately, being an armchair expert is as far as a lot of men are prepared to go.

There are exceptions, of course, but sadly these are pretty rare, for whilst every man wants to be regarded as a 'great lover' few are selfless enough to go to the lengths of, say,

Casanova, or even Prince Aly Khan. Which is a shame, because if they did give more time, care and attention to their women's needs, they'd find that not only would their efforts be rewarded a thousandfold, but they would have far less reason to complain about all the things women do wrong in bed.

[Prince Aly, the present Aga Khan's late father, was apparently renowned for his legendary sexual prowess. Moreover, it's reputed that he took his reputation so seriously, he seldom allowed himself to climax lest it impair his ability to 'service' his daily quota of 'several' women.]

And so the arguments rage on, with women complaining that men want it too much, too quickly, and with too little love, whilst men counterattack by accusing women of not wanting it enough. Will we ever get it right? Probably not, but we can at least attempt to make it better by learning to understand the way men and women functon on a sexual level.

Men's orgasms vary but not as much as women's

In *What Every Woman Should Know About Men*, Dr Joyce Brothers explains that the average single man has around 1500 orgasms before marriage compared to a single woman's paltry 250, a large proportion of which are likely to be solo experiences for both.

A woman's orgasms, however, are far more dependent on factors such as mood, health, environment and how she feels about her partner at that particular moment. And whilst fatigue, health and anxiety obviously can affect the quality of men's orgasms too, theirs don't vary in quality nearly as much as women's do.

Men, Dr Brothers claims, can have a minimal orgasm (what one of her interviewees described as a 'jerk and a dribble') or they can have a 'strongly pulsing ejaculation'. But, as *on average* they tend usually to have between ten and twelve contractions (with the first contraction always being the strongest), one orgasm is likely to feel very much like any other. Men's strongest and longest orgasms usually occur after a period of abstinence, two days without ejaculation being sufficient to produce a really strong orgasm in men aged between 20 and 30 (an extra recovery day needs to be added for each decade thereafter). The fact that abstinence makes their orgasms stronger is, Joyce Brothers maintains, the main reason why many men believe the myth that the longer a woman goes without sex, the more desperate she's bound to become. In fact, not only is the reverse more likely to be true, but the quality and strength of women's orgasms are in no way related to the length of the gap in between them.

Once is not enough

One woman I know never reaches orgasm during sex, but when she masturbates she usually needs at least three orgasms before she feels anywhere near replete – and more often than not the last one is usually the strongest of all.

Others report that, whilst they can be happy with only one when they masturbate alone, it can often take up to six orgasms to satisfy them fully during sex. But then, unlike men, the quality and sheer strength of women's orgasms can and do run the whole gamut from 'damp squibs' – those that promise fireworks but usually peter out after a minor shudder and a small contraction or two – through the fairly pleasing 'that'll do nicely' everyday variety – all the way up to the explosive 'Oh my God!' blockbuster-type whose eight or twelve contractions have the G-force impact of a Cruise missile. Although the latter type are often (sadly) more elusive than the other kinds, this in itself makes them so very special that every man ought to make it his aim to witness at least one during his lifetime, if only because the very sight of a woman rendered gibbering-wreck-like by what can only be described – with glaring inadequacy – as an apocalyptic experience, will do such wonders for his 'fragile male ego' that he will automatically exempt himself from ever needing to suffer performance-anxiety again!

Do men worry about their sexual performance?

In the words of a very dear male friend of mine (who also happens to be a psychotherapist): 'Does a bear shit in the woods?'

Women are very vocal about their insecurities. They'll happily confide all their (and your) embarrassing little moments to their friends, and they can spend hours discussing such riveting topics as 'the most exciting positions', 'the quickest way to make a guy come', 'the surest method of ensuring he doesn't', as well as swapping stories about their best and worst performances. That's how women learn about sex, about men's likes and dislikes, and it's also how they learn to build their confidence.

But the same does not apply to men. Remember the Monty Python team and the craze they started for the phrase 'nudge nudge wink wink'? Well, that's precisely how men pass on to each other their own misinformation about women and sex. Now, by that I do *not* mean to suggest that all men have the dirty minds and lewder habits of a sex-crazed oik. Rather that most of their conversations about sex consist of vague references, allusions and implications which other men interpret according to what male culture and conditioning processes have taught them to believe.

When men get together they'll often talk about sex in general terms, they'll tell jokes about it, and, on occasions, they might even compare spurious notes on who's had who, or who'd like to have who. But men don't like discussing *details* – particularly their own *personal* details, so beyond allowing a dirty laugh or a sheepish grin to imply, 'We're all bastards together when it comes to women', no man ever really gets to discover the truth, which is that every other male is as riddled with precisely the same sexual insecurities and doubts as himself.

Lee Eisenberg, the American editor-in-chief of British *Esquire* magazine, thinks that while men are far more in touch with their emotions now than they were 10 or 20 years ago, they're still not *talking* as women would like them to. 'Women assume that men are in touch with their own abilities and proficiencies sexually and that they talk about nothing else,' Eisenberg explained in a recent magazine interview. 'But most men really have very little idea as to whether they are any good in bed. And contrary to the great cultural myth, men don't really discuss women in graphic detail. For a man to share that with another man is far too intimate. It's almost as if the second man has jumped into bed with the first.'

Surprising as it might seem, not all men are as sexually uncomplicated as myth would have us believe, for many profess to feeling every bit as vulnerable as women when their sexual defences are down. Toby, a 25-year-old singer confides:

> Every time I pluck up the courage to ask a girl out, I'm putting my self-esteem on the line. Do women realize how much nerve it takes to risk constant rejection like that? And whenever I make love to a girl for the first time, I really have to work hard at not letting her see how shy, nervous, and vulnerable I feel. I know people think I must be super-confident because I sing with a band, but that's just an image. Once you take your clothes off and there's just you and the girl alone together, you can't help being aware that she's expecting you to make the earth move for her, and there you are thinking, 'Jesus, what will she think of me or say to her friends if I don't?'

In a rare moment of honesty, Dean, a 25-year-old advertising executive admitted that he too is often at a loss:

We're all supposed to be so sure of ourselves, none of us ever dares admit to needing pointers on sexual technique. But we're not born with a map of a girl's erogenous zones inside our heads, and girls' bodies don't come with directions indelibly stamped all over them instructing us to 'touch here, stroke there, then press that spot'. So the only way we can learn is through experimentation, and because it's obvious you're going to make mistakes when you first start out, you can't help but wonder sometimes whether girls think you're a hopeless prat. I'm convinced lots of men must worry just as much as I do, but you try getting any of them to admit to it.

Dean's older brother, Steve, had his first sexual experience at the age of 14:

> I thought I was Jack the Lad, and acted like it too, until something happened which made me have my doubts. I met this girl I really liked, but the first time we went to bed was also the last. Just when I was really getting into the swing of it she suddenly started begging, 'Touch my clitoris, touch my clitoris, *please*'. I didn't have a clue what she was on about. 'Um, er, yeah, okay then,' I said, fumbling around a bit. Then I spoilt it all by blurting out, 'Uh … er … what is it? *Where* is it?' That killed it stone dead. It took a long while for me to get my confidence back after that. I can tell you.

At the age of 30 Tony appears to have everything: a successful business, his own home, and a beautiful and very sexy girlfriend who has multiple orgasms every time they make love. But is he happy? No, he's not:

> I sometimes think it must be terrific to be a woman. Imagine being able to come five, six, maybe even more times, in one session! I couldn't believe Sharon was for real the first time we made love. I

felt sure she must be faking it. But she wasn't. I'd never come across a woman with such a prodigious capacity before, so it made me feel really good for a while. But lately I've started having my doubts about whether it's really got anything to do with my ability after all. If I was the first guy with whom she'd had such a great time, I wouldn't mind. But she says sex has always been terrific for her, and she's always wanted it a lot. That makes me wonder. Does it mean that *anyone – or anything* – would satisfy her just as well as me?

Less sex, more love in the nervous nineties

Once, it was assumed that the only thing that mattered to single men was keeping up their 'scoring' average. Now, however, things have changed. The threat of Aids is largely responsible for much of the fear we're all now experiencing. But it's not only Aids that's putting more and more of today's singles off casual sex. Many experts are saying that we've been veering towards the adoption of a more sensible, conservative attitude about sexual relationships for some time now. And my own research has given me no cause to dispute this. But whether this is due to the entirely natural forces that occur when the pendulum inevitably starts to swing in the opposite direction, the terrifying prospect of Aids, or even the fundamental change in consciousness that has followed in the wake of feminism, remains to be seen.

Whatever the cause, the result is that men are definitely, but slowly, beginning to change. And whilst some are indeed electing to retreat from relationships altogether, others, such as Sean, Gerald and Keith, have now reached the conclusion that 'screwing' is out, and making love is in.

Sean, a 30-year-old print production controller, says:

Admittedly, when I was in my teens and early 20s, all I thought about was 'the next screw'. But most men realize, sooner or later, that 'scoring' just isn't enough. For me that moment came when, faced with another meaningless romp, it suddenly hit me that I'd far sooner go home alone and satisfy myself than have to endure all the bullshit preamble and then feel like a heel in the morning.

Gerald, 32, says his moment of enlightenment arrived when he drove one of his colleagues home after last year's office Christmas party:

I'd only recently broken up with my fiancée. We'd been together for four years, so I suppose I was a bit out of touch with how much things have changed. Everyone at the party was getting well into the Christmas spirit, and there was all the usual tomfoolery going on, with the most unlikely people pairing off in the stationery cupboard and all that sort of thing. When I announced I was leaving to the group I had been talking to, one of the girls, Serena, who's only about 24, asked if she could have a lift home. To say I was gobsmacked when she asked whether I'd like to 'come in and fool around a little' is an understatement. Although we had worked together in the same department for several years, I'd never thought of her in that way. All sorts of things passed through my mind in the space of about 30 seconds, from 'Why not?' to 'I'm damned if I'm going to behave like some performing seal'. In the end I just made some pathetic excuse. Since then Serena's avoided me like the plague. I haven't been totally celibate since my break-up, but one-night-stands just don't seem to do anything for me any more. Of course I miss sex, but there's not much point in it when there's no feeling there.

Keith, who works as a borough surveyor, got divorced at the age of 29 after being married for seven years:

Being single again came as a real culture shock to me. I just couldn't believe how many women now seem to think sex is obligatory on a first date – not that the onus is on *them*, but on me! And you wouldn't believe how angry or upset some of them get when you politely decline. 'Course, my married mates think I must be mad to turn them down, but frankly I can't handle the pressure. It's not sex I'm after, it's a worthwhile, loving relationship.

Sean, Gerald and Keith are just three of the men I interviewed who confessed to having recently experienced a complete turn-around in their views about casual sex versus relationships. The irony is, alongside this change of heart sits a newly discovered fear of women using *them* as 'superstuds'.

What a ridiculous situation we're in. On the one hand there's a whole segment of male society accusing women of holding too much back, whilst on the other there are those who confess to being terrified of women who are too bold. And women are just as bad; far too many complain that men are incapable of being considerate in bed, but what can they expect when, by lying to their partners, they're simply conspiring against themselves?

3

Hookers, Whores and One-Night-Stands

SOME YEARS AGO an experiment was conducted with American college students to assess how many of them would be prepared to sleep with someone at first meeting. Not surprisingly, 75 per cent of the men who were approached with an offer accepted, whilst *all* of the women who were propositioned declined.

Obviously the sexual climate has changed considerably since that particular experiment was undertaken, but whilst that gap between the typical male and female attitudes to casual sex does appear to have closed in the last few years (i.e., single women today are less reluctant to consider the odd one-night-stand or two), historically it always has been, if not always understandable, at least acceptable, for men to feel more comfortable with sex purely for the sake of it.

However, whilst women undoubtedly do seem to *accept* the notion that anonymous sex – in the form of strip shows, stag nights, casual sex, and even sex with prostitutes – is a peculiarly male interest, they still can't fully comprehend wherein the attraction lies.

Prostitution, they say, is the world's oldest profession. If its birth can be dated, then it probably coincides with the very same day that Adam and Eve were banished from the Garden of Eden for having tasted the forbidden fruit. And from the moment sex was discovered, there have been women who have been prepared to sell their bodies for profit. Of course, like any other industry, prostitution depends on the law of supply and demand: the only difference being that prostitution is recession-proof, fashion-proof, and timeless.

What satisfaction – apart from the very obvious, that is – do men derive from impersonal sex? Can those few minutes of less than idyllic, mechanical sex really be worth the money they're charged? And what pleasure do men get out of visiting seedy clubs – purely to ogle women who divest themselves of their clothes to a monotonous rendition of 'The Stripper', and who, not to put too fine a point on it, are rarely ever dazzlingly beautiful specimens of perfect womanhood – particularly when they have to pay such exorbitant prices for the privilege of doing so?

Stag shows and strip clubs

'Men who enjoy going to stag shows and strip clubs aren't men – they're animals!' spat Kerry, 26, a young wife and mother who was so disgusted when her husband bought a ticket to a charity stag show staged at his local rugby club that she took both her children and left him.

'I've heard what disgusting things go on at stag shows – men get up on the stage and have sex with those filthy women. "Well," I told him, "I don't care how many of your mates are going, if you go, I'm leaving." He went. So I left. *I'm* not putting up with that sort of perverted behaviour in *my* marriage.'

Kerry did go back eventually, but it took a lot of persuasion on the part of her own family, as well as a lot of convincing from her husband Trevor that nothing untoward had happened. 'Why couldn't she understand?' asked Trevor, when he gave me his version of the event. 'No bloke I know goes to these things to get involved with whatever's going on up there on stage, we just go for the drinks and the laughs.'

There are several reasons why women get upset and feel threatened by these occasions. First, they've usually heard several lurid – and probably vastly exaggerated – tales about stag shows and strip clubs. Second, and perhaps not unreasonably, they do have a tendency to feel threatened by any traditional 'male only' pursuit that excludes them whilst at the same time involving other females. And third, the idea that *their* man should gain amusement from anything that both debases women, and the sexual act itself, is not only deeply upsetting and humiliating on a personal level, but also it raises all sorts of uncomfortable questions about his character and nature that they may not wish to confront.

On several occasions during my own career I've found myself mentally reassessing various male colleagues after having heard them proudly regaling all and sundry with tawdry tales of their exploits during 'boys' nights' of this nature. And, frankly, if their wives and girlfriends ever were unfortunate enough to be appraised of the knowledge I've been privy to in the past, I'd have said these men would only have themselves to blame if all hell broke loose. The fact is, whilst every woman can accept that camaraderie is the glue that holds male society together, and that much of that camaraderie tends to be expressed by a reversion to stereotypically schoolboyish behaviour (toilet humour, sexist jokes, dirty songs, etc,), *no* woman likes to think that *her* man is morally weak, immature, or so easily led that he'd allow himself to be coerced into doing anything that, to her mind, smacks of degradation.

Philip, a 27-year-old single advertising sales executive, is privately so ashamed of some of the things he's done at 'men only' Christmas parties, he wouldn't allow me to use his real Christian name for fear of being identified:

> In my business, we get involved in lots of client entertaining, particularly at Christmas, when media buyers and the bosses of companies who

advertise direct in our publications are traditionally 'treated' to an all-expenses-paid session at a well-known strip club.

The food's indifferent, the drinks are over-priced and under-strength, and the tab my company has to pick up is enormous. But what we're really paying for is what the clients want: girls who are so obliging and attentive to their needs that they're guaranteed 'a good time'.

Last year, which was my first year in this job, I got so rat-arsed, I ended up as part of the floor show. I don't actually remember much about it, but everyone else does – and they've never let me forget it. Apparently I let one of the girls strip me naked and perform one or two unmentionable acts on me. Then, I'm ashamed to say, I apparently had full sex with her. I also threw up and passed out, which, of course, gave everyone the perfect opportunity to do all sorts of awful things to me and generally have a good laugh at my expense.

When the guys told me about it the next day I didn't believe them at first. They all thought it was hilarious. To be honest, I actually cried with humiliation later, but I never told them that. They all seemed to think it was a really manly thing to do. For weeks afterwards whenever I had to visit one of the clients who had been there, I'd be slapped on the back, taken out to lunch or to the pub for a drink, and generally treated as if I was one of the boys.

I hate that attitude, but if I said so they'd all think I was strange. I'm dreading this year's 'do'. If I can find a way out of it, I will. But if that proves impossible, then I'm going to make real sure I don't get drunk.

Well, what can you expect? When there's a group of people misbehaving, everyone feels better about their own misdemeanours if they can point the finger at someone whose behaviour is far worse. Moreover, when a crowd gets carried away on a tide of alcohol, it doesn't take much for mass hysteria to develop to the point where people forget we're meant to be a civilized race. And believe me, that can apply just as easily to women as it does to men.

Philip's experience aside, most of the men I questioned on this point were in agreement that, for them, the main attractions of a stag show were the comedians and 'sharing a laugh with the guys'.

'At their best, they're a harmless bit of fun,' said Jonathan, 33, who organizes two or three a year for his football club. 'And at their worst, they can be so tedious and tackily pretentious, they're still amusing. I've certainly never been to, or even heard about, stag shows that involve the audience and the stripper in any form of sexual act whatsoever, apart from a guy being invited to pull off a stripper's gloves, or undo her bra. That's as far as it goes in my experience.'

Women can be just as bad

In 1972, after leaving *Forum* magazine, I was commissioned by its editor to write an article about one of the first ever 'hen' nights that took place in the east of England. To say that the behaviour of the women who attended this event was an eye-opener is an understatement of immeasurable magnitude. By the time the main attraction, billed as 'The Savage Apache', gyrated teasingly onto the dance floor and commenced to stomp barefoot around his fake camp fire to the strains of the Rolling Stones singing 'I Can't Get No Satisfaction' (a rather unwise choice, in the event), a whole clutch of respectable married housewives – who'd got so carried away by the coy teasing of the supporting acts they'd long ago dispensed with all claim to the adjective – were gathering at the edge of the floor ready to pounce.

From my vantage point of safety behind the manager, who was growing whiter by the second, I watched with mingled fascination and horror as the raucous crowd of female vultures swooped down upon the poor man and lifted him bodily off his feet. Within seconds they had divested him of his loincloth, his minuscule 'posing pouch' and the feathery 'willie-warmer' concealed underneath. And they didn't stop there. For they then proceeded to man-handle (woman-handle?) him in such an outrageously familiar manner, no one – least of all he – had any doubt but that they fully intended to provide him with the very thing his theme tune had indicated was missing in his life.

Needless to say, by the time the manager and his dozen burly bouncers had managed to restore order, every inch of that poor 'Apache's' face and body was so red (whether from embarrassment, the vigorous clutching of a hundred or so female hands, or the imminent threat of an apopletic fit brought on by fear, I never could tell) he would have had no difficulty passing himself off as a real red indian.

The point is, whilst obviously there are *some* people who, given the right circumstances, will always go over the top, it's both foolish and unfair to assume *all* men and women do.

If it's any comfort to Kerry, and any other woman who has similar fears about stag shows, very few companies who organize these events would risk being prosecuted for breaking the law. And if that's not enough to allay their fears, perhaps the following testimony will.

At 26, Amanda has been working full time as a stripper for six years. At weekends she works at a club in London's West End. Three or four evenings a week she travels around the country performing her act on the stag show circuit.

> Just because I take my clothes off in front of men, it doesn't mean I'm a whore. And neither are any of my mates in this business. None of us would ever do that other stuff. We're just girls who happen to have good bodies and don't mind showing them off. Besides, most of us have got boyfriends who

travel around with us, so we're hardly likely to get up to anything we shouldn't, are we?

In order to fully comprehend why men are more attracted to these forms of entertainment than women, we need to understand more about male society itself.

Rites of passage

In primitive times, the roles of male and female were clearly delineated. Man was the hunter, the provider, and woman was the nurturer. Older males in a tribe or group took on the full responsibility for training, educating and preparing young men to take their places in male society. Boys were taught how to handle the bows, knives and other implements that were their tools of trade, and when they reached the age at which they were deemed to have attained 'manhood', some form of initiation ceremony was conducted to mark this rite of passage. A boy learned not only how to conduct himself like a man, but also precisely what it meant, in his particular culture, *to be a man*, from all the other men of his tribe who were his role models.

Today, few males in the western world – apart from those of the Jewish faith who have their *bar mitzvahs* – undergo any discernible form of initiation ceremony to celebrate their transformation from boyhood into manhood. This, according to many experts, could well be the main reason why men have evolved certain 'rituals' that, by tacit agreement, have come to be recognized, accepted and approved as definitive male pursuits and behaviour.

In *Malespeak*, Irma Kurtz describes how and why the physical transitions a male makes as he passes through puberty to manhood are rarely as traumatic as the female's. His first nocturnal emission, the sudden cracking of his voice, the growth of body and facial hair, as well as his penis, are all likely to be pleasurable experiences for him, explains Kurtz. And though he might experience some anxiety about his first sexual experience, once this has been successfully accomplished it is viewed as a victory; something he has gained.

Compared with the female's progress into maturity – the first blood of menstruation which may be accompanied by discomfort and pain; the losing of her virginity, which is more often to be regarded with a feeling of sadness, of having lost rather than having gained something; pregnancy, labour, birth, the cessation of periods at menopause, all of which are milestones invariably marked with physically obvious changes – the male's progress appears to be far less emotionally and psychologically transformative.

Thus, Kurtz says, 'The male ego is compelled to invent mutual, shared ways in which men can assure themselves and indicate to others that their progress is normal, they are not alone, and they have not failed.' And it is precisely *because* men are forced to invent their own rites of passage that the only way they can persuade themselves of their own maturity is to persuade others of it first.

'Men,' asserts Kurtz, 'clamber for rank, symbols and insignia to show off their position in the male hierarchy or, more likely, to show others where they fancy themselves worthy of being. They inherit rank rather than prospects, they drive symbols instead of cars, they wear insignia, not clothes. In a man's world, to own the best is to be seen as being the best, and to take a chance on anything at all that is odd or out of the ordinary is to risk failure and derision.

Men, far more than women it seems, are publicly compelled to conform, to herd together like sheep, grazing only in those metaphorical pastures that male culture decrees are representative of all that is traditionally and quintessentially male. Unlike sheep, however, the human male must forever jostle with other males for supremacy and strive continually to demonstrate a position of status in the hierarchical pecking order of maledom. Because status is what male society is all about.

The key to men is status

A man's status in the eyes of his fellows is of supreme importance. What does it matter whether his woman believes him to be the best lover, the best husband, the best father, if his peers do not accept him as equal or superior to themselves? The truth is, it's the acceptance, the admiration, and the approval of *other men* that men crave above all else. For male society – not female – is the true testing ground of machismo. That's where a man's self-image is first formed, nurtured, and continually reaffirmed.

Where once man competed in the arena, he now competes in pubs, clubs, bars and on the field; the skilfulness with which he wields his tongue has now replaced his muscles as a weapon of war. Corporate coups, sporting triumphs and bedroom braggings are the modern-day warrior's route to claiming the spurs of manhood. For it's only through conversation and his sporting skills that he now can vie with his fellow men to establish himself as a man of worth. Here men will swap jokes, each wracking his brains for the dirtiest, the funniest, the wittiest, most sexist, racist or the most up-to-date on a given topic. Because the one who gets the biggest laugh, the one who tells the one that tops them all, is the one who has succeeded in establishing himself as having (however temporarily) superior status within his peer group. And underlying men's shared passion for airing their knowledge about sex and sport is a desperate need for compensation for their failures at both.

If you think I'm being unfair or harsh, the next time you find yourself in the company of a group of men, observe the ritual for yourself. Then test it further by noting equally the nature of what is *omitted* from men's conversations. They do not, for instance, discuss their business fears or failures, their sexual fears or failures, or anything that in any way diminishes their status. And if, perchance, the conversation turns to tales of 'the ones that got away' (whether it be a fish, a football match, a female or a financial coup), wry humour or a touch of modest self-deprecation will be used to subtly twist and transform a story of 'failure' into one that will be perceived as a tale of triumph.

In male culture, lying to one's brother is tantamount to committing a criminal offence. (Lying to women, on the other hand, is not only considered highly commendable, on certain occasions it's mandatory, particularly when they do it in order to 'protect their women'!) So, because there is a general consensus in male society that the man who lies automatically reveals himself as inferior in status, quite simply, men do *not* tell lies. Rather, they make minor 'adjustments' to the truth; a little judicious editing here, a small patch of embroidery there, and hey presto, once again they emerge *status intacto*.

Generally speaking, therefore, women have nothing to fear or mistrust about a man's interest in strip clubs, stag shows and other entertainments of that ilk. (Would they feel more reassured if I said that to fear such things is to make an undeserved mountain out of a mere molehill of male ego?)

Forget the offensive jokes at which he's guffawing, the considerable quantities of beer he's quaffing, and even the women whose bodies he is undoubtedly ogling; these are largely meaningless. The *real* attraction is nothing more sinister nor personally threatening to you (in fact, it has *nothing* whatsoever to do with you, and *everything* to do with himself) than a golden opportunity to align himself alongside the other chaps as a healthy, macho male, doing what healthy macho males are traditionally supposed to do. It is also to safeguard and further stoke the fire that keeps his male ego burning by reassuring himself that his stature within his group is all that his self-esteem requires it to be. Deprive him of that opportunity, however, and who knows what price you might have to pay, because, remember, the human male has a fundamental need to build and reaffirm his ego *outside of your relationship, and wholly within the world of men.*

If you still need further proof, let me remind you of one final, incontrovertible fact: a male's self-esteem is derived solely from his perceived status within his peer group. Likewise, all his insecurities have their foundations in a terrifying fear of failure. *Is it likely, therefore, that any normal man would willingly take the risk of shaming himself by failing in front of the very people he most needs to impress?*

Who needs hookers?

Apart from psychologists and sociologists, whose knowledge at best can only ever be theoretical, there are only two groups of people who are adequately qualified to answer the question: 'What, apart from the obvious, do men get out of sex with a prostitute?' These are a) the men who, for whatever reason, feel compelled to purchase their services and b) the women who profit from these men.

The transsexual, Stephanie Anne Lloyd, once found herself in the position of having to offer her own personal – and sometimes very unusual – services as one of the latter:

> Every prostitute who has ever gone on record about her profession has likened herself to being a combination of whore, sister, mother, agony aunt and social worker – and I guess I feel just the same, for it gave me great pleasure to be able to solve people's problems for them.
>
> I lost track of the sheer numbers of men who wanted to don female underwear or babywear, or be tied up and spanked. I can understand why prostitutes are so much in demand when regular girlfriends and wives are reluctant to do anything outside the 'norm'.

Certainly the majority of my customers were outwardly happily married men, but the very fact that they needed to indulge their more secret fantasies with me often made me wonder how *happily* married they might really be, were it their wives who were catering to their special needs, out of love, rather than a hooker who did it for cash.

Not surprisingly, therefore, the feminist argument that, as well as being unacceptably exploitative, prostitution, strip clubs, stag shows and pin-up magazines denigrate women is one that Stephanie Anne Lloyd takes issue with: 'It's extremely difficult to feel that women are being exploited by men when men are the ones who part with large sums of money in return for what often amounts to exceptionally short periods of work!'

Precisely how many men use prostitutes is difficult to quantify. Not surprisingly, men are rather reluctant to confess to this need. However, when the British edition of *GQ* magazine surveyed a national sampling of more than one thousand men on a variety of issues, 15 per cent of their respondents said they had 'slept with a prostitute'.

[Although the sample ranged in age from under 20 to 40 plus, 56 per cent were between the ages of 25 and 34; 64 per cent were single, but 24 per cent of those were in a long-term relationship. Socio-economically, these men fell into the ABC1 group of high-earning 'decision makers'.]

What kind of men use prostitutes?

Some men use prostitutes for no other reason than that they simply do not have any other means available to them for finding sexual relief. Other men, when questioned, have confessed to turning to prostitutes when they need specific acts or services that they feel might either distress or horrify their wives or, alternatively, which their wives have refused to perform for them.

Some men don't even bother to find out how accommodating their wives might be. Often these are the ones who, during their formative years, have absorbed distorted ideas of sexuality, inasmuch as they regard sex as being permissible only when it's sanctified by procreation, and, therefore, as sinful or dirty at all other times. And, according to psychotherapist Dr Robert Young, some men are attracted by the idea of the straightforward, honest, business transaction type of deal. In reality what these men are paying for is the right to remain in control; money is merely a currency they use to absolve themselves of all responsibility for and obligation to the person who services their needs. Whether married or unmarried, these men definitely do *not* want to become involved. Anonymous, impersonal, but above all discreet sex with a prostitute is, for these men, on a par with paying to eat in a restaurant when they're hungry. Or, as one habitual 'punter' summed it up in a recent anonymous press interview: 'Prostitution isn't an emotional thing. It's like having a boil and squeezing it.'

There are rich, sad, money-no-object, jaded old men who wouldn't be seen dead with your average, ordinary run-of-the-mill hooker, because their fires can only be rekindled at the expense of very young and very beautiful flesh. And, of course, there are those whom we invariably wind up feeling sorry for, the ones who unfailingly come unstuck when their secret vice is revealed in two-inch headline exposés in the tabloids. Goodness knows why we should feel any sympathy for this type of vice-girl user; he's usually rich, powerful, prominent, occupies a position of enormous responsibility, and is often 'very happily married' to a nice middle-class woman who is ill-equipped to deal with either the sordid nature of her respectable husband's secret vice, or the scandal, shame and prurient interest of the tabloid press.

Why do these men do it? More to the point, why do they seek to do it with bottom-of-the-rung girls who tout for

business in seedy red light districts, instead of paying for
the safer and more discreet services of a call girl? Particularly when, as one vice-squad officer recently pointed out,
'so many of the street girls are known to be drug addicts
suffering highly contagious diseases, including Aids.'

Despite the public denials, the carefully worded statements from 'spokesmen' or 'aides' claiming that the punter
was suffering from stress, amnesia, or a wholly uncharac-
teristic but medically certifiable temporary aberration,
these men's behaviour usually can be summed up in one
sad but simple sentence: they crave the excitement of
flirting with danger, and the more they have to lose, the
bigger the thrill. Or, as that same vice-squad officer said:
'It's as if they hit the self-destruct button.'

And as for the women they pay to do it with? Here again,
women's reasons for resorting to prostitution are as varied
as the services they offer. Some girls turn to prostitution
when they have no other means of financial support. Some
are forced into it by unscrupulous 'boyfriends' or 'min-
ders'. A number see it as the only way to make money to
support their drug habit. Whilst others just regard it as an
easy way to make money – period.

'My body is a commodity,' said Barbara, who classes
herself not as a common or garden prostitute who'll go with
any old Joe, but rather as a 'high-class call girl':

> I'm young, attractive, educated but, apart from
> being able to speak five languages fluently, I do not
> have any skills which would pay me enough to live
> at the standard I enjoy.
>
> I've been doing this for four years. It started by
> accident, when a friend asked me to accompany
> her to a 'business' dinner with two wealthy
> middle-eastern men. Both men were erudite,
> charming, sophisticated and very presentable
> indeed. Perhaps I was naïve, but when the
> gentleman I was with invited me to his hotel room,
> I was attracted enough to agree.

I stayed with him all night, and in the morning when I left he discreetly slipped an envelope into my handbag. It contained £1000. I was too overwhelmed to feel insulted. I've been in love with men who have enjoyed my body for free and treated me very badly. Now I'm in control. I only sleep with the men I want to. I've never experienced any problems. I have a few regular clients who pay very good money for my time and company when they're in town. I get to visit wonderful clubs, restaurants, and the very best hotels. All in all, I think I have a wonderful life. I certainly don't have anything to complain about.

To the girls on the street, whores of Barbara's calibre have it made. To Barbara, the ones who can be considered truly to have made it are the very few women who live, surrounded by splendid luxury, at the expense of one regular patron who is prepared to pay anything up to £150,000 a year for the exclusive right to visit his 'woman' at any appointed time of his choice. The attractions of such a life become obvious when you learn that these women receive only three or four calls a year from their patrons.

In 1990 *Marie Claire* magazine published an extraordinary and fascinating interview between writer Patrice Chaplin and one such woman who devotes her entire life to tuning her body and mind for one thing: 'concentration; utmost concentration on the client', wrote Chaplin. 'She gives him everything and he gives her quite a lot.' Her routine, when not with one of her clients, consists of daily massages, reflexology, lymph draining and shiatsu, all of which are designed both to keep her body at the peak of perfection and to delay the ageing process. For one week every month she leaves her Swiss mountain-top home to spend a week at a health farm.

'She has given up screwing,' explained Chaplin, 'and changed to S & M (sado-masochism). This is not just a question of wielding a cane; it takes imagination and timing. She can work out what a man really wants – buggery with special equipment, a scenario where he is gay, pain more cunning than simply beating him. Her cunning is special, her methods impeccable, and she is absolutely discreet. And it makes a lot more money.'

When asked whether she likes men, she simply replies, 'I use them'. And when counselling a distressed friend who's complaining she cannot get money from her lover to keep her for the rest of her life, she offers the following advice: 'They don't give life insurance. They want you just as a frivolity. It's your business to arrange your last years behind their backs. Life insurance reminds them of their wives. Ask for something they can see and enjoy. A boat? He may die before you.'

Clearly there's a world of difference between the experiences of women like Barbara (or even the one whose interview appeared in *Marie Claire*, both of whom chose of their own volition to make capital out of the sexual needs and/or peculiar desires of wealthy men) and her sadder sisters at the bottom of the pile who are forced to sell their bodies and souls for other reasons.

Certainly, there undoubtedly exist many cases which are truly deserving of our tolerance and sympathy but, as the feminist writer Kate Millett pointed out in her book *The Prostitution Papers*, the gulf that exists between 'respectable' women and those designated by virtue of their professional lack of virtue as 'non-respectable' is too vast to be easily breached. Besides, despite their bravado, a prostitute's self-esteem is usually so low that both our sympathy and our interference would likely prove unwelcome.

As for the men who use prostitutes? What are we to make of them? Are they pathetic wimps deserving of our pity? Self-indulgent bastards who deserve all they get? Or perverted animals who should be avoided at all costs? Who really knows? And so the argument of who is really exploiting whom rages on.

As I make no claims to being an expert on this subject, I am as ill-qualified as anyone else to judge the morals and ethics of both parties. Ultimately, therefore, the only comment I feel I can make is, so long as these men are not inflicting harm on anyone, and so long as they aren't personally menacing you, me or the horses, perhaps we ought to let them just get on with their business of taking – and paying for – their pleasure, in peace.

One-night-stands – and the call that never comes

Of all the things that women say they do not understand about men, the one that probably infuriates and confuses them the most is the time-worn phrase: 'It was great. I'll give you a call.'

'Why do they always say that?' raged Cathy, who's 28 and has lost count of the number of nights she's sat at home waiting by a phone that never rings. 'If they don't want to see you again, why don't they just say so?'

'Yeah,' agreed Maria, 26. 'But I'll tell you what's worse than that, it's when they let you think they really like you, so you wind up in bed together, and everything's great, with them telling you what a wonderful person you are, and what a great time they're having, and how they'd love to take you out again, and then … zilch. Because all they really wanted all along was a one-night-stand. Only you don't get to know for several days that that's what you've just had.'

'It makes you feel such a fool,' said Maria's cousin, Amy. 'There you are walking around on cloud nine for days, wondering when he's going to call. And then a couple of weeks go by and when you've still not heard a word you start feeling let down and sorry for yourself, 'cause you feel like you've been had – literally!'

'What really annoys me,' chipped in 25-year-old Gill, 'is when you've already decided you don't want to see them again, but you don't get the chance to let them know that because they're the ones who are supposed to say, "I'll give you a call, shall I?" and we're supposed to be all polite and say "yes". I've wanted to say no on lots of occasions, but I was taught to be polite, so I don't. Instead I think I'll make an excuse when they call, but when they don't call, you don't get the opportunity. And then you're the one who's left feeling shitty, because they think *they've* dumped *you*.'

Without realizing it, Gill has hit the nail right on the head: because, not surprisingly, men find it just as difficult to be forthright as women do. Of course they know they're lying if they say 'I'll call you' when they don't have any intention of doing so at all. But the fact is, they really don't want to hurt your feelings. At least not whilst they're still around to see it. And as they can't bear confrontations of any kind at all, they daren't risk one *now* (*especially if they've just crawled out of your bed*), so they do what their culture and conditioning processes have taught them is the safest, easiest and politest thing to do: they salvage their pride and your ego by offering you the little carrot of the mythical, non-appearing telephone call.

Is that really any different, or any worse, than what women do when they smile sweetly, agree that they, too, have had a simply wonderful evening and feign equal eagerness for a repeat performance by offering up their telephone number with an insincere 'Mmm, yes, please do'?

And as for honesty, well, all I can say is, I pity the man who's foolish enough to take a woman at her word this early on in the game. Just imagine how she'd react if he were brutally honest enough to say something along the lines of 'God, that was such a boring evening, I think we might as well dispense with the courtesies right now and agree not to have an action replay, don't you?' And what woman's ego could survive the searing humiliation of a comment such as, 'You were a great lay, baby, but as I'm not into bullshit, or bonking the same bird twice, I won't take your number, but I'm bound to see you around'?

Honesty? If women expect honesty on a first date, I'm afraid they're expecting far too much too soon. That's not to say, however, that there isn't another option open to them. After all, to seize control of the situation all they need do is smile sweetly, feign eagerness, and simply say: 'Why don't you give me *your* number, and I'll call *you … in a week … or three.'*

4

Saints and Sinners

To THOSE OF us born in the 20th century, romantic love has become the single most desired experience of life. And because of this, adultery has not only become one of the most feared experiences in any relationship, it's also come to be seen as the ultimate betrayal.

Prior to this century, adultery was regarded as the exclusive preserve of men, and those who chose to commit the act did so with impunity, whereas any woman who was unfortunate to be caught in the act ran the risk of being punished in a variety of ways which ranged, according to her culture, from being 'put aside', i.e., divorced, to being put to death. Primarily there were two reasons for this; first, before the advent of the DNA test (which now provides conclusive evidence), paternity could, at best, only ever be a matter of trust, and second, traditionally wives were considered to be the sole *property* of their husbands.

To many people the term adultery applies only to the act of sexual intercourse by one married person with someone other than their legal partner, whilst to others even the mere *thought* of some kind of lascivious liaison is enough to constitute the act.

When Jimmy Carter was President of the United States he publicly confessed to having committed adultery purely on the basis of having had 'impure thoughts' about someone other than his wife.

Some men – and women, too, it appears – believe that so long as they stick to one-night stands, they're not adulterers; therefore, they are not guilty of doing anything to harm their relationship or marriage.

What drives men to adultery?

What is it that drives a man to infidelity? Is it love? Lust? A need for danger and/or excitement? Or is the real cause likely to be more complex and obscure than all of these?

In her book *How To Keep Your Man Monogamous*, Alexandra Penney argues that men don't necessarily stray because of something their partner has or perhaps has not done, so much as to fulfil certain basic, primary needs within themselves that are not being met. These range from a need for acceptance and a need for variety to intense sexual frustration, sheer boredom or simple curiosity.

When nature appointed testosterone as the primary hormone governing the male sex drive, she not only assured the tendency towards polygamy in men, she also granted them a possible cause – though not necessarily an excuse – for their ability to separate the physical act of sex from their emotions. And though, undoubtedly, there are many men to whom fidelity – both their own and their partner's – is of supreme importance, I doubt there's even one who wouldn't succumb to the temptation if it were guaranteed absolutely that he should never be found out.

'But it didn't mean anything, darling.'

Women will never understand the essential dichotomy that exists between men's hearts and their loins. Likewise, men will never truly comprehend how much infidelity devastates their women. When men protest 'But it didn't *mean* anything', or 'I only *slept* with her, I don't *love* her', they genuinely do seem to believe such words are sufficient to excuse their flings.

'I don't think one-night-stands count as adultery,' said Jim, a long-distance lorry driver who confessed to having had so many during the ten years he's lived with his girlfriend, he's lost track of the actual number. 'I wouldn't seriously cheat on Jeanette, because I don't think that's fair to her. Besides, I couldn't cope with all the hassle. But one-offs are different – they're no worse than wanking; if you don't actually get caught doing it, you don't have to worry about feeling guilty, do you?'

Ah, well, that's all right then, isn't it? In which case we can safely assume Jim wouldn't have any complaints if Jeanette adopted his credo, too!

'Too bloody right I would. I'd kill her! It's not the same thing at all,' he complained.

Why not?

' 'Cause men have stronger sex drives, that's why. And we ain't expected to behave like saints all the time.' And therein lies the rub. For the irony is, when it comes to actual divorce, or the severing of a relationship, men are far more likely to cite their partner's adultery as the main reason than women are! Women, traditionally, have always feared the younger, more beautiful or nubile girls with whom their men come into contact, and never has this fear been more pronounced than it is today. Witness the many women who are so obsessed with maintaining a lycra-tight form, and features tautly frozen in a fabrication of youth, that they rush to worship at the altar of the surgeon's scalpel as religiously – and as greedily – as they would gulp from the mythical fountain of youth were it found to exist.

It's not how good you look, it's how well you stroke his ego

Contrary to what most women believe, whilst many a middle-aged man has indeed been known to have his head (not to mention other parts) turned by the stereotypical young, blonde bombshell of a secretary at his office, a significant proportion of men who leave their partners do so for love – or lust – of someone who, on the face of it, appears to have less to offer in terms of beauty or intelligence than the woman they've left behind. But then when men seek diversion, physical attributes often don't figure very highly; it is how the other woman makes him feel, and how much attention she's prepared to pay to him, which do.

When Bjorn Borg left his young blonde wife, Marianne, it was for a much older and far less pretty dark-haired woman. Similarly, when rock star Bruce Springsteen's affair with his raunchy backing singer, Patti Scialfa, hit the headlines, few people could understand what was so attractive about a woman who was not only almost a decade older than his own beautiful actress wife, Julianne, but whose figure was in no way comparable to hers. And who, even now, could possibly comprehend what magic lured John Lennon away from his first wife, Cynthia, into the arms of Yoko Ono, a woman of diminutive size, eccentric tastes, a totally different culture, and who was seven years his senior to boot?

Time and time again we read about men who have become so besotted with new loves that they've abandoned their families and disrupted their careers at the mere drop of a bra strap – or, more likely, a mere stroke of the ego – without apparently even so much as a backward glance.

Why is it that some men can become so enslaved by their libidos that they are prepared to risk their existing relationships for the excitement of a quick, or even a slow fling with another woman? The answer is: because men rarely set out with the intention to start an affair, consequently it rarely occurs to them they are risking anything at all. And by the time that thought does rear its ugly head, they're either too involved or they under-estimate their ability to control events.

Not all men develop a wandering eye because they're

short of sex, some just seek novelty and variety. Or, as the sex theorist Albert Ellis once said: 'Men get fed up with the monotony of marriage. They find it a bore. Monogamy is not for humans, it's for angels.'

If you put together man's need for variety, his ability to become easily aroused (particularly by something or someone new), his emotional vulnerability, and his (virtually constant) innate sexual insecurity, the only ingredient preventing him from baking his cake *and* eating it is *opportunity*. Solve that one, and the result, more often than not, will be infidelity.

If there's such a thing as a chronic adulterer, then Anthony, who's 45 and married to his fourth wife, proudly stakes his claim to membership of this dubious order:

> I can't help it, I just love women. I told all my wives before I married them, I'm a lousy husband, but I'm a perfect lover.
>
> I married my first wife, who was pregnant at the time, when I was 20. In my job as a sales rep I spend several days a week on the road away from home. I wouldn't say I'm irresistible to women, but they do seem to be attracted to me in large numbers. And, frankly, I just can't resist them.
>
> Shereen, my first wife, threw me out when my second wife, Karen, told her we were having an affair. I had nowhere to go, so naturally I moved in with Karen. When she got pregnant and insisted on getting married, I did warn her I might not be able to stay faithful, but she still insisted on going ahead regardless.
>
> Six years later, after several one-night-stands in between, I met Laura. By then I had three kids, two by Shereen and one by Karen. Of them all, I guess it was Laura I loved the most. When I told Karen about her she tried hard to keep the marriage together. She even let me go on seeing Laura on the side. But I thought I wanted to be with Laura all the time. I didn't look at one other woman in all

the time I was seeing her. But when we got married, the old wanderlust came back, and within months I found myself having a bit on the side again.

The thing is, women are great when they're your girlfriends, but once they become wives something seems to happen to alter them. Knowing my history, Laura was extremely suspicious the whole time we were married. That's what spoiled it for me. Every time I came home it would be like the Spanish Inquisition with her grilling me about where I'd been, which customers I'd seen, what hotel I stayed in, etc. On and on it went. She even used to ring up the hotels to confirm that I had actually stayed there, and whether I'd booked into a single room or a double. Once or twice she rang my hotel room in the early hours of the morning to make sure I was in my own bed, and, presumably, to spoil things if I was in it with someone else. From a sweet, sexy, loving girl, she changed into a suspicious, sneaky old harridan. I soon got tired of that. Then I fell in love with Kim, and I found I just couldn't take any more of Laura's persistent questioning, so I moved out and into a rented flat on my own for a while to give myself a breathing space.

I seriously considered not marrying Kim because I really didn't want to hurt her. I told her all about myself, and also that while I loved her I still might get tempted from time to time. She said as long as I didn't fall in love with anyone it would be okay, but she'd rather not know about anyone I might sleep with on a casual basis. But it's just a bit of fun, something to relieve the boredom. I mean, I've never ever seen any of my women while I'm actually staying at home, that time has always been devoted exclusively to my wife. So I don't feel that I'm cheating them out of anything that's theirs. But when I'm away from home doing my job, that's *my* time, you see. I'm not seeing anyone on a regular basis at the moment, and I haven't in all the four years I've been married to Kim. But I have had lots of one-nighters.

Why do I do it? Well, like I said, it's only fun. I don't mean any harm. I just like a bit of excitement, a bit of variety. You know what it's like; just because you can afford steak all the time, you still don't lose your taste for pie and chips, do you?

There's more to adultery than meets the genitals

One cannot help wondering why men like Anthony, who experience this overwhelming need for variety and excitement in their lives, don't remain single. But, for most chronic adulterers, the issue underlying their propensity to stray is, in reality, far more complex than at first meets the eye, or, indeed, the genitals.

According to Caroline Buchanan, who wrote *Caught In The Act*, a fascinating account of infidelity from all three sides of the triangle, there are only two reasons why men stray; either there is a problem within the marriage itself, which may or may not have something to do with sex, or the root cause lies somewhere in the man's background. 'In most cases it can be related back to the family. Either the man is the son of a womanizer, or he's responding to generations of learned behaviour which has influenced him to believe that it is all right for men to indulge in extra-marital affairs, or he's reacting against his mother; i.e., he has a deep lack of trust in women because of a damaged relationship in his childhood.'

What Caroline Buchanan discovered during her own research was that many adulterous men often marry a woman who will collude with them. Some women collude consciously inasmuch as they turn a blind eye to their husbands' flings because it relieves the sexual pressure on themselves, whilst others, who profess to be shocked and devastated by the knowledge of their men's philandering, collude unconsciously by refusing to acknowledge anything is wrong until they're forced to. Which usually means when they're confronted with the actual evidence.

Of course, collusion of this nature is hardly a new

phenomenon. In her book, *Adultery – An Analysis of Love and Betrayal*, Annette Lawson divides adultery into three main types: Parallel, Traditional and Recreational.

Parallel adultery – an act of collusion?

'Parallel adultery,' Lawson writes, 'is usually known to the wife who may condone it by her silence even if she does not approve or enjoy it ... Sometimes the wife does approve and even enjoys her husband's adultery; it may leave her with greater freedom to lead her own adventurous life, or, perhaps, to ensure she is "bothered less" – an important way, at least in past times, to render herself less likely to bear another child, risking death with each birth.'

The history books are full of examples of Parallel Adultery. Take royalty, for example, for whom the keeping of mistresses was almost obligatory. Undoubtedly one of the most libidinous kings in British history was Charles II. In addition to his legion of long-term favourites (Nell Gwyn and Barbara Castlemaine were just two of these), Charles II was reputed to have bedded a cast of 'extras' that ran into thousands. And, like hundreds of other wives both before and after her, his Queen had no say in the matter.

More recently, the high profile professions of show business and politics have emerged as the ones in which a certain amount of blind-eye-turning on the part of wives and long-term girlfriends is most likely to take place. And for every 'famous' wife or girlfriend who would rather sever her relationship than condone her partner's flings – Priscilla Presley, Alana Hamilton Stewart (ex-wife of 'Rocking Rod') and Anjelica Huston, on-off girlfriend of Jack Nicholson for 17 years, are but three well known examples – there are two or three others who, in the face of yet another tawdry peccadillo made public, have been known to set their faces stonily to the wall and carry on regardless.

And who knows how many ordinary wives and partners are behaving in precisely the same way?

Who's got the power?

If Simon had been aware of these three categories of adultery, he probably would have assumed his own to belong either to the traditional or the recreational type. Certainly he freely confesses that, throughout the last 18 months of his two-year affair, he not only viewed it as 'a diversion; merely a private bit of fun on the side', but also a good deal of his kicks were derived from feeling that he must be a clever and ingenious fellow to be able to deceive his wife so easily. In reality, however, Simon's infidelity belonged in part to all three categories of unfaithfulness. For he discovered to his shock, when the final *dénouement* came, that his wife had not merely been aware of his affair all along, she'd been colluding with him all the time by allowing it to continue:

> For the first six months of my affair with Sonja, I was riddled with guilt. Every time I came home I felt sure my guilt was written all over my face. But the more you get away with cheating, the more relaxed you become about it. That's not to say you start taking stupid risks, or let your guard down at all, but you can't help taking it for granted that if you've got away with it so far, there's no reason it can't continue for as long as you want.
>
> Of course I reckoned without Sonja's determination to get me. She got one of her girlfriends to ring my wife, Maria, and tip her off. I guess she imagined if she forced the issue Maria would throw me out and she and I would then live happily ever after. But Maria told me she had known about Sonja almost from the beginning.
>
> I couldn't believe it. She wasn't even angry with me. In fact, she was more annoyed with Sonja for bringing the whole thing out into the open

between us. 'Why didn't you say something?' I asked. Do you know what she said? 'Because after the initial shock had worn off I assessed the situation and decided she wasn't enough of a threat.' She was right, of course, there's no way I would have left Maria and our three kids for Sonja, no matter how besotted I was. But how could Maria have been so sure?

You know how it made me feel? Like a little boy who had been caught with his hand in the cookie jar. There wasn't much point in continuing with Sonja after that. As her plans had obviously come to nothing, she couldn't see any mileage in continuing the affair. And there wasn't any fun in it for me, feeling as if I was only getting away with it because Maria *allowed* me to.

For many unfaithful men, the whole point of adultery is not so much sex with someone other than their wives, but the *frisson* they get from flirting with the dangerous and forbidden, and, of course, from injecting a little variety into their lives.

Once the glamour and allure of these two factors has been removed, however, the attraction often dies. As has been proven by the number of cases in which men leave their wives for their girlfriends, only to come running back as soon as they discover that inside their mistress lurks a woman remarkably like a 'wife'. After all, what man needs a new wife when he's already got a perfectly comfortable one at home?

In Simon's case, his wife had a better understanding of the likely root cause for his infidelity than he had himself. But it would be a mistake to assume that, since Maria was aware of the affair and, perceiving no threat in it allowed it to continue, no lasting damage has been done to this relationship.

Some couples have found to their surprise that, occasionally, there can be a positive side to an affair; but only when each partner is brave and honest enough to view their crisis as an opportunity to examine both themselves and their relationship, in order to discover wherein their true problems lie.

Unfortunately papering over the cracks, as Simon and Maria appear to have done, doesn't usually provide a long-term solution. Through courting excitement and danger, Simon was able briefly to fulfil a subconscious need to exercise power and omnipotence; both of which, according to many experts, are underlying causes for many episodes of adultery. In this particular case, however, the true power resided with Simon's wife who could so easily have dispelled his illusions at any time of her choice. In revealing this to Simon, Maria has merely reinforced the lack of self-esteem that motivated his infidelity in the first place. Sooner or later, Simon's twin emotions of shame and suppressed anger are likely to be overtaken by a need to redress the balance, and thereby regain the feeling of power and omnipotence he so obviously craves.

Traditional adultery – filling the gaps

Lawson's second category, Traditional Adultery, covers those relationships which, if revealed, definitely would be considered as a breach of the marriage. Those involved in this kind of liaison usually go to great lengths to keep the affair secret from their partner, though often they might admit a very close friend or relative into their confidence. Moreover, the underlying cause has less to do with a need for danger or risk-taking, and more to do with filling in any gaps that exist in the marriage and/or the need of the individual to bolster his sense of self-worth.

William's experience is a perfect example of this type of adultery. At the age of 49, William was passed over for promotion to the Board: a position his whole working life had been geared towards achieving. His children were both married, and his wife had returned to her former profession of teaching. William's disappointment coincided with his wife's promotion to Deputy Head Teacher, a job which not only entailed quite a bit of responsibility, but involved many extra hours of work, too:

Naturally I was pleased for Greta and proud of her, too. But the more involved she got with administration, the more neglected I began to feel. If she wasn't attending meetings at school in the evening, she was closeting herself away with her charts and books. She also started studying part-time for a degree in Sociology, and that means the occasional weekend away from home at special tutorials.

It felt as if, just as my life had started taking a downward turn, hers was shooting up and off the graph. I felt lonely, discontented, unappreciated, and, I suppose, there was a bit of resentment and self-pity mixed up in there too. I started sniping and bitching for no apparent reason, and though Greta normally has a lot of patience, I could see she was getting irritated.

One night she snapped: 'For goodness sake, William, I'm almost beginning to believe that when you say you're proud of having such an independent, articulate and intelligent wife, you really only want me to be those things when it suits you.'

Well, she was right, wasn't she? I didn't mind what she did when I wasn't around, but I wanted her attention to be all on me when I came home. I know I sound selfish, but that's the way it always had been when the girls were young and Greta stayed at home.

For my birthday, Greta bought me membership to a sports club. I'd always enjoyed tennis and squash, but I hadn't played in years. Instead of being pleased about it, though, I resented the implication that I needed to get into shape, and that Greta's only thought was to get me embroiled in something so that I would no longer be a nuisance to her. But I went along anyway. And after a couple of months I began to meet a whole new circle of people. I soon got asked to join both the tennis and squash teams, and for the first time in all our married life I went to social events without Greta.

You can imagine what happened, can't you? Before long I developed a relationship with a much younger girl. Of course she can't compare to Greta in any way ... except, that is, as far as their bodies go. Greta's had two children, she's 45, and though she's still beautiful to me, her body has gone to seed; whereas Carol, who is only 27, has a superb body. The funny thing is, although sex with Carol is good, there's something missing. I don't know whether it's the comfort I feel with Greta, or merely guilt getting in the way. But in another sense Carol makes me feel so special, I'm afraid I'm becoming addicted to her. She looks up to me, asks my advice, admires me and so obviously sees me as a suave, older, successful and knowledgeable businessman, it's a powerful and very heady combination.

It's been six months now. I don't think Greta has a clue, but the double life is driving me insane. I don't know how much longer I can cope with it. It's going to be hell at Christmas when the girls come to stay and I won't get to see Carol for the whole week. I just know something's got to give ... somewhere ... soon. But I don't know what. I love Greta, I can't give her up. But equally I can't bear to think about losing Carol. She's given me so much in such a short time. The truth is, I want them both. And if there was a way I could keep them both, then I would.

Half of me dreads the future, the other half just wishes something would happen now to resolve the whole situation. I've lost over a stone. I can't concentrate at work. Frankly, I'm experiencing hell ... and yet it's like being in heaven, too. For the first time in my life I feel totally and completely fulfilled, but it's taken two women to make me feel this way. I know I'm being utterly selfish, and that I'm playing a very dangerous game, but I just can't stop myself.

William's adultery is typical of many affairs that fall into the Traditional category. Though it's no excuse, many men are vulnerable to affairs at certain crisis points in their lives. Becoming a father and assuming a role of responsibility that they're often not as adequately prepared for as they think can be one such crisis point. Very often men feel additionally vulnerable at this time as, quite naturally, their wives are deeply involved with another human being and consequently have less time to devote to their husbands' needs. It has to be said, too, that because men aren't very good at dealing with, or even recognizing, their own emotions, they experience great difficulty in articulating their feelings, and, therefore, in eliciting the help and loving support that is so crucial at such a vulnerable time.

Birthdays with noughts at the end (30, 40, 50, 60 etc) are another landmark, with 40 often hitting particularly hard since that's the age at which men tend to evaluate their lives and career progress, pessimistically assuming that if they haven't attained their career goals by now, they'll be marked as a failure. Losing a parent, particularly their own father, is another such crisis point, because, so long as our parents are still living, we can avoid the thought of our own mortality.

If I were asked to make an assessment of William's dilemma, I'd be tempted to tell him that, though he might not recognize it now, if he could find a way to repair and rebuild his relationship with Greta, his yearning for Carol would disappear. Just because he's not getting all his emotional needs fulfilled at home right now doesn't necessarily mean that Greta is incapable of fulfilling them at all. Moreover, I'd hazard a guess that, with professional help of some kind, William would soon realize that most of his problems have very little to do with his wife, and a great deal to do with his own current image of himself as a man.

Recreational adultery – a bit of fun on the side

The third type of adultery, that which Lawson terms Recreational, is more concerned with satisfying the individual's desire to seek out pleasure for the sheer sake of it, to play and to have fun. People who commit this type of adultery, Lawson maintains, not only seek to avoid or sidestep the moral dilemmas involved, but also are more likely to favour further extending the boundaries of play by seeking to introduce other parties into the game, as with threesomes, wife-swapping, and group sex. What marks this type of adultery as being different from the other two kinds is that here the partner is often involved and not excluded. Not surprisingly, men are far more likely to express a desire for Recreational Adultery than women.

How common is infidelity? Far more common than many adulterers would care to admit. Or, for that matter, than many cheated partners would care to acknowledge. It has been estimated that as many as 75 per cent of men will have been unfaithful to their partners by the time they reach the age of 55.

Author and Agony Aunt Deirdre Sanders once reported that, according to a survey she conducted involving 5000 men, two out of three husbands who confessed to their own infidelity admitted to having had between one and three affairs, with the top two attractions being phrased thus: 'Affairs are more interesting than marriage, and/or they simply provide extra, although not necessarily better, sex.'

[62 per cent of unfaithful husbands in her survey had had affairs which lasted under one year, whilst one third described theirs as being 'extremely short-lived', i.e., one-night or even one-day-stands. 20 per cent had experienced affairs which had lasted between one and four years, 8 per cent between five and ten years, and 2 per cent had continued for more than ten years!]

Of course, not all men go around with one eye firmly fixed on the door of opportunity. But when opportunity confronts *them* (and it can do with alarming frequency), the ones who are least likely to resist the temptation are either those whose marriages contain unresolved problems or conflicts, or those whose past history has provided them with a role model for this behaviour.

'Some men', says Caroline Buchanan, 'have an innate lack of trust or a desperate fear of intimacy and closeness. Having flings or affairs is a way of putting emotional distance between themselves and their partners. Others fear change; for them flings are a means of not having to confront or resolve what is wrong with the marriage or themselves. The danger lies in thinking that you can keep an affair away from and not threatening to the marriage.'

There's no such thing as a harmless fling

Journalist Jan Etherington, writing in *New Woman* magazine last year, stated that there is no such thing as a harmless fling. 'Having an affair is the most calculated piece of deception and the worst example of bad manners that one person can show to another,' said Etherington scathingly. Moreover, excuses of the 'it just happened' variety merely compound the deception because, as Etherington so rightly pointed out: 'It never just happens. It is not possible that you "just happen" to share someone else's bed and body without ever having the opportunity to say, "Stop. This has gone too far," unless it is genuinely against your will – and that is not an affair.'

Whether we are male or female, when it comes to adultery human nature decrees there can be no fence-sitting. Regardless of whether we're male or female, which side of the fence we sit on entirely depends upon whether we are the one doing the cheating, or the one being cheated on. If we're the former, we will naturally seek a way to expiate our guilt and justify our actions by hanging a label on them. 'This thing is bigger than both of us,' we might claim dramatically, implying that love is a force so powerful, no mere mortal could possibly resist it. Alternatively, we might respond to our partner's rage at our betrayal by attacking to defend; blaming *their* real or perceived inadequacies for having driven *us* into another person's arms. We might even profess to having been momentarily bewitched, like Titania in *A Midsummer Night's Dream*, whose eyes were brushed with pansy juice. But, however we choose to defend ourselves, the one thing we never will be honest enough to admit is that *we simply felt like doing it*. And for the betrayed no amount of excuses, pleas for forgiveness or vitriolic attempts to shift the blame on to them will ease the pain and devastating humiliation of knowing that, for whatever reason, a partner *wanted* to share themselves, their time, their thoughts, and their body with someone else.

Of course I need hardly add that *every* man I quizzed (both the faithful and the unfaithful) deplored the idea of having the tables turned on them. 'It's different for us,' said Rick, a 33-year-old welder who admitted to having had two short extra-marital excursions and several one-night-stands. 'It's sort of expected, in a way. We're only human, after all. But women aren't supposed to do it.'

Why not? Are we not human, too? 'Well … it's just that … well, women just aren't … I mean they just don't, do they?'

And if all men believe *that*, all I can say is they've got a big shock coming to them when they read chapter 5!

Adultery changes a relationship for ever

'Adultery stinks!' said Irene, who has been the victim of it more than once in her life. 'It's the worst thing any man can do to someone he's supposed to love. And no matter how much you love your partner, or how hard you fight not to let it spoil things, in the end it always does. You might say you forgive him, but you never, ever forget.

And that knowledge is like a cancer eating away inside you; it eats your trust, and consumes your faith. Eventually you become withered and stunted. Part of you withdraws into a safe little hidey-hole within yourself, and life can never be the same again. *You* are never the same again.'

Irene should know. As I said, it's happened to her more than once. On the first occasion, her husband had an affair with her best friend. But, despite doing all the right things to save their marriage, like severing the relationship, moving home and seeking marital therapy together, Irene found it impossible to regain her trust and faith in him. The second incidence occurred when Irene was living with her boyfriend of four years:

> I couldn't allow myself to totally trust him. I tried hard, and I told him that I did, but something made me hold a little bit back. But I did allow myself to hope. When I discovered he'd had a drunken one-night-stand on a stag night, I went to pieces. He begged me to stay with him, saying he wasn't like my ex-husband, and that it had only happened because he'd been so plastered. But I couldn't do it. I just couldn't take that risk again. I wanted to, I really did. But I knew that I'd never be able to let him forget it, and sooner or later, I'd let it come between us. Once it's there, you see, you can't ever wipe it out. I didn't want to face years of misery, always wondering, never being totally sure. And I didn't want to put him through that either. So I just cut it dead there and then and walked out of his life.'

Revenge is sweet – but caution is safer

When faced with their husbands' infidelity, wives have been known to devise the most ingenious ways of expressing their fury by retaliating in a manner which they know is guaranteed to hurt the most. One woman I know ran up a five-figure bill on her husband's American Express card. Another systematically cut every single one of her man's very expensive designer suits, shirts and ties into such tiny little pieces they resembled confetti by the time she was finished. A third became so enraged she bundled her husband's treasured – and valuable – stamp collection into a black plastic sack and deposited it at a local jumble sale. For her, though revenge (she said) was exceedingly sweet, it was also decidedly brief – his feeling of contrition soon evaporated and now war has been publicly declared in one of the dirtiest, bitterest, most acrimonious divorces it has ever been their friends' good fortune to witness.

Generally speaking, however, whilst every woman can recognize the kind of intense emotion that fuels such furious displays, and some might even applaud the fearlessness of those who indulge in them, most women will keep the true extent of their rage under wraps so long as there might be a chance of saving the relationship. Of course that doesn't prevent them from exercising their imaginations by conjuring up diabolical fantasies of revenge (boiling him in oil, permanently and painfully separating him from his prized appendage, having a retaliatory fling, were just some of the milder punishments many of my interviewees confessed to having mentally toyed with), but generally that's as far as they're prepared to go. Because, no matter what their man has done, nor how badly he might have behaved, three very important considerations will hold them back:

- First, regardless of what a faithless rat they now recognize him to be, he's still *their* rat, and they (probably) still love him.

- Second, and especially if they have children, they've not only invested a considerable amount of emotional currency in him, there's a significant financial investment at stake, too.

- And third (and possibly most important of all), somewhere inside their heads a little voice is responding to a lifetime of cultural conditioning by whispering the classic words: 'Are you *really* sure that somehow, in some way, you're *not to blame?*'

'Adultery livens up life at home'

Of all the excuses men use to justify adultery, this is undoubtedly the one that irritates – and insults – women the most. Yet Julian, a 36-year-old businessman and entrepreneur, claims this is the *only* reason he strays outside of his ten-year, live-in relationship:

> None of the usual reasons, like neglect or lack of sex, apply. I just do it because I enjoy it. I love my girlfriend, I can't imagine ever wanting to commit myself to anyone else. But, after ten years, sex does get boring. Once that magic has gone, no matter how good or satisfying it is, and no matter how often you plan little treats or surprises in an attempt to recapture it, it's never the same as it was in the beginning. Once your partner becomes a known quantity, passion diminishes.

Does Julian ever feel any guilt or sense of betrayal?

> Never. You see, although I know she would never accept this, I actually do believe that having other women from time to time injects new life into my existing relationship. It makes me appreciate my girlfriend more. If I didn't have this outlet, I know from previous experience that eventually I would become restless, bored, and my sex drive would decline. I wouldn't stop loving her, or wanting to stay with her, but it definitely would spoil things.

In fact there is some evidence to suggest that, from a purely biological point of view, novelty and variety do indeed provide a boost to a male's flagging libido.

Certainly this has been found to apply with male rats (who, according to many women, are only one step away from being related to the human variety, anyway), as well as monkeys, in a number of experiments which revealed that the males of these species are far more attracted to the smell of new females than ones with whom they have recently mated.

Likewise there is also some biological evidence to suggest that men like Julian and Anthony might not be quite so much in control of their actions as they believe, as it's possible they could be responding to an addiction they're not even aware they have.

Adrenalin, the fight or flight hormone which is produced by the adrenal glands at times of extreme stress, excitement or danger, is known to be highly addictive (this has been confirmed with athletes and joggers who say they're hooked on the phenomenon known as 'runner's high'). When they're secreting adrenalin the adrenal glands also release cortisone which, when prescribed medicinally, has the side-effect of producing an increased sex drive and feelings verging on wild euphoria.

Furthermore, it has now been proven that there is a link between men who have high sex drives and those who are particularly successful, powerful, have a strong driving ambition or appear to be high achievers. The key is to be found in the level of the male hormone testosterone. For testosterone is not only responsible for making men male, it also governs their libidos and their aggressive streaks. Hence, when a man experiences a sense of accomplishment or achievement, whether it stems from scoring a winning goal or pulling off a major business deal, testosterone levels in his bloodstream will rise and so also could his desire for sex.

What happens biologically is that when a man faces danger, stress, threat or any other potentially tense situation, adrenalin floods into his bloodstream to provide him with the impetus for fight or flight. If the stressful situation is both short-lived and one from which he emerges victorious, adrenalin is then replaced by the hormone noradrenalin, which has been found to have an effect similar to a spark plug in that it stimulates the brain's pleasure centre and sparks off the production of testosterone. The more dangerous, competitive and frightening the situation, the more adrenalin, noradrenalin and testosterone a man will produce.

Phenylethylamine (PEA) is a chemical produced in the brain that has exactly the same effect on us as amphetamines. When we fall in love or even when we simply receive approval, it has been found that the production of this chemical is greatly increased. This could provide another explanation for the fact that an abundance of approval and love are such vital factors to our sense of happiness, emotional security and well-being. Therefore, it's logical to assume that, with some men (and women, too, of course, but we'll concentrate upon them more fully in the next chapter), a propensity towards infidelity might possibly be explained as being nothing more nor less than a predictable outcome of an internal chemical chain reaction. In other words, if a man's partner isn't supplying sufficient emotional security and approval, he'll be driven to seeking some form of 'topping up' from elsewhere.

But, as Zelda West-Meads of *Relate* (formerly the British Marriage Guidance Council) has said in the past, pointing to the animal kingdom, and the way in which males of other species are biologically programmed to behave, just isn't a good enough excuse any more. After all, human beings are *supposed* to be intelligent, rational and civilized. Likewise it simply isn't good enough for men to use their wives' or girlfriends' inadequacies as an excuse for their own failings. 'I'm not knocking religion,' said Zelda, 'but all we hear is that Eve was to blame for giving Adam the apple. No one blames Adam for *eating it*.'

In the final analysis, no amount of scientific or biological evidence will ever justify, excuse or explain away the sheer havoc, hurt and terrible damage that infidelity can wreak upon a couple's relationship. And whilst it might be true that a high proportion of marriages do survive a husband's infidelity (mainly, I have to say, due to the wives' heroic efforts to keep the family together), no matter how seamlessly the cracks appear to be papered over, there *always* will be one unanswerable question hovering silently – and accusingly – in the background of a woman's mind: *Why didn't you simply say no?*

On the other hand, it's only fair to say that unfaithful men aren't solely and totally to blame. For as Caroline Buchanan says: 'It's very dangerous to shift the blame totally onto another person. Whatever your own position in the affair, everyone must take their share of the responsibility for what is going on. And though in many cases a wronged wife might only be five per cent or even one per cent to blame, if *both parties* aren't brave enough to work out together why the infidelity occurred, they never will be able to solve their problems.'

No matter which way you look at it, adultery *is* the ultimate act of betrayal, although as I said earlier, it is *possible* that, with courage, it can result in two people developing a better understanding of themselves, and of each other. Without that kind of courage and commitment to the relationship, however, it's undoubtedly the most destructive act a man can commit.

Yet so long as women refuse to confront the true underlying causes for their men's infidelity, their men will go on lying, cheating and deceiving them. Similarly, so long as men refuse to acknowledge, confront and learn to deal with the *true* underlying cause for their own philandering, not only will they *never* be capable of finding true happiness in any relationship with the opposite sex, but also they'll never convince women of their claim to be the stronger, more superior sex.

And if that's not enough to convince men of the demerits of adultery, perhaps they should try on this sobering thought for size: men are three and a half times more likely to suffer a heart attack during sex with a mistress than a wife!

5

Wives and Other Lovers?

TO HEAR WOMEN talk about adultery, you'd think it was something peculiarly exclusive to men. And yet, according to the results of one particular survey which was conducted amongst 600 white, middle-class women, it was estimated that 40 per cent of women under the age of 33 will have had an affair within four years of marriage, compared with only 25 per cent of their husbands.

Obviously the behaviour and attitudes of 600 women of a particular socio-economic group can hardly be said to mirror the likely behaviour of *all* women. But when these results are added to those of several other surveys, a clear and startlingly radical behavioural trend appears to be emerging: women in the 90s are having *more* affairs, whereas men are having fewer.

In *Adultery – An Analysis of Love and Betrayal*, author Annette Lawson writes: 'The idea that sex might be enjoyed purely for pleasure has permitted women as well as men to claim that sexual relationships can be enjoyed separately from profound (intimate) love and from any durable commitment. And women, too, have begun more often to use another argument stressing similarity rather than difference between the sexes: women, like men, have sexual needs to be satisfied separately from any emotions they may have.'

Lawson goes on to explain further that as it is women's

sexual behaviour which has changed so much in recent years (not men's), not only are they now having sex with more partners, but also it's possible that they're having at least as many, if not more, adulterous affairs than men. On the other hand, it's entirely feasible that women aren't necessarily committing adultery any more than they were before; they may simply feel much freer to *talk* about their marital indiscretions now.

What makes a woman unfaithful?

What makes a woman unfaithful to her man? Is it because of emotional deprivation, as we have been led to believe? Or is this apparently increasing tendency merely a reflection of women's changing status in society? After all, improved contraceptive methods have virtually eradicated the biggest fear that has traditionally kept women monogamous: the fear of unwanted pregnancy and, consequently, the fear of foisting another man's offspring on their husbands.

Moreover, the rise in the numbers of working wives has meant that women are not only less financially dependent on their husbands than previous generations, but they also have greater opportunities both in terms of the number of men with whom they come into contact and the amount of freedom they have outside of their family life.

Judy has had two affairs during her six-year marriage to Terry. The first lasted for six months, the second is still continuing after two years. Why does she do it?

> Because it's exciting. Don't get me wrong, sex with Terry is great ... when he can summon up the energy, which only seems to be at weekends now. But I'm not really doing it for the sex. It's for the thrill of being courted, being treated as if I'm a girlfriend again. Terry works so hard, I don't get to see much of him. I know his career means a great deal to him, and that I benefit from it in many

material ways, so I certainly wouldn't want to stand in his way or start sounding off like a whingeing wife. But I do get lonely when he's working late or he has to go abroad on business.

But doesn't Judy find it difficult to juggle an affair, a job, a husband and a home? And what about her conscience? After all, women are supposed to be the irrational, illogical sex, the ones who are assumed to be less adept at keeping their emotions on a tight rein.

My first affair was difficult. I felt very guilty and I was always worried that I'd give the game away. To be honest, that was the reason I ended it. Well, that and the fact that my lover got too involved and started pushing for more.

But the affair I'm having now hasn't been a problem at all. Maybe that's because Jack is married, too. I don't know whether what I feel for Jack is love or some sort of very deep bond of friendship. It's hard to define. He makes me feel good about myself in a way that Terry doesn't. I know Terry adores me, but after six years of marriage I suppose it's natural that you make less of an effort and start taking your partner for granted. He seems to forget that I need conversation, I need to feel significant as a person in my own right, and not just as good old reliable Judy who can always be counted on not to nag, to understand and to accept that Terry's needs come first. I feel like an extension of Terry, as if by marrying him I've somehow lost my own identity.

And yet when I am at work, I feel totally different. I'm me, a person who is seen as efficient, clever, intelligent, someone who has some value. I work with Jack and because he's always seen me in that light it's easy for him to recognize the qualities in me that Terry's forgotten exist.

And what would Judy do if Terry discovered her affair with Jack?

He won't. I'm too clever for that. I cover my tracks
so well he'll never know. And if Jack starts getting
so deeply involved he becomes a threat to my
marriage, I'll finish it. I know it sounds rather cold
and selfish of me, but I do love Terry and I intend
to remain married to him. All I'm doing is relieving
some of the pressure which might otherwise have
a detrimental effect on my marriage.

What's interesting about Judy's rationale is how
remarkably similar it is to a man's. But then so is Sally's.

Sally and George recently celebrated their silver
wedding anniversary. To their family and friends they're
that rare combination: a perfectly suited and happily
married couple, an assessment Sally herself would not
take issue with. And yet Sally has been conducting a
liaison with Reg for eighteen years!

It started when my children were small. I was
bored with being at home all day and I suppose I
used to take it out on George when he came home.
To be honest, I think I begrudged him the
excitement of having something to look forward to
each day. Of course I loved my kids, but they're
hardly what you'd call a mental challenge, are
they?

I met Reg at the school gates. He worked nights,
his wife worked days, so he would collect the kids
from school in the afternoon. We got chatting, as
one tends to do, and when my son became friendly
with his, I thought it might be a nice idea to invite
Reg and his boy back to our house for tea.

George has a managerial job. Reg works in a
factory. In every conceivable way they're streets
apart. But I liked Reg, he made me laugh.
Gradually, over a period of about nine months, one
thing slowly led to another, and soon Reg was
giving up his sleep to come round in the morning
when the kids were at school.

Although we don't see each other quite as often

as we used to – I have a job for one thing – Reg and
I meet when we can. Sometimes we'll make love, if
we have somewhere safe to go and we both feel
like it, but mostly we just sit and talk. I suppose
you could say I love him but I'm not in love with
him. Never was, in fact. He just made me feel good
about myself, stopped my mind from vegetating,
and gave me something extra at a time when I
needed it. I think he feels the same way about me.
Does George know? Good heavens, no! Neither
does Reg's wife. I think my daughter suspects, but
she seems to find it amusing. She sometimes
comes shopping with me on a Saturday morning,
which is when I usually meet Reg in a coffee bar.
Obviously she remembers him from school, but
I've told her we're just friends and she seems to
accept that as being perfectly natural. She jokes
about Reg being my lover, and she always gives
me a knowing kind of look, but she's never ever
told her father about my meetings with Reg, so I
suppose she must think something's going on.

What's nice about my relationship with Reg is
that neither of us wants more than we have. It's
comfortable, it's affectionate, we trust each other
implicitly, and neither of us feels it detracts in any
way from what we have with our partners. The
only way I can describe it is to compare it to that
Alan Alda film, *Same Time Next Year*, in which a
couple met for one weekend every year for about
30 years. The only difference is Reg and I meet
once a week or so.

When it comes to the likely causes for adultery, experts
seem to agree that men are more likely to be unfaithful
due to boredom, a need for variety or sexual deprivation,
whereas women tend to be unfaithful when they're
feeling emotionally neglected.

When Annette Lawson asked her subjects what were
the benefits of adultery, the words 'sexual fulfilment' were
the most commonly mentioned ones. However, one

important distinction emerged between the genders: while men rated 'sexual fulfilment' top of their list of benefits, and also considerably higher than the second most important feeling they derived from their affairs, women rated it as being equally as important as 'friendship' and the feeling of 'being loved'.

When men use sexual boredom as an excuse for philandering, no one seems to be particularly shocked or surprised. It's almost as if there's an absurd secret consensus which allows that wives who fail to keep sex exciting for their husbands deserve all they get. And yet the same allowances still do not seem to be offered to wives who are sexually bored or deprived. Which rather seems to imply that, despite the sexual revolution, society still hasn't quite shaken off the notion that, for men, sex is a perk, whilst for women, it's still seen as a duty.

Women get bored too

Sheer boredom and/or a need for excitement precipitates far more women into affairs than is generally assumed.

During my own research, I spoke to 40 or so women who either had been or were being unfaithful to their partners. Of these, 18 quoted boredom and/or 'a need for excitement' as the spur, six said they had done it for revenge, whilst 14 described 'a need for some form of emotional fulfilment' as the lure. Only the remaining three or four used the word 'love' as their justification for betraying their marriage vows. What I found particularly enlightening, however, was the knowledge that, regardless of why they had commenced the affair in the first place, no less than nine of my interviewees had been successfully juggling their affairs and their marriages for more than ten years! And Sally's affair with Reg was by no means the longest-surviving.

Gilda is a 54-year-old manager of a nursing home for the elderly. Her relationship with Cyril has not only been going on for 23 years, but has actually survived the death of Gilda's first husband and a subsequent marriage to her late husband's brother. What's even more remarkable about Gilda's experience is that her lover has never been married himself, which in itself poses some very interesting questions, such as why didn't Cyril and Gilda take the opportunity to legalize their union when Gilda's husband died? And how did Cyril feel when, after only 18 months of widowhood, Gilda married another man?

'Oh well, we did discuss the possibility,' said Gilda, surprisingly matter-of-factly, 'but, to be perfectly blunt, we both enjoyed it the way it was. Cyril's not what you would call a domesticated man, he's far too busy running his companies to want to be bothered with what he refers to as "life's petty little details". So we decided to leave things as they were.'

But wasn't Cyril jealous when Gilda married Robin? I asked, intrigued. Didn't he feel in the least bit betrayed? Quite frankly, Gilda's apparently genuine insouciance about her very strange situation was a revelation to me. And what about Robin? After all, it's one thing to cheat on your husband after some years of marriage, but to be cheating on your intended both before *and* after the wedding ... well, it does seem rather unusual, doesn't it?

'Why?' said Gilda. 'Where does it say that you can't love three men? I loved my first husband, Dennis, but I've always loved Cyril, too. And I've always been attracted to Robin. He's kind, thoughtful, loving, etc. In fact he's probably a better husband than Dennis was, and he's certainly a better one than Cyril could ever be.'

So why didn't Gilda do the decent thing and renounce Cyril when she married Robin? 'Because I didn't want to,' she answered simply. 'Why shouldn't I have them both? Robin's happy with me, far happier than he was with his first wife. And what he doesn't know can't hurt him, can it? Besides, I don't see that I'm depriving him of anything that's rightfully his. He's got all of me that he needs and wants. And I've got all of him that I need and want. If Cyril had been a different kind of man, one who could

have settled for the cosy companionship of marriage, I'd
have married him. But he's not, so it wasn't an option –
and neither was I going to give him up. He's mine, he's
always been mine, and I certainly wasn't going to give
someone else the opportunity to have him. As far as I'm
concerned it's quite simple: I've loved three men in my
life, two of whom I still love. I can't say which one I have
loved or do love the most, because they're all different.
I've never been forced into the position of having to
choose, and it's highly unlikely I ever will. Life's far too
short to worry about "what ifs".'

When we talk about the differences between men and
women we can only ever generalize. Obviously there are
women who frequently do have affairs with all the casual
abandon that is generally considered to be a male trait.
Equally there are women who say that they would never
have an affair under any circumstances whatsoever.

Female adultery, however, is still considered (generally)
to be a far more heinous crime – certainly by men and,
possibly, still by some women. But women have always
possessed the potential to be as unfaithful as men; the
only difference now is that they have also attained a
measure of the same freedom as men. And whilst
sociologists might argue that the decline in female sexual
morality is a present-day phenomenon – a legacy
bequeathed solely by female liberation, a more permissive
society and the Pill – it's difficult to make the argument
stick.

Take the Second World War, for instance. Granted,
women did have greater social freedom (and, therefore,
the opportunity) during that period. How could they not
when, with most of the able-bodied male population away
fighting for King and country, women were the only ones
left to keep industry and the war machine from grinding
to a halt? But even allowing for the removal of these two
prohibitive factors, women still had to contend with the
most major one of all: the fear of unwanted pregnancy.
Yet, according to all the reports and statistics compiled

around that time, vast numbers of women are known to have thrown all caution to the winds. This suggests that, by and large, women do have the *potential* to be every bit as sexually permissive as men but – and this is where the essential dichotomy lies – *their motivation for doing so invariably arises out of a vastly different set of needs*.

And this is where we find that there is a fascinating paradox to be explored. The differences between the genders can be broken down into three areas: physical, mental and temperamental. Measured against each other we find that, on the physical level, the characteristics associated with the male gender are greater size, strength and the capacity for short-term energy output, whereas the female has a greater capacity for physical endurance.

On the mental level, men have better spatial and mathematical skills. This ability to perceive and judge space and distance more accurately than women is, scientists now believe, the main reason why men tend to be better at technical projects such as architecture, and also why they make better drivers. On the other hand, women have better verbal and social skills and they're more empathetic than men. Temperamentally, the characteristics associated with men include dominance, rank-related aggression (the preoccupation with status rearing its ugly head again), independence, psychopathy, sensation-seeking, sexual initiation and exploration, whilst those associated with women include submission, defensive aggression, attachment/nurturance, anxiety, security-seeking, sexual selectivity and relationship-seeking.

[Source: Symons, 1979; Seward and Seward, 1980; Ellis, 1986.]

Men and women are different. Our bodies are different, our abilities are different, we have different strengths and weaknesses, even our thought processes – and our brains themselves – are different.

The right hemisphere of the male brain develops earlier than that of the female; the female's left hemisphere develops earlier than the male's. The left hemisphere governs verbal, language and reading skills, and it processes information in a logical, step-by-step manner. The right brain governs spatial abilities and processes information, not step-by-step, but in pattern form.

However, whilst it's certainly true to say that the male brain is more specialized than the female's, and men use the right hemisphere of their brain more efficiently than women do (men use the right brain for dealing with spatial problems and the left for verbal problems), many of the abilities governed by the right side of a woman's brain are also duplicated in the left. And this is what gives women two very important advantages: their ability to employ both sides of their brain not only makes them far more perceptive about people, they're also far better at intuitively deciphering the differences between what people say and what they actually mean, and at reading all the subtle nuances of behaviour which can reveal a person's true feelings. (Another advantage is that this also apparently makes them less vulnerable to accidents than men – but that's another story.) So now we know why women not only are so very good at picking up on another woman's attraction to their man, but also where their apparently uncanny ability to 'know intuitively' when their man is harbouring thoughts of an illicit affair comes from.

When it comes to sex and procreation, women are inclined to believe that the biological scales are weighted in favour of men. Theoretically, one male could fertilize literally hundreds of women in the course of a year, whereas each female is only capable of being fertilized on average once a year, and only for a limited number of years. On the face of it, therefore, it's not unreasonable for women to assume that men have all the sexual advantages: because they have been biologically endowed with the inclination and the wherewithal to indulge in sex as often as possible with as many partners as possible, sexual selectivity doesn't even figure in their mating equation.

But the sexual scales aren't quite as unevenly balanced as women believe. For their own biological programming has provided them with one very weighty advantage: their need to bond with, nurture and ensure the survival of their offspring is so powerful that they are driven to be *extremely* selective about whom they choose to mate with.

Consequently, whilst men might appear to be eager and willing to indulge in sexual activity whenever, wherever, and with whomever they choose to do so, the actual decision about *whether* they do so *rests entirely with the woman*. Which means that, when it comes to sex, in the natural order of things it is the woman – not the man – who occupies the driving seat every time.

To take this argument – and the foregoing evidence – one stage further, I would go so far as to suggest that, despite the twin primary factors of emotional make-up and biological programming which incline women towards sexual monogamy, once circumstance propels a woman beyond these boundaries, she will actually cope with all its practical aspects far better than any man ever could. Or to put it another way, whilst a woman may think longer and harder about all the various implications of having an affair, once her mind has been made up, she'll plan it better, conduct it more efficiently, and become both more adept at the art of compartmentalizing her emotions and feelings about it, and at keeping it separate from the rest of her life.

Caroline Buchanan, author of *Caught In The Act*, confirmed this belief when she said: 'There are a lot of women who can have an affair and not only don't want it to affect their marriage, but *won't let it*'.

What's more, I suspect that men have long been aware (albeit on an unconscious level) that, given enough reason and the right circumstances, women's innate facility to be ruthlessly practical far outstrips any ability they might fancy themselves as possessing in this area. And because men are *not* particularly adept at sensing the subtle nuances that so easily could give the lie to what women say and do, this makes them far more emotionally fragile and susceptible to love (they'll hang the label 'love' on all sorts of feelings that are anything but), and also *far more susceptible to being deceived*.

Hell hath no fury like a man betrayed

Whilst men might well have reason to believe that there's more than a grain of truth in the old adage, 'Hell hath no fury like a woman scorned', any woman who's ever been caught out in an affair would counter that cliche by equally asserting that there's no more terrifying sight than a man who's been cuckolded.

Women, it has to be said, are far more likely to forgive, or at the very least come to terms with, their husbands' infidelity than the other way around. True, a woman will undoubtedly express shock, rage and fury on discovering that her husband has been lavishing time, money and love (which she, quite naturally, sees as belonging to her) on another woman. But more often than not she will forgive him. She may never forget, and she may well make sure that *he* never forgets his betrayal either, but ultimately a woman will fight tooth and nail to keep her marriage together.

Conversely, when a man discovers that his wife has been unfaithful to him his sense of outrage, horror and indignation is likely to be so severe, his sense of betrayal so immense, that physical violence will often result. Moreover, unlike a woman, a man will rarely ever be moved either to forgive or to forget. Why? Because, in addition to all the usual emotional and psychological effects one might expect all betrayed partners (men as well as women) to experience, there is another facet to adultery which, apparently, applies solely and uniquely to betrayed men: their *reputations*.

According to the evidence garnered by Annette Lawson, one of the reasons for men's apparent inability to come to terms with their wives' adultery is the threat it poses to their reputation. At the same time, however, Lawson found that adulterous men hardly ever experience any concern for the effects their own infidelity might have on the reputations of their wives. Which is precisely the kind of inequity that gives fuel to many a feminist argument and offends many a wife's sense of injustice.

As unfair as this might appear to be, the fact is men have had literally hundreds of years of cultural conditioning to influence the way in which they both experience and relate to a wife's infidelity. And no matter how intelligent, rational or progressive a man might appear to be, the moment he perceives his ego, status and reputation to be under threat, it's inevitable that he will instinctively revert to uttering the same primeval howl of pain that has emanated from the egos of all cuckolded men throughout history.

For, sadly, no matter how unjust it may be, when a woman is unfaithful to a man, she's not only guilty of betraying his love, she's also guilty of annihilating every single aspect of his nature that, to him, confirms his masculinity. But the female has always instinctively understood that the task of keeper of the flame (and stoker of the male ego) is hers alone, and that's why so many women have learned to develop, hone and perfect their innate ability to camouflage the aspects of themselves that threaten the male ego, and why so few women are ever foolish enough to confess. Unless, of course, they consciously (or even unconsciously) have an ulterior motive for doing so.

Can monogamy work?

Whilst the evidence and case histories outlined in this and the preceding chapter might dishearten and depress many people who regard monogamy as being an essential component of a happy relationship, the one thing we can take comfort from is the knowledge that it isn't quite the impossible ideal that many of us believe it to be.

The fact that fewer men appear to be committing adultery today compared with 30 years or so ago is one hopeful sign. So, too, is the fact that women and men nowadays are, on the whole, far more interested in gaining knowledge about what makes the opposite sex tick. The more we know about each other, and the more we understand each other, the better able we will be to put right the things that often go so disastrously wrong in our relationships. Most experts agree that, discounting those cases of adultery which stem from the need to find specific kinds of sexual activity which are denied by the partner, and those whose adultery masks a deep-rooted psychological problem, the majority of men and women become susceptible to straying only when certain fundamental emotionally derived needs are not being met.

For example, one of the most interesting and enlightening aspects that emerged from Annette Lawson's massive research into the subject of adultery highlighted the fact that, in virtually every single case, the prime benefit adulterers gain from their illicit affairs is a feeling of 'being alive'. In other words, it isn't necessarily sex which is the prime motivating factor, it's the excitement that comes from feeling appreciated, from being lifted outside and above the normal humdrum routine of everyday life, and of being able to feel that one is attractive, unique and significant; three things which invariably are the first to suffer under the weight of our daily routines. After all, let's not forget that one of the main goals of sex is orgasm, and if that were all that was required, there are very few individuals who cannot take care of that for themselves. Not only would it be a lot safer and far less of a risk on all counts, it's guaranteed to do the job with the minimum of fuss or potential embarrassment.

Sex itself, then, is not so much a cause for adultery, rather it's a secondary factor to and the by-product of a fundamental urge to fulfil a wholly selfish need to recreate within ourselves that little spark of excitement that makes us truly know we are gloriously, vibrantly *alive*. And that is something that each man and woman in a relationship has the unique ability to create for themselves and their partner.

What women need to understand is that excitement, novelty, and variety are as vital to a man's sexual appetite as food is to his life, and that appreciation, admiration and all the other little signs that make him aware he is valued and important to his woman are equally vital to his sense of emotional well-being and self-esteem.

Likewise, men must learn that the key to a woman's heart (and her unswerving loyalty and devotion) is to take care of her emotional needs, and this can only be achieved if he is prepared to share his thoughts with her, to talk to her in a way that makes her know her opinions are valued, to show appreciation for all the considerable efforts she makes to keep his home-life running smoothly, to be interested in what she has to say (no matter how boring or trivial it might sound to him), and, above all, to make her *truly* feel that she is loved, admired, protected, and cared for.

None of these things is impossible to achieve. In fact, they're remarkably easy to achieve. All it takes is a modicum of unselfish thought, a little attention to detail, and a great deal of tolerance.

6

Men's Secret Fears

'THERE'S ONLY ONE thing men fear, and that's not being able to get it up,' scoffed Vikki, a 27-year-old marketing executive who's become so battle-scarred and war-weary that cynicism flows like a waterfall from her tongue.

Surprisingly (or perhaps not so surprisingly, given that, as so few men confide their innermost fears, all women have to go on is their own, and other women's, experiences with men, and the stereotypical images of men that society fosters in them), the majority of women I interviewed tended to agree that, if men do have secret fears (and many women doubted that they had), then they probably would be tied up with sex in one way or another.

They were wrong. That's not to say, of course, that men don't worry about sex; they worry a great deal about impotence, premature ejaculation, and not being 'big enough' or 'good enough' in bed (more of which later). But they also worry about many other aspects of themselves, too.

It might surprise women to learn this (and doubtless it will be the cause of some shock to men, too), but men are born insecure. That statement is neither my own, nor an original one. Rather, it's simply a conclusion that many psychologists, anthropologists, sociologists and other experts on human nature have reached as a result of extensive research.

Dr Joyce Brothers explains this as being directly traceable to what she terms the Eve Principle: that 'every embryo would be born a female unless a number of connections were made at exactly the right moment'. By which, of course, she means that male insecurity begins in the womb.

Dr Walter J Ong, a professor of Humanities in Psychiatry at St Louis University, expanded on this theory in Dr Brother's book, *What Every Woman Should Know About Men*, when he described it thus:

> The embryo has to fight to be masculine. He is conceived in an environment in which he is totally dependent, yet which is partly hostile because it is feminine. The male embryo has to start quickly secreting his own male hormones. In order to be a man, he must in the beginning have his life dominated by a woman. And he spends the rest of his life proving himself – asserting the masculinity he fought so hard for at the outset. Because of this, males are always ready to fight. Contest is the pattern of their lives. It is different for the female. The female does not have to battle to assert her femininity. That is why females are fundamentally stable.

To say that men are fundamentally insecure might seem to be an odd statement, particularly when you take into consideration the fact that, historically, it always has been, and very largely still is, a man's world. Or the fact that men always have considered themselves to be the superior sex, the ones to whom women look for protection, succour, love, emotional fulfilment, and on whom they are dependent. And to say that men are biologically inferior to women will, no doubt, be construed as an inflammatory remark. Nonetheless, according to the experts, that's precisely what men are.

Biologically men *are inferior to women*

Before I go any further, let me stress that the phrase

'biologically superior' has little, if anything at all, to do with gender *equality*, which is something else entirely.

Men, it seems, are far more vulnerable to infection than women, they're more prone to contracting certain types of killer diseases, they cope less well with illness, trauma and pain, and they die at an earlier age than women.

[Apparently, the X chromosome is the one which contains the gene that helps protect against disease. As the female pattern is XX, and the male XY, women naturally have greater immunity potential.]

Despite all these apparent advantages, however, you'd be hard pushed to find even one heterosexual male who would actually want to be a woman. And who could blame them? After all, to be a man is to have virtually every obvious advantage our society places such a premium on. Men earn more money, their career prospects are better, and even today they are still accorded greater professional status and respect by virtually every member of our society. And yet, time and time again we read, hear and even see the evidence that men have a deeply rooted subconscious fear of women.

What is it about women that men fear so much? And why?

'Male chauvinism should be understood for what it is – a male defence against women,' says Joyce Brothers. 'It is also an offence, but that is secondary. Many men actually dread women and feel equal to them only in their dreams. In everyday life, women make them feel inadequate.'

Women are fond of complaining that men attack and undermine them in a myriad different ways, and they believe that when it comes to blind prejudice, men are the worst offenders. They're right, of course. But what women tend to forget is that a woman's mind and emotions are alien to men's more functional, less intuitive brains, and their efforts at understanding women's irrational thought processes often result in a mental state bordering on brain fatigue. And so, on the grounds that ignorance is supposed to be bliss, they very quickly abandon the attempt. The problem is, ignorance, as we know only too well, is anything but bliss; it results in prejudice, prejudice leads to fear, and fear engenders attack. And we all know what attack is, don't we? *It's our first instinctive method of defence.*

Sadly, fear is something that the male has in abundance. It begins in the womb and is reinforced in the arms of the one woman who has total control over him during his most formative years: his mother. When mother puts him to her breast she is attending to his fundamental needs in the most exquisitely sensual manner. When mother pets him, strokes him, cradles him against her shoulder and murmurs soft words of love in his ear, that tiny little man's entire body and soul thrills with extreme pleasure: he is loved, he is approved of, he is worshipped.

The tragedy is, his very first experience of himself as a subject of divine worship is also his last. Throughout the rest of his life, every single thought and action will stem from a deep subconscious desire to recreate once more the ultimate certainty within himself that the all-powerful little man of his babyhood has become a fully grown, omnipotent man.

Throughout time and throughout virtually every culture, the male has been prized and exalted above the female. The twin notions that a man is not deemed to be a man until he has fathered a son, and that a woman has not fulfilled her maternal duty until she too has produced one, still exerts its powerful influence.

In her book *The Rites Of Man: Love, Sex and Death in the Making of the Male*, Dr Rosalind Miles reveals the 'startling degree of favouritism' with which little boys are treated. Boys, she says, are more willingly breast-fed by mothers, weaned later than their sisters, given almost twice as much time at the breast, and their greediness at suckling is actively encouraged, whereas 'greedy' girls tend to be frowned upon. Moreover, a boy is 'more readily allowed to go naked, or loosely clad. He is allowed to explore more freely than a girl, play more adventurously, make messes and get dirty. Most important of all, as an infant he will be permitted to play with his genitals, which will be a source of complimentary jesting, pride and attention in adults, especially the mother.'

Meanwhile, or so Freud believed, the baby boy is responding to every touch with an unconscious arousing of his sexual instinct. Mother is the source of his security and his self-esteem, and he and mother are indivisible. Imagine, then, how bereft, abandoned and confused this baby feels when he learns first that he and mother are *not* one, and second that he has an unconquerable rival for her affections. Or of the damage his ego sustains when he discovers that the power he has over mother is nowhere near as great as the power *she* has over *him*. And, perhaps even more importantly (certainly in the long-term), that there is a terrible price to pay for the continual approval he equates with his parents' love.

'Don't cry, son. Only babies and little girls cry, not big boys like you.'

'You're not frightened of the dark, are you lad? Only cissies and scaredy-cats are afraid.'

'Scared of the bullies at school? Good grief! Toughen up, boy. What are you, a man or a mouse?'

From the moment he is born, society's influences begin their subtle and subversive work, denying a man the right to display, and possibly even experience, his own emotions. As he grows, he's taught to be competitive, manly, tough. He's encouraged to believe that 'winning' and 'scoring' are the name of the game; that overt displays of emotion are signs of weakness, and, therefore, abhorrent.

Denied from boyhood the kind of expression that is actively encouraged in girls, why are we so surprised that, by the time they're grown, many men feel isolated in – and very often from – their inner emotions? Particularly when one of the first lessons a man learns is how to dissociate his emotions from his reason, then emotion from sex and, ultimately, emotion from love. Winning, whether it be at sports, in business, or with women, rules his life, *not* because he wants it to, but because he has been taught that losing is anathema to all true men.

Out of the 54 men with whom I conducted personal interviews (whose ages ranged from 16 to 57), 47 ranked 'failure' as the thing they feared the most. None of them actually used the word 'failure' – its connotations being far too painful to contemplate – rather they used phrases like: 'not being able to attain my goals', or 'not succeeding at … ', and even 'finding that I can't … ' But in every instance, the word they so studiously avoided employing hovered in the air, a far more accurate description of the nameless but omnipresent spectre that haunts the metaphorical feast of each man's manhood.

But what, precisely, constitutes failure? Does it have different meanings for different men?

'To me, failure means not being as good as or better than other men,' said Greg, a 43-year-old journalist and father of five children. 'If I could not support my family I would consider myself a failure. If I failed to keep my wife happy, or sexually satisfied, I'd be a failure. If I can't afford to stand my round of drinks at the pub, or be considered at the very least adequate – but preferably more than that – at all the things men are supposed to be capable of, then, in my own estimation, and I am sure in the eyes of my friends, I would be a failure.'

'Not being able to pull the birds, or keep the one I want to keep,' said Ian, a single salesman aged 25. 'I don't mean being blown out on the odd occasion, that's bound to happen from time to time. I mean suddenly discovering that none of the birds I make a move on want to go out with me. That's failure.'

Graham is a 33-year-old single doctor:

> My father always drummed it into me that being a
> man meant being strong. Not only physically, but

mentally and emotionally, too. I think that's why I chose medicine as a profession. In the eyes of patients, doctors are God. They come to you with their problems, their illnesses, and their fears, and they look to you, with all your vast superior knowledge, to wave a magic wand and release them from their fears. They don't expect me to be nervous, or to be weak, they want me to be almost inhumanly tough and strong. So in a way, I guess I'm acting out my fantasies of being everything that I secretly fear I may not be.

Four years ago, at the age of 49, Roland, a printer, was made redundant from his job:

I used to pride myself on being strong. I never doubted my manhood. I'd been married for 29 years, I'd fathered two sets of twins, one boys, one girls. I'd been a bit of a lad in my day, and even had a few little bits on the side over the years. I used to play football, and rugby, and I enjoyed being in the works' darts team and my evenings out with the boys.

Then me and most of my mates were made redundant. For six months we picketed the plant, and though money was tight, I felt good knowing that I was standing up for what I believed in and showing my solidarity with my mates. But after a while, people began to drift away as they gradually got fed up with the situation, or found themselves other jobs. That's when I began to feel strange, you know, as if I was all alone; on my own.

Suddenly, it wasn't worth getting up. I didn't have anywhere to go or anything to do, and no one was expecting me. My confidence began to disappear, I started getting depressed, and when my wife got herself a job as a school dinner lady, I felt ashamed that she should have to go to work to support me.

I was out of work for 18 months, and if I'm

honest I can't say that I felt like much of a man for
the last 12 of them. When you can't support your
family, and when no one needs your skills, you
start to feel as if you're a nothing. It makes you lose
all your self-respect.

My wife was a regular diamond. She never once
complained. She always encouraged me, and did
her best to make me feel good about myself. She
even used to give me the money to go to the pub
on a Friday night, bless her, so that I could still
have a game of darts and a pint with the lads. But
after a while I stopped going. I couldn't handle the
look of sympathy I'd see in their eyes when they
knew I still hadn't found myself a job.

To be the object of sympathy is one of the worst things
that can happen to a man. To men sympathy is
indistinguishable from scorn and, in turn, scorn is what
men feel for their inferiors, not those whom they regard as
equals.

A man's real mistress is his work

According to Joyce Brothers, men regard what they do for
a living as a measure of who and what they are. It doesn't
matter how genuinely nice a man is, or how well-educated
he might be, the job he does, and the position he holds, is
what other men – and women – inevitably judge him by.

Conduct a survey amongst men on what happiness is,
and undoubtedly most will equate happiness with their
work. In fact, to be unhappy in his job, or worse, to be
without a job for any length of time, is one of the worst
things that can happen to a man, as Joyce Brothers
confirmed when she said, 'Men's happiness, their
physical and mental well-being, is so dependent upon
their work that more men commit suicide when they are
fired than when their wife or child dies. Getting fired
shakes a man to his very foundation.'

Furthermore, we only have to look at the medical

statistics to know that men are far more likely to suffer from depression-related illnesses, impotence and loss of libido following a prolonged period of redundancy, than at any other time in their lives – including bereavement and divorce. Or glance at the figures pertaining to male mortality which reveal the higher incidence of male deaths that occur within two years of retirement, to recognize that a man with no useful work to do will ultimately perceive himself as having lost all status in life. And a man with no status is often a man who would rather be dead.

The fact is, a man can live without a female partner – he'd rather not, of course, because there's no denying he feels less comfortable in every sense of the word without a woman in his life – but nonetheless he will survive. But deprive him of his work and status (for more often than not the two are inextricably entwined) and you could be depriving him of his reason for living.

Obviously there are some men for whom this is not so, like Keiron, for instance, a 35-year-old single father who is bringing up his daughter alone. Keiron is a plumber and though he loves his job, he consistently refuses all offers of promotion when it is offered to him:

> If I'm doing a job and it goes well, I'm happy. If it doesn't, then I do get a bit uptight with myself. But I am a Trojan, I'll keep going on with whatever I'm doing until I get it right. But that's as far as my interest in work goes. I don't want more responsibility. I don't need the respect of my workmates. I suppose that's because I know I already have it. What's really important to me is my woman.
>
> Losing my woman's love is the one thing I fear most in all the world, because I love her, and I am working towards the end that we will be together. Love is the most important thing in the world, and if you don't have that, or feel that, then you are missing out on something wonderful, you're missing out on life itself.

Equally there are others who, having failed to achieve any real status or level of authority at work, make up the shortfall by transferring all their energies and their desire for success to the one aspect of their life they feel they can control: presiding over their family. Providing their desire for control is tempered with benevolence and genuine love, they should be applauded for doing so, not just because they are satisfying safely a deep inner need of their own, but because their loved ones will undoubtedly benefit, too.

The only danger is, some men have such a desperate need for authority and control that the only way they can satisfy it is by wielding power over their wives and families with far more sinister, subversive and potentially dangerous (if not physical, then almost certainly psychological) effects.

What else do men fear? 'Weakness,' said Gordon, a 33-year-old anaesthetist:

> I don't know how to show my emotions so I keep them locked away inside me. At my hospital I have a reputation for being cool and controlled, but I'm not really. It's just that I don't feel comfortable about displaying any signs of weakness. I know why I'm this way, it's because my father used to ridicule my sensitivities as a child.

Phil is a 44-year-old divorced engineer who freely admits that, while life is fairly good at the moment, he's keenly aware of an underlying emptiness which, he feels, can only be filled by a woman he truly loves:

> Off the top of my head, I guess I would have to say there are two things that constitute failure for me. One is impotence, and the other is less easily defined but definitely has everything to do with work.
>
> I need and want the respect and admiration of the men I work with. That's why, when I joined

this particular job through an unusual route, I put myself through three years of torture studying for an ONC in electronic engineering. I was already doing the work so it wasn't as if I needed the qualification for the job, but I needed it for me. I wanted to be the other men's equal, not ridiculed for my lack of formal knowledge. I hated having to study. From the first year I wanted to give up, but something inside wouldn't let me. I suppose the idea of failure has something to do with survival. It's that inner core inside you that makes you go on and on trying to succeed even when you feel that something is hopeless or impossible. If that's true, and it's only just occurred to me as we are speaking, then you also have to acknowledge that true failure is when you don't even *want* to try any more.

Phil mentioned that he didn't like being ridiculed. Well, who does? But men, I believe, have a deeper fear of it than women. That's why men are particularly bad at confiding in other men, and, though it almost goes without saying, in women. It's understandable, because confiding one's weaknesses both makes one's self vulnerable and gives an advantage to the other person. The only way we have of balancing situations like these is if the person you've confided in is encouraged by *your* own confidences to confide similar weaknesses in return.

Confiding is something women find far easier to do than men. Not because they are necessarily any better, or superior to men, but simply because, as women are more interested in people and emotions (whereas men are more interested in abstract concepts, problems and 'things'), confiding is a natural and inherent part of a woman's nature which is allowed free expression, and even actively encouraged, from birth.

Back to Oedipus

According to Dr Rosalind Miles, many men spend their childhood and adolescence fighting to break free from the bonds of maternity without ever realizing that the child within themselves dreads both abandoning mother and being abandoned by her; to be without mother is to be isolated, unloved and alone.

At the same time, however, she says that 'very many men look back from adulthood with painful memories of the destructive power of the mother's love'. And that's why men need to feel that they are successful with women; partly in order to assuage their unconscious need to regain that early never-quite-forgotten closeness they had with their mother, partly in order to satisfy their self-esteem (and, of course, their sexual needs) and more than partly in order to convince their fellow men that they, too, are 'all man'.

Men seeking love

As far as forming relationships with the opposite sex is concerned, men have innumerable fears.

Men worry about their looks. They may not display their concern in an obvious manner – that implies vanity, and vanity equates with, yes, you've guessed it, weakness – but worry they certainly do.

Men will spend hours worrying about hair loss. Never mind all the old clichés about baldness and virility, a man would rather have his hair any day. He'll spend a small fortune on every kind of lotion, potion and miracle-cure cream advertised, and an even larger one at clinics specializing in hair-weaving. He'll endure excruciating pain to transplant what little hair-follicle-carrying skin there might be at the back of his head on to the front of it. He'll even devote endless hours to raking each specially grown long strand across his dome in a vain attempt to disguise his shame. And when all else fails, he'd rather suffer the humiliation of wearing an ill-fitting 'rug' (and take his chances that it might not withstand a force eight gale) that would barely fool a myopic two-year-old, in preference to displaying himself in all his natural hairless glory. Few men are immune. Burt Reynolds isn't. Bruce Forsythe isn't. Elton John isn't. Paul Daniels wasn't, but sensibly he eventually saw the light – and so, now, does his pate. Interestingly it was his wife, Debbie McGhee, who, to her credit, finally convinced him of the one fact all men should know – women prefer men who are both natural and *confident* enough in themselves not to worry about how they look.

All mean fear sex to some degree. Young boys fear they might never get an opportunity to do it. When the opportunity presents itself they fear they may not do it 'right'. And when they finally do it they fret, fear and worry that they might not get a chance to do it again. Grown men live in fear of premature ejaculation or, worse, impotence. They also fear they may not be 'good enough' at it to satisfy their partner. And regardless of whether they satisfy their partner or not, they all suffer agonies that a feckless woman might spread the word around that 'he wasn't much good, after all'.

Men worry about size. They cannot bear the idea that their 'best friend' doesn't measure up to their best friend's. Apparently, single men worry more than married men, and uneducated men, as well as those lower down the socio-economic scale, worry more than other men. Men think bigger is better. I don't know where they get this erroneous impression from, but all of them have it (don't listen to him if he says *he doesn't*, because believe me, he does) and they all *believe it*.

When I was working at *Forum* magazine, we were inundated with letters from men of all ages begging for reassurance about the shape, length, girth, and even the texture, of their 'tackle'. Should it bend to the left, or to the right, they'd ask. Was three inches enough? (They never did say whether they'd measured it erect or flaccid.) One boy even wrote in asking whether 15 inches were sufficient to satisfy a woman, but something told me he was probably lying!

Why do men think *theirs* is never as big as other men's?

According to Joyce Brothers the answer is both logical and obvious; it's simply a matter of perspective: 'When a man looks at his own penis, he is looking down. A four-inch penis is pretty unimpressive when you are looking down at it. When you look across to another man, a four-incher appears very adequate,' she says.

Women should understand that when men mention their member, they are seeking reassurance. But there's no need to lie, for as Joyce Brothers advises, there's more than one way to skin a cat. For example, you could mention that it almost doubles in length when it gets hard, or even that the circumference is the same as your wrist. On the other hand, you could adopt an ingenuous expression and repeat what one of Joyce Brothers' interviewees always used to say: tell them that it's bigger than a gorilla's. There's no need to enlighten them further. In fact it would be wise not to, as apparently a gorilla's penis is about the same size as the average female's little finger!

What men need most

Status and success
More often than not a man's self-esteem is dependent upon these two factors. His status at work and the financial rewards it brings will, not always, but probably mostly, rank higher than success in his personal life. Witness the many high-powered businessmen who, regardless of their innumerable marriages and/or disastrous love lives, nonetheless gain enormous satisfaction from their corporate achievements.

A sense of security
Men need to know that they belong someplace. It could be in the corporate world, in society, or, failing these two, within their own small community. But given the choice, the first two will always be preferable to the last.

Independence and autonomy
It doesn't matter whether we're talking personal freedom (the kind that allows him to make his own decisions about his social, sporting and work activities without first having to seek permission from his wife or girlfriend), or whether we're talking about his level of authority, control and autonomy at work. No man likes to have decisions made for him, or to feel as if he is forced to follow the dictates of someone in a more powerful position than he.

Excitement, action, challenge
'Man,' a much-loved former man of mine once said, 'is essentially a problem-solving animal. Take away his "problems" and he will become so thoroughly miserable, bored or apathetic that he will have to create problems for himself to solve.' The same need that drives men to seek novelty and variety in their sex lives also drives them to seek excitement, stimulation, action and challenge in their daily lives.

Sex
And preferably lots of it. But it also needs to be inventive, exciting and varied.

Reassurance
On every single one of the above.

What men fear most

Rejection
Men find it very hard to cope with being turned down or dumped. Women have no idea how much courage it takes for a man to walk across a crowded dance floor and break into a group of girls to ask one of them to dance with him. Men find rejection excruciatingly humiliating. It doesn't matter how good the reason is, his ego will interpret it as signifying he's 'not good enough'. This applies right across the board, from dances right through to dates and

jobs. And if the rejection is made in public, then the humiliation is compounded.

Not fitting in

All men aspire to being 'leader of the pack'. But if they can't achieve that, the next best thing is simply gaining *admittance* to the pack. To be an outcast, a misfit, or unapproved of by 'the boys' ranks highly on every man's list of secret fears.

Vulnerability

Women complain that men often shy away from marriage or emotional commitment because they don't want to give up their freedom. And they're right. Men do, indeed, dread the prospect of being tied down, restricted, hampered, under the thumb. The very idea makes them feel enormously vulnerable. That's why clever women know that, contrary to popular opinion, the route to a man's heart isn't through his stomach at all, it's through respecting his need to retain his freedom and to remain master of his own fate.

Confiding

Men hate being made to look a fool. That's why they find it so hard to confide in people (especially women). They also cannot stand the thought of being betrayed or let down. And that's why they find it so hard to forgive two-timing girlfriends and unfaithful wives. (If you've ever wondered why they also have an innate dislike and mistrust of 'girlie gossip sessions', it's because they're terrified that *they* are going to be the subject of discussion.) Few things are guaranteed to upset a man more than finding out that his wife or girlfriend has been sharing *his* most intimate bedroom secrets with all her friends.

Divorce

It's by no means a coincidence that more divorce proceedings are brought by women than men (around 75 per cent). Men hate the idea of divorce and the very mention of the word is enough to dredge up every single fear they have: failure, betrayal, humiliation, rejection, loss of public face and status. There are only two things that will provoke a man into instituting divorce proceedings himself. One is knowing that he's got a better, more exciting woman waiting in the wings (though, as most mistresses will confirm this is pretty rare). The other is when he knows that he'll lose more face if he stays.

Fatherhood

Though men take great pride in becoming fathers, it's also a source of great fear. The moment a man becomes a dad is the moment he knows he no longer can play around like an irresponsible boy. He's head of a family, and as such he must now both grow up and face up to all the responsibilities this entails. And, of course, there's another reason why men fear fatherhood: now that their wife has a baby of her own, who's going to mother him?

Women

Make no mistake, men fear women far, far more than they will ever admit. Partly because they fear being 'taken over', but mostly because they *do not understand what makes women tick*. I personally know quite a large number of single men in their late 20s, 30s and even in their 40s, who've become so confused about (and scared of) what women want and expect from them that, rather than risk making the wrong moves, they make none at all. It's also why they laugh like drains at sexist jokes, such as the one Groucho Marx once made when he declared: 'Women should be obscene and not heard.' The implication being, when a man puts a woman on her back, he feels like a king. Stand her on her feet, however, and it's very likely that the only way he will regain that feeling is by doing verbally what he'd like to do to her literally: put her down.

Mothers make misogynists

Poor mum. Since time immemorial she's taken the blame for everything that appears to be wrong with men. And whilst we have to acknowledge that mothers do, indeed, wield far more influence over their son's psyches than they recognize, what about dad? After all, dads too must have a crucial role to play in moulding their sons' minds and attitudes, and yet their part in the process has largely been overlooked. Until now, that is.

In his book, *Men: An Investigation into the Emotional Male*, Philip Hodson, a well-known author, broadcaster and marriage counsellor, says that in many cases an emotionally distant father 'broadcasts a powerful warning message about the incorrectness of intimacy'. Moreover, asserts Hodson, the very real and acute male identity crisis many men are now experiencing can *only* be resolved when fathers start providing their sons with *real* role models.

Robert Bly, author of the book, *Iron John: A Book About Men*, agrees that what men lack today is a model of how to be a man. In a recent interview published by *New Woman* magazine Bly said:

> Men have very little confidence in themselves today. They've lost their sense of purpose. It all started in the Industrial Revolution some 200 years ago, which took fathers out of the home and into the factories. Since then men have suffered from the absence of the father. Also, the father has become a figure of fun – you can see this in TV sitcoms and in advertisements – and when he sits down at the table he really has no authority.

So how does Bly propose men should change? First, he says, they must look very closely at their own lives, and second, they must then develop *real* relationships with other men as well as women. Real relationships, according to Bly, are not those which merely involve a bunch of guys kicking a football around, or shooting the breeze in the pub on Friday nights. They're ones in which men truly connect with each other through learning to talk about their vulnerabilities, their insecurities and their emotional feelings.

'Inside every man,' maintains Bly, 'there's a Wild Man – a kind of representative of our animal inheritance and the time when we were hunters. The Wild Man is in touch with the strength and vigour of his maleness, but he's very different from what I call the Savage Man. All men have been wounded – perhaps by their father's absence – but the Wild Man is aware of his wound and so doesn't wound others. The Savage Man, however, hides his wound with bluff and bluster and he often hurts other people.'

Two or three decades or so ago, women were being exhorted to believe that *all* men are Savage Men intent only on perpetrating their age-old conspiracy to 'keep women down'. Which, of course, means keeping women for ever dependent upon them.

Today men such as Robert Bly are claiming that whilst they do believe that women's liberation is important, 'some feminists have gone too far in shaming men'. The implication being, of course, that women have only served to increase men's secret fears.

And so they probably have. But then men aren't entirely blameless in both the creation and the reinforcement of women's secret fears, as we shall discover in the following chapter.

7

Women's Secret Fears

'AT THE HEART of every woman,' said a male friend of mine, 'there's supposed to be a soft centre. It's a lie. To draw an analogy between us and chocolates, you could describe men as being more like a product from your average, ordinary box of chocs – a soft, mushy strawberry cream encased in a thin veneer of crisp chocolate coating. But women are like those expensive Belgian confections – deceptively soft and enticingly creamy on the outside, only when you bite into them you risk breaking your teeth on a rock-hard brazil nut hidden in the centre.'

It's a nice analogy. What's more, it's one which, in my experience, contains more than a kernel of truth on both counts. But in defence of my own sex and without any sexist intent, there are a number of very good explanations for (some) women's ability to develop a hard, inner core. Some have a historical and biological foundation; others are the result of more recent changes in female culture and society in general; but all are fundamentally defensive in origin.

Traditionally, women always have needed men. First to provide their seed, second to provide food, protection, and a safe haven in which they can nurture and raise their young, and third, for love.

Nowadays, however, female liberation and the advances of medical technology have effectively ensured that women don't actually *need* men for anything other than their seed, and they don't have to even come into contact with them for *that* if they do not wish to. On the other hand, no amount of cultural, social or technological development can eradicate a woman's natural need for love. *And love is the source of all women's secret fears.*

Little girls dream of romantic love and happy-ever-after relationships from a very early age. By the time they become adolescents, their desire and need for love are so great, their deepest fear is that they will be the only girl in the whole wide world who cannot attract a boy. When this fear proves groundless, they immediately resurrect the one which they imbibed with their mothers' milk: all he really wants them for is sex. And then, when they've finally got their man to commit himself, all their initial fears are transmuted into dread: a combination of angst and sheer terror at the prospect of some day in the near, or even in the distant future, losing him to another woman.

Love me love my body – but when you do I won't believe you

When women aren't worrying directly about men, they worry about their physical shortcomings. Which means, of course, that they're still worrying – albeit indirectly – about men. Even the most highly intelligent and rational women worry about their looks and their bodies, and the media, advertising, fashion and dieting industries get rich reinforcing women's fears.

Don't let yourself get fat, women are being constantly exhorted, because men find fat women physically repulsive. Which doesn't say much for all those men who are perfectly content to marry their larger than average loves. It certainly does nothing to explain why so many men deliberately sabotage their woman's attempts at dieting out of an unconscious fear that should she become slim, she will either no longer find *him* quite so attractive, or he'll be driven mad with jealousy by the hordes of other men who will come in hot pursuit of his newly confident, slim wife.

More recently, a new twist has been added to this old refrain. Being slim is no longer quite enough. After all, what good is being slim if you don't have good muscle tone? Or soft, silky skin? And slender thighs are worthless if they're tainted by even a teensy bit of cellulite or one tiny wayward stretch mark. And God forbid you should allow one minuscule stray dimple to escape the hawk-like eye these industries have invested small fortunes and long years in ensuring we've all become neuroticized into developing. *Quelle horreur!*

No, a female cannot truly consider herself worthy of the accolade 'woman' until she's pared, honed, and ruthlessly re-modelled every inch of man's temple of delight by vowing a lifelong commitment to low-calorie foods, and punishing herself with a daily regime of exhaustive workouts in the gym, supplemented by five sessions a week on the toning tables. And that's just for starters.

What's the point of it all, you might well ask. Particularly when, by the time she's starved and whittled her body to within an inch of its skeletal (but nonetheless beautifully defined and tautened) frame, she's likely to have become so brainwashed by the 'thin is beautiful' brigade, and so neurotic, that she won't believe what you and her mirror tell her anyway.

The point of it is, whatever a woman is born with, she will never believe it's good enough bait to first capture and then keep a man. And even the fortunate few, those stunning icons of catwalk and cinema screen whom we lesser females continually strive (but fail abysmally) to emulate, are not immune from the syndrome. Show me just one female star or high-profile society beauty who swears she's happy with her looks and her body, and I'll show you a woman who's lying through her beautiful, expensively capped, artificially whitened teeth.

Take fitness freak Goldie Hawn, for example, who was recently reported as saying: 'If I'm making love to Kurt

[Russell, her long-term lover] I take far more pleasure in the act for having done sit-ups the day before.' Since when was exercise critical to orgasm, or even sexual pleasure, for that matter? Or the once-beautiful and lithe Kathleen Turner whose alleged love-hate relationship with food has led to umpteen battles of the bulge and more than a few unkind comments from the press, not to mention quotes (from so-called friends of hers) like this one: 'Her frumpy look is a million miles from the screen goddess Jay Weiss married. But at least she won't be the focus of other men's lust now.' Some friend!

Even the gorgeous Michelle Pfeiffer admits, 'There are times when I think I'm positively ugly!' But who can blame her for having hang-ups when her career is in the hands of movie moguls (most of whom, incidentally, happen to be men) who have the power, and the nerve, to issue decrees demanding body stand-ins for the likes of Kim Basinger, Geena Davis, Jane Fonda (yes, surprisingly, even the fitness guru herself has had a body stand-in), Catherine Oxenburg and Julia Roberts, because all these women's bodies are *not considered to be 'perfect enough' for nude scenes*. And if that lot (some of whom are considered to be amongst the most beautiful women in the world) aren't deemed to have sufficiently good bodies, it's no wonder the rest of us are riddled with body neurosis.

The fact is, any woman born within the last 50 years was born into a society which greets every new female with the dubious gift of a major handicap; henceforth her mind will be manipulated until it becomes constitutionally incapable of being content with what nature saw fit to endow the body which houses it. And it doesn't stop there. For before we're even half-way through our tubes of 'Zit-Blitz', and still obsessed by worries about acne and teenage problem skin, we're bombarded with cosmetic ads promoting the message that it's never too early to declare all-out war on wrinkles. The implicit punch-line being, of course, that men are only attracted to nubile, blemish-free youth.

Believe me, it takes a very strong woman indeed to resist this kind of conditioning. And the curious thing is, if a beautiful woman dares to tell us that she *doesn't* worry about her age, her weight, her looks, or men, we smother our envy with bitchy cries of 'Arrogance!' or 'Who *does* she think she is?' But when an obviously imperfect woman, like 51-year-old fashion designer Vivienne Westwood, is quoted as saying, 'I've amazing confidence in my looks. I think any man is either mad or stupid who wouldn't prefer me to every other woman in the room wherever I go', we gawp with admiration at her confidence.

And it's no use men telling us we're wonderful, or that our self-perceived blemishes are invisible to their love-lorn eyes, because it's *too late*. For when you've been force-fed a daily diet of neurosis since the day you were born, it's a miracle if you've managed to retain even one single gram of self-confidence by the time you're grown.

Men need to know this. They also need to know that women *never* tire of receiving compliments about their looks and their bodies. In fact, they can't get enough of them because compliments only have a shelf-life of about three and a half hours.

Why else are more and more women going for younger men nowadays, if not for the fact that it feeds (briefly) their self-esteem? Why briefly? Because before long all the taboos society places on such an association will rise up in her mind to fuse with all the insecurities she has about love, looks and age. And that's when she will start questioning her young lover's motives for wanting *her*.

Pat is a 53-year-old divorcee with three grown-up children. Five years ago she met David, who's 38, at a local one-parent family group:

> We got to know one another as friends first, so the age difference didn't become an issue until our friendship developed into something more. Then, despite the fact that I know I could easily pass for 43, and David looks much older than he really is, I

began to worry. What does he see in me? Is he looking for a mother-substitute? Why doesn't he want someone of his own age? I'm three stone overweight, I'm nowhere near as attractive as I was in my youth. He says he wants to marry me, but what's going to happen in ten years time when I'm in my 60s and he's still in his 40s? He won't want me then. Men don't want older women, do they?

Well, that's what women have been brought up to think, and, believe me, with a message as powerful as this one, it's mighty hard not to believe it. In fact its power is so great that even though there's been a recent radical swing in favour of the older female, women still find it impossible to come to terms with reaching 'a certain age'.

Whilst newspapers and magazines deluge us with the evidence that nowadays it's acceptable for women in their 40s, 50s and even their 60s to dress, look and act younger than their chronological age, there's still a sneaky little voice whispering its doubts and its 'yes-buts' into the ears of ordinary women, reminding them that it's all right for the likes of Joan Collins, Cher, Jane Fonda or even Liz Taylor to be seen cavorting with younger men, but *they* don't have to run the gauntlet of the neighbours' gimlet eyes, do they? Or face the humiliation of being subjected to the same kind of scorn (or worse, pity) your friends and acquaintances would probably heap upon you should you dare be brazen enough to cruise the aisles at your local supermarket with your toyboy in tow.

No, David may not understand Pat's reservations about formalizing their arrangement, but we women certainly do. And we've all the more sympathy for her because she's having to fight society's conditioning processes on two fronts: the aforementioned one of our instinctive prejudice about age, *and* the fact that she's fat, both of which (we have repeatedly been told) classify her as unacceptable, undesirable and, therefore, decidedly unlovable.

Paradoxically, more and more often these days the media is focusing on the unique qualities that make older women attractive to men. Older women are more interesting, they tell us. Okay, so they may no longer glow with the peach-bloom-freshness of youth, but look at that sparkle of sensual knowingness that experience lends to their eyes. And so what if their hormones are no longer burgeoning with erstwhile abundance or the promise of ripe fertility? After all, freedom from the fear of pregnancy and a yearning for motherhood are known to instigate an amazing renaissance in a woman's sexuality, aren't they? And aren't older women also presumed to be more relaxed, both with themselves and with men? As well as wise enough not to begrudge men their little vanities but instead to soothe their fragile brows and stoke their monumental egos with endless tolerance, eternal forgiveness and total understanding?

Like hell they are! The fact is, women are far too focused on their own man-made fears and insecurities to concentrate on stoking any ego other than their own. And the dread prospect of menopause (as well as the onset of all the other horrors that stalk it) only serves to compound those fears a thousandfold.

For many women, the only beginning the menopause heralds is *the beginning of the end*. Good grief, if we are angst-ridden about our bodies and our looks during our prime, how could any man make the mistake of assuming that maturity (a word that equates with all the D-words we hate, like degeneration, drabness and decay) and experience will eradicate or even alleviate any of our fears?

Particularly when female humorists like Joan Rivers keep reminding us of man's innate fickleness with quotes like this one: 'Trust your husband, adore your husband, and get as much as you can in your own name.' Or when legendary connoisseurs such as the much-married and allegedly many-times-artificially-rejuvenated Zsa Zsa Gabor warn us that, 'Husbands are like fires. They tend to go out if unattended.'

If the rich, the successful and the still-beautiful-despite-their-age aren't immune from the fear of losing their man to a younger, more beautiful woman syndrome (actress Angela Lansbury, 66, recently revealed that she felt compelled to resort to the surgeon's knife because, 'I had to do everything possible to beat the clock'), what hope is there for the rest of us?

What's especially revealing – and perhaps there's a lesson to be learned here – is that the only women who profess to have found true contentment and confidence are those who have finally stopped perceiving themselves in relation to the current state of their relationships with men. Like Shirley MacLaine who said in her recent autobiography, *Dance While You Can*:

> It seemed pointless to long for another to ratify one's own identity. What was wrong with the one I already had? To be fair, I was not the only Hollywood star experiencing the 'lifting' of sexual pressure ... I was beginning to realize that we had previously been sexual victims of a product-selling, profit-and-loss culture whose very basis was dependent on sex addiction. If some of us had found that sexual non-addiction was more peaceful and satisfying, we were decidedly out of the mainstream. Perhaps I should take heed from the characters I was playing and recognize, without pressure, that in one's 50s and 60s a manless existence would really be state-of-the-art living, because the women themselves were more fabulous than ever and the men were the ones missing something.

For women, confidence can only be won at the expense of something else and more often than not, that 'something else' is likely to be of equal importance. For example, many girls nowadays regard academic achievement as being vital if they wish to pursue a career. But they dare not flaunt either their qualifications or their interest in studying because it's generally supposed that boys don't like 'swots'.

That's why many a grown woman (with every reason to feel proud of her own career successes) will not only frequently avoid talking 'shop' when in the company of men, but actually play down her accomplishments and knowledge virtually to the point of self-abnegation. And even as the voice of her intellect is busy berating her for having compromised her integrity and her 'self', for playing the game of pretending she's less than she really is, some good old-fashioned, conditioned reflex learned in childhood will still be compelling her to adhere assiduously to the dutiful lesson of diminishing herself in the eyes of men.

According to authors Sally Cline and Dale Spender, reflecting men (which also happens to be the name of a book they wrote) is a ploy that women learn (or are forced to learn) to use in order both to place the male at the centre of attention and to reassure him of *his* significance. The phrase 'reflecting men' (first used by Virginia Woolf in a discussion of women's self-realization entitled *A Room of One's Own*, written in 1928) is one which Cline and Spender felt summarized remarkably aptly the enigma they were investigating: namely, why it was so important to women to make sustained efforts to boost the egos of men. 'Women,' Woolf said, 'have served all these centuries as looking-glasses possessing the magic and delicious power of reflecting the figure of man at twice its natural size.'

Why, asked Woolf, and Cline and Spender after her, do women 'possess this *power*'? And whilst these writers' answers are multi-stranded, in essence the nub is this: throughout their lives the message that is hammered home into the female collective unconscious more effectively than any other is that 'males come first'.

Thus, according to Cline and Spender, women's biggest fear is: what will happen to us if we should stop reflecting men at twice their size? It never occurs to them to ask: what will happen to *men* if we should stop?

That women fear men, or rather, the power that men

have over them, is unarguable. It permeates every facet of female society. Women who militate against men are unpopular. Successful assertive women are often accused by male colleagues of being 'pushy', 'domineering', 'aggressive', or 'ballbreakers'. But they're the lucky ones. The less fortunate are those who work with and for men whose sense of superiority is so threatened by women's encroachment into *their* territory that they resort to using sexual harassment as a tactic to ensure they stay on top of the situation.

Married women who stand up to or defy their husbands at best risk losing their man to a more amenable, less confrontational rival, or at worst being subjected to and subjugated by physical violence. Single women who display their independence by adamantly refusing to commit themselves to one man risk being misunderstood as 'difficult to please', 'demanding', or even 'a dyke'.

Strong women threaten men. That ought to make women feel powerful, but it doesn't. Instead it makes them fearful. As actress Greta Scaachi recently confessed: 'I've still got to learn a few lessons in not threatening men. You have to cajole and it's awful to find that it's up to women to be devious, to use their intelligence to make the guy feel okay. In the most demonstrative ways, men are afraid of women and they have somehow got it in their power to punish women. It's around us so much even the nicest guys don't realize they are doing it.'

Clever women frighten men. So the *really* clever ones soon become adept at concealing their cleverness – they'd sooner be taken for 'less intelligent' than not be taken at all. And independent women scare men, so in turn, many independent women learn to feign dependence.

The irony is, when you tug at the root of nearly all women's fears, you can't help but discover that they're not women's fears at all, for when we trace the source of all that makes women fearful, it leads us right back to men: *women fear making men fearful of them!*

What else do women fear? Well, apart from frightening

men off, many women also fear the very weaknesses they have been taught to believe are an inherent part of every man. Like his sexual appetite and his desire for novelty and variety which, supposedly, no one woman could ever satisfy fully, or even adequately, for the next ten years, let alone the rest of his life.

Women also fear:

Being hurt and used by a man
And even when she *knows* that it's his problem and not hers (because he has a reputation for being the kind of feckless charmer who automatically uses all women) she'll still convince herself that if she had been a better, slimmer, sexier and far more attractive woman, he wouldn't have been able to prevent himself from falling madly in love with her and allowing her to reform him.

Pregnancy
Because if she's fat and unattractive he's bound to stop fancying her, and then he'll become vulnerable to the passing charms of every other woman he meets.

All his previous lovers
It makes no difference who ended his previous relationships, or why, a woman in love will always wonder whether he's secretly hankering after a past love.

All his female friends
Because she doesn't believe in platonic relationships between the sexes, even though she has several platonic relationships with men friends of her own.

All the ones who got away
Because she believes there's nothing so attractive to a man as the ghost of a woman he's always fancied but never had.

His mother
And it doesn't matter how good or how bad his

relationship with his mother is; if he doesn't get on with her she'll convince herself he's a secret misogynist who one day will turn all his pent-up anger and resentment and hatred on her. But if he adores his mother, she'll for ever suspect him of secretly being a 'mummy's boy'.

His friends

Because a man's friends will always cover up for him. And when they're not covering up for him, they'll very likely be leading him astray.

And finally, it doesn't matter how successful, ambitious, independent, or dedicated a careerist a woman might imagine herself to be, one of her biggest fears is love itself. For when push comes to shove in a relationship with a man she loves, she's only too well aware of the enormous demands that having a career and a family entail.

8

Men's Secret Sexual Fantasies

WHEN A MAN makes love to a woman, regardless of whether she's a one-night-stand or a familiar and much-loved partner, his performance will always be, to some extent, precisely that: a 'performance'.

Whether he's out to impress with his sexual versatility and prodigious capacity, or whether he's genuinely concerned about his partner's enjoyment, his lovemaking virtually always contains an element of judicious editing, of holding back, of not allowing himself total free rein; because partners can put constraints on sexual behaviour. They might not mean to, they might not even be conscious of the fact that they are doing so, but nonetheless their personal preferences, dislikes, inhibitions, and certain sexual taboos will communicate themselves, with the result that a man will monitor his performance accordingly. Then there are external constraints, the ones imposed by society's attitudes towards what is considered to be 'normal', permissible sexual behaviour, and that which is known to be illegal or regarded as a 'perversion'.

But when a man *fantasizes* about sex, he's free to release the brakes of propriety, concern, fear, even love, and really let himself go with a vengeance.

Fantasies apply no restrictions to a man. He can't be laughed at or reviled for them, and he certainly can't be arrested because the obscenity laws don't apply to the visual imagery conjured up inside a man's head. That's why they're so much fun.

In his own imagination a man can be the greatest lover in the world, or even the coarsest and crudest. He can bend his fictional partner to his will and put her through every conceivable contortion – and more than a few that might seem inconceivable – and vent his lust in a gloriously unfettered ritual of primitive passion designed and orchestrated solely by himself in order to achieve one supreme aim: to create an illusion of his own omnipotence.

And he will succeed every time. Because in a man's fantasies he will *always* prove infallible. No one will refuse him, and no one will pull back with fear or horror because, for once, he is totally and utterly in control. Or as Irma Kurtz phrased it in *Malespeak*, 'Plain unadulterated fucking is maleish and quite a few men manage to pull the deed off; very few men, however, in feminine estimation, are better than boring lovers.'

For men, sex is predominantly about lust. For women, it's predominantly about love. And because of this difference, men have come to know that, more often than not, lovemaking requires them to give as well as take. Fantasies allow them simply to take.

'Sometimes, when I'm in the mood for sex, I choose not to call one of the regular girls with whom I sleep,' said Doug, a single businessman of 36. 'That doesn't mean I don't enjoy sleeping with these women, but there are times when you just can't be doing with all the hassle of the preliminaries; the wining, dining, chatting routine you have to go through to make them feel that you don't want them just for sex. Or you begrudge having to spend half an hour or so on foreplay in order to get them aroused. Again, it doesn't mean I don't enjoy all that sometimes, but there are definite occasions when you're feeling so horny all you want is a good, basic and instant, no-holds barred fuck. And then there's nothing to beat your best fantasy and your own right hand.'

Male fantasies come in as many different varieties as there are positions for making love. Some men can get turned on simply by imagining what they would do to this month's centre-fold in *Penthouse*, or at the mere glimpse of a length of shapely thigh striding past in a mini-skirt. In fact, almost anything can turn a man on. In *The Great Sex Divide*, author and psychology lecturer Dr Glenn Wilson reported the results of a survey conducted in 1987, in which large numbers of men and women were asked to describe in written, narrative form details of their favourite sexual fantasy. These revealed that group sex, or sex with two women was by far the most common element to figure in male fantasies.

[31 per cent of men fantasized about group sex compared with only 15 per cent of women (Wilson 1987).]

The second most common theme involved some form of voyeuristic (i.e. visual) stimulation relating to various items of clothing such as black stockings and suspenders, sexy lingerie, leather, or school girl and nurses' outfits.

Not surprisingly, sexually frustrated men (those without regular partners and married men with unsatisfactory sex lives) tend to have more fantasies than men who reported their sex lives as being satisfactory. But *all* men fantasize some of the time. And what each woman should understand is that, whilst her man's fantasies might often not feature *her*, this doesn't necessarily signify that it's a reflection on her, for it appears that men are far less likely to incorporate a regular partner into their fantasies than women.

Other predominantly male elements that emerged from this research appeared to underscore the fact that men are more visually oriented than women. More men were found to include details of the bodies, age or race of their fantasy partner, as well as descriptions of the type of sexual activity they liked to imagine themselves engaging in.

As one might expect, only a very small number of men (four per cent) included the type of romantic elements normally associated with female fantasies, i.e., those involving exotic settings such as beaches, forests, waterfalls and even, strange as it might sound, heaven. The same number also reported a desire to be raped by a woman (though given that rape would be almost impossible to accomplish in the absence of an erection, I imagine 'seduced' would be a better description), whilst only a 'few' fantasized being totally submissive to a female partner.

Glenn Wilson's research also revealed that the correlation between fantasy and actual conversion of the fantasy into activity was very high, although, as one might expect, women are more successful at turning their fantasies into reality. But then, as Glenn Wilson points out: 'Supply and demand in the sexual market-place works in such a way that for women an activity is little sooner desired than done, whereas men often have to settle for pornography and masturbation as outlets for their redundant libido.'

Obviously there are a number of differences between what men and women fantasize about, as well as some overlaps. But, again not surprisingly, more women fantasize about their regular partner, or someone who is known to them, than do men.

[According to a recent survey conducted in America, the most common male fantasies include nude or partly clothed female bodies, sex with a past lover, making love with two or more women, watching their wife or girlfriend making love with someone else, having sex with a younger woman, and being considered a superstud.]

But perhaps one of the most interesting things about men's fantasies is that the women who feature in them invariably appear to have stepped straight out of a scene from the film, *Stepford Wives*. (In which all the wives in the town of Stepford were gradually subjected to a horrific – well, it was supposed to be a horror film but I found it hilariously funny – de-humanization process which transformed them into caricatures of the kind of ultra-feminine, down-home, cherry pie-baking, ever-acquiescent and wholly subservient housewife whose sole function was to fulfil every one of her husband's desires.)

Poets and pornographers

Men, it seems, rarely fantasize about *real* women. Unless, of course, the real woman is an unapproachable heroine whom they lust after from a safe distance, and around whom they can weave their own safe, erotic scenarios.

Contrary to what many women believe, men can be wonderfully romantic. Some of the world's greatest and most romantic poetry has been written by men in the grip of a *grande passion* for a woman they have worshipped from afar, and wouldn't dream of pursuing into bed. Men have a tendency to put their women on pedestals, to endow them with qualities no mortal female ever could live up to. And in their romantic fantasies, their love for these ethereal creatures of their own creation can grow to such spiritually pure heights, there's no question but it transcends way beyond carnal desire. But there is one thing these mythical dream-queens who inspire men with 'pure' love do have in common with the women who inspire their sexual fantasies with pure lust: they're both unobtainable, they're both abstracts, and they both represent two opposing but enduring male ideals: the raunchy and the romantic.

For most men, sexual fantasies are nothing more than a harmless form of escapism, a way of letting their imagination take flight, and of conjuring up all kinds of variations on themes that, given the opportunity, they would probably baulk at turning into reality. Men like sexual fantasies because they are safe, they're legal and, most important of all, they can write their own endings.

According to many of the men I interviewed, that's what pornography represents, too. Most of these men said hardcore porn (movies and magazines depicting unnatural sexual acts, some of the more weird kinds of perversions and fetishes, and acts involving animals) did nothing for them sexually. But films and magazines depicting sex between men and women, or lesbians, were exciting. 'It stimulates my imagination as well as my appetite,' said Tim, a 45-year-old lecturer. 'And when they're accompanied by masturbation, they're a quick, handy (no pun intended), safe, and purely functional, means to an end. There's nothing sinister about them. And there's certainly nothing in our interest that women should find threatening in any way at all. In fact, the reverse is probably true. After all, I've often wondered what some men would do if they didn't have access to these kind of outlets.'

When men look at photographs of a naked girl, they're not interested in her as a person, or what her life is like, because to them, *who* she is is irrelevant; it's what she *represents* that is important. This is precisely what bothers some women, such as Adele who, in common with many others, regards pornography and pin-up magazines as humiliating to women. 'They degrade us and depersonalize us,' she complains. 'How would men feel if women pored over pictures of naked men, making remarks like, 'Who-hor, I wouldn't mind giving him one?' To which her boyfriend, Charles, a 28-year-old single stockbroker, replies, 'Why do you get so upset about this "sex object" thing? After all, it's not as if we're grabbing hold of real people, having our wicked way, and then tossing them in the waste bin when we've finished. Pin-ups and girlie mag models are nothing more than a focus, that's all.'

Eddie is a 42-year-old divorced telecommunications engineer whose hefty collection of *Playboy*, *Penthouse* and *Forum* magazines dates back to the early seventies:

Admittedly I sometimes use them to fuel my fantasies when I masturbate, but my interest in them isn't purely a pornographic one. I don't consider them sleazy at all. Sometimes I get ideas from *Forum* of something new to try. Sometimes I just like looking at the pin-ups, as one might admire a pretty girl in the street or in a newspaper. I don't get turned on by them all the time, it depends on the mood I'm in.

I've had girlfriends who say they think they're disgusting, but all the same they like to flick through them and I've noticed one or two definitely get turned on, though they won't admit it.

One lover got quite angry with me, accused me of being a pervert, and for a while it even began to affect our sexual relationship. But what women don't seem to understand is that there is making love and there is screwing. I don't need to fantasize when I'm making love, only when I'm screwing or masturbating. And I don't always masturbate out of lust, either. Sometimes, I just do it to relax, or to help me get off to sleep. But the main point I want to make is, we're all – men as well as women – a lot more like animals than we care to admit, and there are bound to be times when the animal side of us surfaces. Why deny it?

Nigel, a 42-year-old father of five, likes to watch pornographic films sometimes before he joins his wife in bed:

My wife doesn't watch them because she says they don't do anything for her, but she doesn't mind me watching them. In fact she often jokes about how much better I am in bed when I've seen one. A lot of my mates pass them around. Some of their wives know about it, others have to view them in secret. I feel sorry for the ones who have to sneak around hiding them from their wives and lying. It's harmless enough. In fact I don't see it as being any different from my wife staying up watching a cookery programme or 'Come Dancing'. I wouldn't want to join her, but if she likes that kind of thing, she's welcome to watch it on her own.

Sometimes fantasies can have a key role to play in forming a successful relationship. Take Mel, for example. At 28, and with one engagement, three other long-term relationships and a succession of short flings behind him, Mel is beginning to despair of ever finding a girlfriend who not only can accept his own particular little fetish, but also will find it as much of a turn-on as he does:

I'm not gay or anything, you understand, but I've always had this thing about wearing women's underwear. I think it started when I was about 12 or 13. I saw my elder sister's clean underwear hanging over the radiator in the bathroom, and I don't know why, the idea just popped into my head to try it on. Curiosity, I suppose. When I looked at myself in the bathroom mirror I looked so strange, I found myself getting quite excited. It was me, but it wasn't me, if you know what I mean. The only way I can describe it is that it was like looking at the feminine side of myself. Over the years I've acquired quite a collection of ladies' lingerie. I like silk best. It's such a wonderfully sensuous and feminine fabric. Anyway, I didn't usually mention it to my girlfriends until we'd been going out together some time and really got to know one another well enough for them to realize that as far as sex goes, I'm absolutely normal. My fiancée freaked out. In fact that's what broke us up. Most girls really can't stand it. One called me a poof, another said I was a pervert. There was only one who said she'd give it a go. She was game, I'll say that for her. But in the end I could see she was only doing it for me and that made me feel a bit inhibited.

All my fantasies feature underwear. I imagine I'm with some beautiful woman who's got really expensive taste. She only ever wears Janet Reger lingerie. And she lets me undress her slowly and then watches me as I put it on myself. Then I make love to her in it. It's perfectly harmless. I don't do anything awful, I just find the feel of it turns me on. Why can't women accept that? It puts me off relationships a bit. I mean, I'd love to meet a wonderful girl and get married, but I don't want to have to lie or keep my fantasies for ever shut up inside my head. I want to be able to include them in a normal love-life. But if I can't find a girl who's willing to understand, what chance do I have of ever getting married? I've thought about putting a discreet ad in a newspaper or something, but I don't know … it could be a bit risky, don't you think?

Contrary to what many people think, an interest in cross dressing (or transvestism) doesn't signify that a man is gay. In fact the majority of transvestites are decidedly heterosexual, and very few of them actually get a sexual kick out of their fetish. Although no one knows why some men develop this particular fetish, Stephanie Anne Lloyd, who was once a man herself and now runs a highly successful chain of shops and a mail order business supplying every conceivable item of a woman's wardrobe in sizes made especially for men, offered a possible explanation when she told me:

Some men find it very difficult to express the softer, gentler, more feminine side of their nature. Wearing women's clothing somehow frees them to do this. I have a customer database which numbers at least 100,000 male customers. Some want the whole works, from hormone creams to extra thick make-up, wigs, false eyelashes, size 12 high heels, you name it, they'll order it. These are the men who find some kind of contentment not only in dressing up completely as a woman, but in actually imagining that they are one for a while.

In my opinion, more men ought to try it; it would certainly give them a valuable insight both into how women are treated and how and why they relate to things differently to men. Many of my customers are happily married, they're not interested in other men, or even in having affairs with other women, and not all of them get sexually turned on by wearing women's clothes, although some obviously do. The ones who are the happiest and most well-adjusted about the whole thing are those who are lucky enough to have understanding wives who help them choose their clothes and advise them on their make-up etc.

In my view, transvestism is perfectly harmless. A man might be a wife-beater, a drunkard, a gambler, or a whole lot worse, and yet no one would doubt his manhood. Believe me, a woman could be a lot worse off than be married to someone who simply enjoys wearing women's clothes.

Hugh has a thing about bondage. He doesn't actually want to inflict pain or harm on anyone, he merely enjoys the sense of power it gives him:

Some women misunderstand it. They think once I've got them tied up to the bedpost I'm going to start whipping them or perform some kind of unmentionable act. But to me it's all about trust. It's knowing that a woman loves you and trusts you enough to put herself entirely in your hands. There's something wonderfully primitive and animalistic about the whole male domination/ female submission thing that really appeals to me. But I've never, ever hurt a woman in my life. I don't have any kind of kink that way, and it wouldn't give me any pleasure at all.

When Ian, a 32-year-old sales representative, met his fiancée, Lara, at a mutual friend's party it was lust at first sight. And when they made love the following evening, he fell head over heels in love:

I can't tell you what it's like to find someone with whom you can have a totally uninhibited sexual relationship. I've always been attracted to strong, independent women, and the moment I set eyes on Lara, who was dressed from head to toe in leather – skin-tight black leather trousers, leather waistcoat, red silk shirt and high-heeled suede boots – I felt this incredible surge of attraction. To look at me, you'd think I was your typical rugby-playing macho man, and I am. But in bed I like being dominated by a woman. I don't mean being whipped, or chained up. I just like the idea of a woman being so turned-on by me that she can't stop herself from going at me like a wild animal. For me it's the biggest compliment in the world to know that she's so excited by me that she simply can't control herself.

When I started talking to Lara at the party there was something wild and untamed about her in the way she looked at me, not coy or flirty the way other girls do, but sort of direct with a speculative look in her eyes as if she was sizing me up. There was also a challenge in them, as if she was daring me to do something.

I couldn't wait to see her the next night. I booked a table at a very expensive restaurant, because she looked like the kind of girl who only appreciated the best, and I planned to take her on to a club afterwards. But when I picked her up at her flat and told her what we were doing she totally floored me by saying, 'No we're not. I've made other plans.' And then she just grabbed hold of my hand, pulled me into the bedroom and threw me (honestly, that's what happened) on to the bed. And she was just like a wild animal, too. She ripped my shirt in her haste to get it off me. She bit and scratched and clawed. It was almost like rape, except that I was a willing partner and I loved every minute of it. At the end of the evening I was totally limp with exhaustion. I've never known anything so wild, or so wonderful. 'You've used me up and worn me out,' I told her. That was it for me. I couldn't let her get away after that, could I? I might never find another woman like her. I proposed within a month, and we're getting married next Christmas. I adore Lara. She's everything I've ever wanted in a woman.

And as far as Lara is concerned, she feels exactly the same way, too:

I can't believe we're so well-matched. All my previous boyfriends found it disturbing. They couldn't cope with my aggression, said I behaved too much like a man! But Ian loves me playing the man in bed. If you ask me, men who can't handle a woman who's dynamic and assertive in bed aren't real men. Ian's the boss out of bed, and I'm the boss in bed. That makes us perfect in my eyes.

In addition to setting the seal of success on a new relationship, sexual fantasies can be used to resurrect excitement and passion when sex has become routine and boring, as Geoff and Colette discovered when Geoff almost had an affair:

After 15 years of marriage, sex ceases to be quite so important. What I mean is, it's still important, but because work, the kids, etc all intervene, you naturally get into the habit of giving it less priority. I still fancied the idea of sex, but actually doing it wasn't half so much fun. When this young girl at work started coming on strong to me, I found it really exciting. I dithered about actually doing anything for quite a while, partly because I was scared and I didn't want to do anything that might hurt my marriage, and partly because I was having such a good time fantasizing about having it off with someone new, and that in itself perked up our sex life at home.

At first Colette liked my renewed interest, then she became suspicious. One night she asked whether I was having an affair, and I decided to be honest and tell her I'd been tempted. She was really good about it. I thought she might get angry or upset, but we had a really good discussion about how we'd let things slide and what we could do about livening things up.

It was Colette's idea. She said that if the thought of an affair turned me on so much, why didn't we have one with each other. She's got such a great imagination, it never would have occurred to me.

Without telling Geoff, Colette booked a hotel room for a day and arranged for a neighbour to collect the children from school. Then she phoned Geoff, told him to take the afternoon off work and arranged to meet him at a restaurant. Geoff's eyes sparkle as he describes what happened next:

> I was sitting in the restaurant, waiting for Colette to arrive, when this gorgeous red-head came up to the table and sat herself down. My eyes nearly popped out of their sockets. It took me some minutes to realize it was Colette wearing a wig and the kind of clothes I'd never seen her wear before.
>
> I still didn't twig what she was up to, but I let her prattle on at me as if we were two strangers who'd only just met. She was amazing; she'd thought the whole thing through, invented a name and a life for herself. I went along with it, pretending to be someone other than good old boring Geoff, and after lunch was over she simply said: 'Would you like to come back to my hotel for the afternoon?' It was bloody fantastic. Like really having an affair with a total stranger.
>
> We do it at least once a month now, and we've

got more and more inventive as time has gone on. We take it in turns to set the whole thing up, so one of us never knows quite what to expect. Sometimes I'll write Colette a letter, pretending to be a lover from abroad making an assignation for his next trip to England. Sometimes we go off for a weekend, and even take separate cars so that we don't arrive together. I never know what she's going to do to surprise me next, but sex has become dynamite again. And I'm far too involved in the game to think about having a real affair.

Clever Colette. Geoff's confession – innocent though he still was at that stage – could have incited a more volatile response. But in spite of the very natural sense of hurt Colette must surely have felt, she chose to respond, first with understanding (every relationship needs a kick of excitement in the sexual pants from time to time), and second by being imaginative and inventive enough to devise an ingenious plan for providing the novelty they both needed. Consequently, she's not only averted a potentially damaging crisis in her marriage, but also has successfully managed to resurrect all the original sexual magic of her and Geoff's early days. In this particular situation both partners have emerged as winners.

However, not all male fantasies are quite so easy to turn into reality. Some, like group sex, wife swapping and troilism (three in a bed), can be difficult to organize, or are likely to damage existing relationships, while others would be considered either so distasteful or weird (fantasies and fetishes involving urination and defecation as well as other far less common methods of gaining sexual satisfaction) that the chances of finding like-minded partners would be pretty remote, to say the least.

Fantasies and fetishes

The difference between a fantasy and a fetish is a very thin line. Fantasies are best described as imaginative scenarios we invent to turn ourselves on. Some men have a whole repertoire they've invented over the years, each of which they use at different times and when they're in different moods. Others have only a few. Fetishes, however, can best be described as individual fixations on a particular object, practice or piece of apparel, without which a man cannot easily (sometimes never) achieve orgasm. While most of us can understand what men get out of fantasies, few of us can comprehend why and how a man might develop a fixation for objects such as ladies high-heeled shoes, rubber wetsuits, or the female foot (a fairly common one, I am told). And as for the more strange predilections some men develop, most of us are either totally baffled or else we tend to fall about laughing at their extreme oddity.

The fact is, some fetishes are very odd indeed. Like the ones Stephanie Anne Lloyd came across during the year she was forced to earn her living as a prostitute, which she related in her autobiography *Stephanie: A Girl in a Million*:

> One day a new customer arrived for his appointment with a very strange request. He asked if I had a very large cardboard box, brown paper, sellotape and some string. Although I didn't have these to hand, I was soon able to get hold of the 'equipment'. My customer stripped his clothes off, climbed into the box and bade me seal it up with sellotape, then wrap the brown paper round it, secure it with more sellotape and finally tie it up with string. After that was done, I had to go through the whole process in reverse, with the strict instruction to jump back in feigned surprise as soon as my 'jack in the box' was revealed. This, apparently, was all it took to stimulate the poor man to climax.
>
> Then there was the man we christened 'Humpty Dumpty' because of his obsession with eggs. When he first appeared for his appointment you could have knocked me down with a feather when

in reply to my usual question: 'Is there any other service you require, sir?' he said, 'Yes. Do you have a dozen eggs?' I thought he wanted me to cook him an omelette! Once we were in the bathroom he asked me to dress him in a pair of my knickers and then carefully place the dozen eggs inside the knickers. Then I had to slap my hands against the eggs so that the shells would break and the gooey mixture would run down his thighs and legs – and that was it!

One customer liked having gooey cream cakes thrown at him so that the light sponge and cream would stick to his body. Another used to like me to dress him up in outsize baby clothes, spoon-feed him with tinned baby food and then allow him to lie curled up in the foetal position suckling a full bottle of milk. I even had one VIP who spent his entire hour with me as happy as a sandboy because I allowed him to clean my oven and toilet clad only in stockings, suspenders and a little maid's cap, with me scolding and berating him for being a naughty boy.

As any prostitute will confirm, men can develop fetishes for the most peculiar things, and in most instances, merely fantasizing about their particular fetish isn't good enough; they need to actually live out the experience in order to attain any degree of sexual satisfaction.

In cases like these, it's not difficult to understand why men seek out prostitutes to help them achieve satisfaction. After all, few wives, I imagine, would be prepared to take any of the above in their stride. On the other hand I'm sure there are many women who would be only too happy to act out some of the more common fantasies men have, if they were to make their needs known. And even if a woman is somewhat reluctant to take part in a particular activity, there is much that a man could do to allay her doubts and fears.

A woman rarely minds her husband or boyfriend

getting turned on, providing she is sure that *she* is the one who is predominantly responsible for motivating his sexual arousal. Because for most women feelings are never far from the surface, and because it's not quite so easy for women to separate their emotions from sex, any man who wants to spice up his love-life a little should always remember that a little encouragement, a little patience, and a great deal of affection will go a long, long way towards removing his woman's inhibitions.

Oh, and by the way, if your love-life is lacking the one vital ingredient you need for lift-off, but you daren't broach the subject of acting out your own particular fantasy for fear of horrifying or upsetting your girlfriend or wife, think again. After all, it's worth remembering that if you think your fantasy is off the wall, there is always someone with a better, more inventive, or even more lurid imagination than yours. And you never know, that person might even be your girlfriend or your wife!

What drives men wild in bed – and why

1) Sexy lingerie, i.e., basques, black stockings, suspenders, nurses' uniforms, bunny girl outfits, French maids …
You name it, they'll go for it, and the more lurid, tacky, and over the top it is, the better. (Makes you wonder how they'd react if you asked them to dress up as policemen or traffic wardens, though, doesn't it?) Why do most men get turned on by black stockings, suspenders and basques? Though no one has yet come up with the definitive answer, it's thought that, for most men, these things have very strong associations with their first erotic experiences. In other words, if he experienced his very first erection whilst looking at pictures of girls dressed in similar garb, that association is likely to remain with him for life.

2) Women who are forthright and honest about their sexual needs
Not only does this save them having to play the exasperating game of 20 questions, it saves an awful lot of

time, to boot. Apart from which, there's nothing so irritating as a woman who's full of wantonness outside the bedroom, and full of coyness within. A certain amount of natural shyness is acceptable and even understandable. Acting like a virgin when you're clearly anything but, not only smacks of insecurity, but you'll also have him wondering why you bothered to agree to it in the first place.

3) *Women who like sex to be fun*
No, not false glasses and funny nose fun, but the kind you can only have when a woman is uninhibited, relaxed and confident enough to enjoy herself, to laugh when things go wrong, and not to freeze at every squelchy noise.

4) *Women who are not afraid to let themselves go*
Ditto above, with the added rider that she should avoid voicing any hang-ups she might have about her imperfect body (real or imagined), fat thighs, cellulite or stretch marks. There's nothing so off-putting as a woman who insists on keeping:
a) the bedclothes pulled up to her chin
b) to one contorted position (because, after months of practice, she's discovered it's the most effective way of holding her bulging belly in, pushing her sagging boobs upright, and keeping the flab on her thighs trapped under her bum)
c) the light off (or worse, slides into her neck-to-ankle winceyette nightie the moment it goes on)
d) holding anything back. And I do mean *anything*. So if you have a tendency to celebrate your moments of ecstacy by singing an aria, swearing like a trooper, or yelling something along the lines of 'Oh God, yes!', 'Mother!', or even 'Father Christmas' (because he only gets to come once a year, too), at the top of your lungs, do it!

5) *Women who talk dirty*
There's only one place in which a woman can swear and behave as crudely as a man – and get away with it – and that's in the bedroom. Don't ask me why sex brings out

the basic in a man, but it does. As the old saying goes, if you behave like a lady in the living-room, a cook in the kitchen, and a whore in bed, he'll love you for it.

6) *Being allowed to act out their fantasies*
Providing they're relatively harmless, I'd say go for it. Though do watch out for the following:
a) men who want to be dressed up as babies and be breast-fed while dirtying their nappies – have you ever tried to buy a man-sized nappy?
b) sadists.

7) *Being surprised … sex games, sex toys, sex when it's least expected*
Because it's 1, 2, 3, 4 and 5 all rolled into one.

8) *Being praised*
Well, we like it, so why shouldn't they? The only rider I would add is, make sure it's sincere.

9) *Just being there!*
Need I say more?

10) *And, finally, the following advice and 'hot tips' are included especially for the benefit of any woman who seriously wants to drive her man wild in bed:*
There's nothing so exciting – or flattering to the male ego – than a woman who cannot restrain herself from seducing *him*. Because men are far more turned on by the purely visual than women are, this is the obvious place to start – and where better than with the eyes? Surveys show that the longer a couple gaze into each other's eyes, the more attracted to each other they are likely to become. Seductive, lingering glances set up an expectation of what promises to be a sensual, erotic, and highly pleasurable experience. So too can anything else which stimulates the other senses of sound, smell and touch.

Aids to seduction include a light, delicate perfume (or

better still, your own clean, but slightly musky, natural scent), soft lighting and harmonious sounds (a little gentle background music can work wonders), slow and sensual cheek-to-cheek dancing and, of course, a romantic candelit dinner for two. Yes, I know it's a cliché, but it works!

Don't be tempted to rush things, a slow build-up can do much to heighten the atmosphere and charge the senses. And don't underestimate the power of gentle stroking and caressing either. Eyes, ears, necks, toes, and even the creases inside the elbow and behind the knees are all highly erogenous areas. Unfortunately, they're also too often neglected on the male body.

Gently massaging your lover with aromatic oils, or slowly running a moist tongue-tip up and down his spine can prove to be relaxing and at the same time curiously electrifying.

Long, deep soul-kisses definitely should be lingered over. Kisses on the palm of his hands and gentle nibbling and sucking on his fingertips can also be incredibly sexy.

The scrotum, every inch of the penis (particularly the head), the area that runs from the groin to the anus, and even the area around the anus itself, are all highly sensitive pleasure zones. And, contrary, to what many women believe, men's nipples are just as sensitive as their own, so don't ignore them.

Oral sex is something that will also turn virtually every single man on. And whilst, for obvious reasons, some women do find this practice distasteful, it has to be said that the more adventurous and unselfish you are when it comes to giving pleasure to your partner, the more he will appreciate the efforts you make.

What turns men off in bed – and why

1) Women who fake it.
A real ego-crusher, this one. So best not to (but if you have been doing it for years, and getting away with it, I guess

he's not likely to find out now, unless, of course, you want him to for some reason).

2) *Women who give orders ...*

No man likes feeling as if he's in bed with the head mistress. Unless, of course, he's got a fetish for mortarboards, capes and canes!

3) *Mindless chatter, or worse, baby talk!*

Although it's possible you might get away with it during the pre-coital ignition phase (some men will put up with almost *anything* when they're raring to go), don't even think about it *afterwards*. In defence of men, I have to say that if anything is at the bottom of their infuriating habit of 'the post-coital kip', this is probably it. Although it's true that a post-orgasm chemical is released which can make men feel sleepy, they don't *have* to give in to the impulse, as after 45 seconds or so the urge usually diminishes. But if you start murmuring inanities, or going 'coochy, coochy, coo', I guarantee he'll not only turn off, he *will* definitely turn over and seek refuge in sleep.

4) *Women who are tactless enough to say: 'Well ... I've never seen one like* that *before!'*

Unless, of course, you don't want to see one like that again!

5) *Women who sigh and say: 'Oh, all right then, if you must.'*

You don't owe anybody any favours – and men certainly don't like being made to feel as if you are doing them a favour – so don't do it. But if for any reason you decide to ignore my advice and do it anyway, remember, *you* made the decision, so keep your mouth shut.

6) *Women who say: 'Have you finished yet?'*

Particularly when he finished ten minutes ago – where *were* you? And if he hasn't, I promise this will deflate him quicker than a pin-prick in a balloon.

7) Women who say: 'Oooh, you're the first/you're the biggest/you're the best!'
Especially those who are stupid enough to say all three – don't you know they're mutually exclusive? That aside, you've already been warned about the dangers inherent in telling sexual lies.

8) Women who use sex to bargain
If you consent to sex with an ulterior motive in mind (like wheedling a new washing machine out of him, a new outfit, or anything else you've been hankering after) you're just as guilty of prostitution as women who take hard cash for their services. If a man wants to make that kind of bargain, believe me, he'd have no hesitation in seeking the real thing!

9) Women who say: 'What are you thinking?'
Because men aren't stupid. They know what you want to hear, and it isn't what they're thinking, you can bet on that! That's why they so often reply, 'Nothing'. They don't actually *mean* nothing, they mean nothing *you* would want to hear about. If fewer women resorted to this tactic, more men probably would speak their minds of their own accord.

What drives women wild in bed – and why

1) Men who intuitively know when they're in the mood for romance (with a capital R)
There's an old joke that goes like this: query – 'What's the Australian man's definition of foreplay?' Answer – 'Brace yourself.' In a nutshell, that says it all. So read the signs. If she's cooked your favourite meal, sends you loving limpid looks across the dinner table, or sits close to you on the sofa stroking your hair, you can bet she's in the mood for romance. And when she's in this mood, responses such as 'Get your knickers off', 'Fancy a screw?' or 'How about it, then?' definitely are *not* what she wants to hear. What she

is looking for is a gentle build-up, soft lights, sweet nothings, and hours of tender loving.

2) Men who intuitively know when they're in the mood for raunch

Yes, women can feel just as randy as men at times. And when they do, they can equally be just as turned on by passionate, rampant quickies as you are. So, once again, read the signals: if her pupils are dilated, if she looks flushed and slightly rumpled, if she's not wearing any underwear, or lets you know that beneath her clothes she's wearing something enticingly naughty, go for it with a vengeance. This is no time for soft lights and sweet nothings, what she wants is to be swept away on an uncontrollable tide of excitement, thrills and gloriously unfettered passion.

3) Hours of foreplay

Women have longer fuses, that's why the more time you devote to foreplay, the more excited they become. And the more excited your woman becomes, the more likely she is to have an orgasm. If she has an orgasm, she'll not only regard you as a wonderful, unselfish lover, you'll also find you'll probably not be able to do any wrong in her eyes for days.

4) Hours of afterplay

But even several minutes are better than nothing at all. To you, it might be a bore, but to her, it's a necessity. So, if you love her, and you genuinely want to please her, stifle those yawns for another 15 minutes or so and indulge her – her need for closeness and warmth afterwards is a genuine one.

5) Men who hug, cuddle, kiss, and show just as much affection out of bed as in

Sadly, some men only seem able to let themselves go when passion has them in its grip. But by and large women are soft and cuddly creatures who, like kittens, will eagerly lap up all the affection you have to offer. A word of warning, though – many women say they love being cuddled, hugged and petted, but when men automatically see this as a prelude to sex, it spoils things. If you're wise, you'll give her as much cuddling as she needs *and wait for her to make the moves*. Restrain yourself, and I guarantee she won't be able to restrain *herself*.

6) Men who can laugh at themselves when things go wrong
And, according to Sod's Law, there's bound to be more than one occasion when it will.

7) Men who believe a woman's satisfaction is every bit as important as their own
Not because you're on an ego trip, but because you genuinely want to give pleasure to the woman you're with.

8) Men who love women just the way they are …
Fat thighs, droopy breasts, sagging stomachs, stretch marks and all. If you saw the film *Shirley Valentine*, you'll understand why.

9) And finally, as I'm well aware that no man likes to think *he* needs any instruction in seduction, the following advice is, of course, only thrown in for the benefit of beginners.

A man who can make a woman feel as if she's not only incredibly beautiful and desirable, but also the *only* woman in the entire world he considers to be worth pursuing and winning is a very rare creature indeed. Woo her, romance her with thoughtful little gestures and surprises, make her laugh and, above all else, make her feel *uniquely special*, and you'll have no trouble in seducing her and having her eating out of the palm of your hand.

When it comes to bed, the more time you take over the preliminaries, the better. Women love to be stroked, petted, massaged and touched tenderly *everywhere*. As skilled lovers know, every single inch of a woman's entire body is potentially an erogenous zone. Kissing in particular can inflame a woman to the heights of passion. So start with her lips and then work your way lingeringly over every other highly erotic centimetre of her body. Her back, earlobes, abdomen, the nape of her neck – especially the little hollow where her shoulder rises to meet her throat – the insides of her arms, wrists, and the backs of her knees. Oh, and don't get so carried away with all of this that you neglect her breasts and nipples (you'd be amazed how many men do!).

And don't ever, ever forget that the most sensitive of all a woman's pleasure zones is the clitoris. The more time you spend on this tiny little protrusion, the more she'll love you for it. And do remember, if she's difficult to bring to orgasm through penile penetration alone, stimulate her clitoris with your tongue, finger or the tip of your penis for long enough and she won't fail to get there in the end.

Oh, and by the way, in case you've heard some rather strange and possibly even unbelievable stories about something called 'the G-spot', let me put the record straight. *The G-spot does exist!* But, contrary to popular opinion (or myth, depending upon what you've heard or what you choose to believe), it has now been discovered that it isn't so much a spot, as a whole band of sensory nerve endings contained within the pubococcygeus muscle that runs right around the whole circumference of a woman's vagina. And the reason why many women fail to gain any sensation from penetration during intercourse (and, therefore, do not give the G-spot theory any credence at all), is apparently due to poor pubococcygeus muscle condition. The good news is, as this is the muscle women are taught to exercise in order to combat stress incontinence, improving muscle tone and control can result in the additional side-benefit of them becoming vaginally orgasmic.

What turns women off in bed – and why

1) Men who come and go … to sleep, that is
See numbers 3 and 4 of the previous list.

2) Men who say: 'It will be better next time, I promise.'
Because if they *can* do better, why can't they do it now?

3) Radio Hams ... you know what they are, don't you? They're
the ones who think nipples are tuning dials – two turns to the
left, two to the right, come in Tokyo, over and out
A woman's nipples are one of her prime erogenous zones.
They're also remarkably delicate things, so don't grab at
them, pinch them, twist them, or bite them. Unless, that
is, she invites you to. Don't assume that because she
invited you to do any of the above last week, she's going
to want it every night – the sensitivity of breasts and
nipples changes with a woman's cycle, so there will be
times when she may not be able to bear having them
touched.

4) Marathon men
Because, sometimes, being 'good in bed' has little to do
with being able to keep going on ... and on ... and on ...

5) Speed freaks
Likewise, sex is not a race in which the fastest man to the
finishing post wins the prize.

6) Men who say: 'But why can't you come?'
And I don't mean in response to an invitation to the
movies, dinner, or even to bed ... but why you can't come
in bed. The problem is, men simply cannot understand
that no matter how eager or willing a woman might be,
unlike his orgasms, hers are dependent on so many
variables that they never can be taken for granted. And
nothing irritates a woman more than a man who either
refuses to understand this, or worse, believes that she's
'holding out' on him.

7) Men who are obsessed with their size ...
To listen to men, you'd think that the only penis worth
having is a jumbo-sized one! But you really shouldn't

worry too much if yours doesn't measure up because the fact is, women aren't the least interested in how much you've got, only in how well you use it! Therefore, the only person to whom the size of a penis is of the least significance is its owner! And whilst it is true that the largest appendage ever recorded measured a whopping 13 inches when erect, even a minuscule two inches is more than adequate, as that's about the depth to which a woman's vaginal nerve endings extend. So, to all those men who take their obsession so far that they feel compelled to utter such turn-offs as 'God, it feels so big ... don't you think it feels enormous?' (I kid you not, countless women have told me about men they've known who really *have* come out with such inanities at crucial moments), my advice is, go ahead if you want to make her laugh, but if you want to make her love you – *keep your mouth shut.*

8) Men who tackle women like they would a rugby scrum
This really shouldn't need any explanation at all ...

9) Men who ask: 'How was it for you?'
If you *feel* you need to ask, don't – you've had your answer!

1)0 Farting, belching, and the pungent aroma of beer
And if you need an explanation for this one, you might as well hang up your spurs and join a monastery right now.

9

Women's Secret Sexual Fantasies

WHEN I WAS semi-retired from journalism 20 years ago due to the imminent arrival of my first child, and in desperate need of a diversion from painting fairy-tale castles on the nursery walls, a rather strange thing happened to me. It was one of those peculiar things that, at the time, don't strike you as being particularly significant or likely to have any major influence on your life, but years later you look back on it as having had far more impact than you realized. Certainly for me, that moment marked a major turning point in my career, sparking off a deep curiosity about and abiding interest in the complexities of human relationships and the differences in the way each sex relates to them.

What happened was this. I received a phone call from my friend and former boss, Al Freedman, the founding editor of *Forum* magazine, enquiring whether I would be interested in taking on a small 'but very interesting project'. Apparently a friend of his, an American female writer, needed someone with a keen eye for detail and a knowledge of writing technique to re-type and copy-edit the manuscript of a book she had just completed. The author's name was Nancy Friday. The book, *My Secret Garden*, which later became an international bestseller, was a landmark investigation into women's secret sexual fantasies.

Women's fantasies in the seventies

I accepted the project with a great deal of enthusiasm and, to be perfectly frank, an enormous amount of prurient interest. Whilst one might think that after spending two years working at *Forum* there would be little that could shock or surprise a 22-year-old writer (particularly one who was both married *and* very heavily pregnant), I must confess to finding myself so utterly fascinated, riveted and yes, shocked, too, by the revelations I subsequently read, that I'm still pondering the subject to this day.

Of course I'd received enough evidence at *Forum* to convince me that female sexuality and women's sexual fantasies were, in contrast to the commonly held consensus during the early 70s, a very potent force in women's lives. But I don't think I'd fully accepted quite how *powerful* a driving force they can be. Or how incredibly inventive and colourful a woman's imagination was capable of being away from society's prohibitive eye. Moreover, not having any particularly significant unfulfilled yearnings or fantasies of my own at that time (in fact, I can't recall having had any fantasies at all!), it certainly hadn't ever occurred to me that women suffered such tremendous *guilt* over activities which – whilst they might raise an eyebrow or two if they were aired publicly down at the young wives' club – only ever took place in their minds! But then, as with men and fear, guilt is something women possess in abundance. Or, at least, back then they did. That's why rape was such a prevalent feature of the sexual fantasies related in Nancy Friday's book.

Women do not actually want to *be* raped in real life, of course, but fantasies of rape can represent a means of evading all responsibility for taking part in and enjoying a particular sexual activity which normally would cause them to feel guilt.

Vera, a thrice-married grandmother of 58, had been a virgin on her wedding night. Never particularly interested in sex, Vera's favourite fantasy is based on a real event which both shocked and titillated her:

When I married my first husband, I knew nothing about sex. Nothing. I didn't have a clue about what was going to happen, and even when it was happening I didn't know quite what it was he was doing to me. I didn't enjoy it either. In fact, I never enjoyed it with him. Sex was better with my second husband, but it still wasn't waves crashing on the sea-shore or eagle-soaring-good. The only orgasms I've ever had have been the ones I have given myself.

I started fantasizing when George, my third husband, was doing it to me as a way of passing the time. When I realized it made me like sex with him better, I got quite carried away with my ability to turn him into all sorts of film stars and other people I've liked. He's been Frank Sinatra, Perry Como, Clark Gable ... but none of them were able to give me an orgasm either. Still, doing it with them was better than doing it with George.

Now I'm on my own, I fantasize all the time. The one I like the best is one that really happened to me. I was being examined internally by a doctor and it seemed to me that he was making a right meal out of it, too. At first I thought he was probably only being thorough, but then I caught him looking at me as he was moving his fingers around inside and I thought, 'Bloody hell, he's really enjoying this!' I didn't know what to say, so I gritted my teeth and just let him get on with it. But once I'd realized what he was trying to do, I suddenly found myself beginning to enjoy it too. 'Course I wasn't going to let him know that. Then another doctor came into the room so he had to stop. I couldn't stop thinking about it. Half of me was really shocked, and half was really turned on. When I got home I lay down on the bed and started playing with myself. Now, I always pretend I'm being examined by him and he's trying to turn me on against my will. I fight it all the way, but he's just so good, he sort of forces an orgasm out of me.

Vera's fantasy is a variation on the rape theme. She doesn't seek the intrusion, but she can't reject it because her fantasy partner is someone who has a legitimate reason for 'examining' her.

At the age of 45 Mary is still a virgin. When she was younger she used to dream about how wonderful losing her virginity would be. Now, though, she says she would be far too embarrassed about still being a virgin at her age to have sex with a man. So Mary plays with herself instead, and imagines she's the heroine in one of her favourite Mills & Boon-style romances:

> I don't know whether I've ever had a real orgasm. When I play with myself I do get some really nice feelings, but I don't know if they're 'it'. I pretend I'm the girl in the book I'm reading, and that the hero is saying all those passionate things to me. I imagine I'm so much in love with him that, though I want to remain pure, my body betrays me and that turns him on so much he can't hold himself back any more. He doesn't exactly rape me. He just loves me so much he gets carried away, and I get swept along with him.

In *Daydreaming and Fantasy*, published in 1976, author and psychoanalyst, Jerome L Singer, related a story about a former patient of his who, throughout her married life, had a recurrent fantasy in which she was repeatedly tortured and threatened with rape by a group of Chinese Communists whose prisoner she had become. She used it to increase her sexual excitement and to reach orgasm whenever her husband made love to her. Needless to say, the husband of this woman remained blissfully unaware of the true cause of his wife's highly ecstatic orgasms.

Guilt-ridden and concerned that her fantasy indicated some form of gross disturbance in her (she was never actually conscious of summoning up her fantasy until after the event), the lady sought Singer's help. However, after a thorough analytic exploration of the woman's sexual experience and marital relationship, Singer deduced that, as there was nothing wrong with either the lady's marriage or her relationship with her husband, her fantasy, which had developed in early puberty, was simply a harmless but essential part of her sexual arousal process.

As far as the origination and development of sexual fantasies is concerned, women, it seems, aren't all that different from men. According to Singer, adolescent fantasies undoubtedly reflect some of the defensive and conflict-laden areas in personality growth; some will simply be used to compensate for what is lacking in real life, and therefore will naturally be discarded when their usefulness is outgrown, while others may well become so indelibly imprinted on the adolescent's mental sexual circuitry that they may form the basis for more lasting 'deviant' sexual behaviour.

Occasionally a sexual interest may become focused on something a little out of the ordinary; a girl might develop a penchant for leather as a result of experiencing her first real sexual thrill while watching a leather-clad rock singer at a concert, for example. Similarly, a boy might develop a lasting fetish for fur if fur was a central component of the first real sexual experience that had an impact on him.

Recent evidence suggests that the direction given to a person's sexual interests by certain early experiences is likely to be confirmed and even refined by a programme of fantasy rehearsal. For example, once a girl has formed an association between leather and sex, every time she masturbates herself to orgasm while fantasizing about leather, she will reinforce the intensely pleasurable associations she has formed between the two. But when it comes to some of the more bizarre sexual deviations, women are far less likely to develop fetishistic fantasies than men. Presumably that's because women are generally acknowledged to masturbate less often than men and, therefore, any fetishistic associations they might occasionally form don't get the degree of reinforcement needed for them to become part of their regular sexual fantasy pattern.

Certainly when *Cosmopolitan* magazine published the results of its 1991 sex survey which attracted 15,000 respondents, objects such as leather, fur, etc didn't appear anywhere on their readers' list of interests. That's not to say, however, that *Cosmo* women don't have adventurous inclinations; 11 per cent of them admitted to fantasizing about violent sex or rape, and while a third like the *idea* of group sex but wouldn't dare do it, 20 per cent regularly incorporate group sex into their fantasies. On the other hand, the *Mail on Sunday*'s sex survey revealed that one in 20 of their respondents actually had indulged in group sex.

Furthermore, 16 per cent of heterosexual *Cosmo* women were turned on by fantasies of gay sex, whereas only two per cent confessed to fantasizing about animals. Tactfully, *Cosmo* avoided enlightening its readers as to the specific part animals played in the latter group's fantasies, but then perhaps the questionnaire was constructed in such a way that there might not have been room for respondents to go into full detail.

Once a fantasy or fetish has become an established part of an individual's sexual arousal pattern it can be difficult, though not entirely impossible, to break the association. Repeatedly substituting unpleasant effects in place of the previously pleasurable rewards is one method that has proved successful in the past. This is what happens when smokers are given aversion therapy, electric shocks, for example, to help break their addiction to cigarettes, but occasionally a fantasy pattern can be broken abruptly by one single unpleasant experience.

Fantasy versus reality

This is precisely what happened to Janine, 29, when, after

years of fantasizing about being forced to fellate a man against her will, she almost became victim to the real thing:

> I'd always had this thing about being submissive, you know, being tied up and having to submit to whatever my lover wanted to do to me. To be honest, I found the whole idea rather exciting. I've always had a few hang-ups about sex, not so much about actually doing it, but about some of the other things like oral sex, which somehow I've always thought of as not being the kind of thing 'nice' girls did.
>
> But that's what I always ended up being forced to do in my fantasies. First he'd make me do it to him, then he'd force me to submit while he did it to me. But I'd never actually had the courage to do it to a man in real life, and no one had ever offered to do it to me, so, up till then I could only imagine what it must feel like. What happened was this guy I'd fancied for ages asked me out. I saw him a few times before we went to bed together, so it wasn't as if he was like a complete stranger. To be fair he didn't get violent or anything, I just think he got a bit carried away. When he pushed my head down on to him I was so surprised I think I just automatically opened my mouth and took him in it. Then he started going a bit wild and it frightened me. I felt myself gagging and I tried to pull away but his hands were pressing so hard on my head, I couldn't move. The more excited he got, the more I panicked and began to choke. When he finally let me go I burst into tears. He didn't actually come in my mouth, but still, I was frightened and I felt sick, almost as if I'd been raped against my will or something. He kept apologizing and telling me how sorry he was, that he hadn't meant to force me to do something against my will, but all I wanted to do was get away from him as quickly as possible. Perhaps it

was partly my own fault, I don't know. But now I
know what it's really like to be forced to suck a
man off, the very thought of it makes me want to
puke! I don't know how women can do it of their
own free will, or how any of them can say it turns
them on!

Needless to say, being forced to comply with anything
against her will no longer figures in any of Janine's
fantasies. And though she never actually sought to act out
her fantasy, the one lesson Janine says she has learned
from her own unpleasant experience (apart from getting
to know a person better before she sleeps with them, that
is) is that some fantasies are best left where they belong: in
the imagination.

This happens to be the same conclusion Cassie, a
22-year-old, self-confessed ex-'groupie', reached after she
too discovered that reality rarely lives up to an imagined
ideal:

I've slept with quite a few fellas in my time. Most
of them have been in rock bands, because they're
the kind of men I'm attracted to, and as I used to go
to a lot of clubs and gigs and things and then get
invited back to parties, it sort of seemed natural
somehow. There was one fella called Andy who I'd
always had a thing about. I thought he was so sexy
with his long dark hair tied back in a ponytail and
these big dark soulful eyes. All the other girls
thought he was pretty neat, too, but no matter how
often I bumped into him, I never seemed to be able
to get him interested.

Sometimes when I was having sex with one of
the other guys, I'd imagine it was Andy who was
making love to me. I just knew he'd be really good
at it, 'cause he looks the type. I'd imagine all the
things he'd do to turn me on, and I'd get so excited
I'd have no difficulty in coming. Then one night,
after one of his gigs, I finally managed to corner
him and show him how interested I really was. He

took me back to his hotel and immediately we jumped into bed. Don't get me wrong, he was good all right, and I really did enjoy doing it with him ... but he wasn't quite as good in real life as I'd always imagined he'd be. Strange, isn't it? And yet, even now if I fantasize about sex with anyone other than my regular boyfriend, it's always Andy I imagine making love to me.

Erica Jong's 'zipless fuck'

Not surprisingly, making love with men other than their regular partners features very strongly in women's fantasies, as do sexual encounters with 'famous' men. 51 per cent of women in *Cosmo*'s survey admitted fantasizing about sex with 'someone else they knew', while 17 per cent enjoyed imagining they were making love with a celebrity. For 28 per cent, however, fantasizing about an Erica Jong-style 'zipless fuck' proved to be a major turn-on every time.

[The zipless fuck is a term coined by the heroine in Erica Jong's novel, *Fear of Flying*, to describe a brief anonymous sexual encounter with a stranger.]

As Nancy Friday reported in *My Secret Garden*, fantasies about having sex in public are not uncommon. Some women fantasize about it with a regular partner, but many like the idea of being taken by surprise by a stranger.

Theresa is a 33-year-old divorced mother of two, who runs her own highly successful business as a publicist. Too busy to form a relationship right now, Theresa, who rates her sex drive as 'high', likes to masturbate herself every night before she goes to sleep:

I have two or three favourite fantasies. They all combine the excitement of being taken unawares by a stranger, and the danger element of doing it somewhere we could easily be caught. The one I like best, and use the most, is the one I refer to as my 'train story'. I'm on a train, one of those inter-city ones with a corridor that runs alongside single compartments. There's only one other person in the carriage, which, naturally, is a first-class one. He's obviously a businessman because he's wearing a smart suit, complete with waistcoat and tie, and he's reading a copy of the *Financial Times*. It's a hot day in the middle of summer and the sun is streaming in through the windows. I ask the man if he minds me pulling down the blinds as the sun is in my eyes, and he says to go ahead. I'm wearing a thin silk suit with a longish skirt, but my legs are bare. After a while I start to feel sleepy and the sheaf of papers in my hand slips to the floor. The man immediately stoops to pick them up for me and I notice that he uses that as an excuse to get a good long look at my legs. 'You've obviously been working too hard,' he says. 'Why don't you take advantage of the journey to rest for a while. You'll feel much better and far more refreshed when you arrive.' I must fall asleep because the next moment I'm aware that I'm lying sprawled along the length of the seat, with my legs hanging off almost touching the floor. What's woken me is a strange sensation I'm feeling in my groin, as if someone is tickling me in a very personal place. I open one eye and there's this businessman on his knees wth his head up my skirt which is partly covering his head. He's performing oral sex on me and it's absolutely wonderful. I pretend to be asleep still, but all the while I'm writhing around and moaning as if I'm having a disturbing dream. The fantasy doesn't stop when I have an orgasm. I like my stories to have nice neat little endings, you see. So what happens is he makes me come, and then about ten minutes or so afterwards I wake up to find him sitting back in his seat reading his paper as if nothing has happened. He doesn't try to make love to me, or get me to do anything to him, he simply can't resist the pleasure of pleasuring me. The train pulls into the station. He smiles, stands up and opens the carriage door for me and says: 'There, you see, I told you you'd feel much fresher and more relaxed for having a sleep.' And neither of us knows whether the other one knows what was happening.

Women still aren't getting what they want

As cunnilingus is one form of sexual activity that can virtually guarantee most women's orgasms, it's not surprising that it should form an integral part of many women's sexual fantasies. What is surprising, however, is that as far as *Cosmo* women are concerned, of the 84 per cent who said they enjoy it, only 59 per cent actually get to participate in it. Contrast that with the figures recorded for fellatio (77 per cent of *Cosmo*'s readers said they participate in this activity, but only 59 per cent admitted to enjoying it), and it appears that there's still a great deal of inequality between the sexes in bed. In other words, women are *still* not getting what *they* want, yet they still feel compelled to do what their partners want, despite the fact that they may dislike what they're being asked to do.

Lizzie, a 43-year-old housewife and mother of two, so resents her husband's continual failure to make any real efforts to please her in bed, she's more or less allowed their sex life to grind to a halt:

He doesn't seem to have much of a sex drive, anyway. When we first met 20 years ago we were at it like rabbits for the first few months. But it didn't last very long. It used to worry me quite a lot. I thought he might have another woman on the side. But frankly, when he does manage to summon up the energy he can only last two or three minutes at the most, so what woman's going to put up with that if she doesn't have to? I did make an effort to inject some novelty into it about seven years ago, and he certainly seemed willing to try a few new things. I've always wanted to try oral sex, not doing it to him (well there wouldn't be much point with him being such a quick-draw-McGraw, would there?), but him doing it to me. So I brought the subject up one night. I led him into it gently, hoping that if I got him talking about his fantasies, he'd ask if I had any. Well, he doesn't, and he didn't. In the end I just came straight out with it and told him mine. 'Ugh!' he said. 'I don't know if I could do that, it might be a bit smelly.' A response like that doesn't exactly give you much encouragement, does it?

Anyhow, a few months later, when we'd had a massive row about something and he was desperate to get back into my good books, he suddenly said in bed one night, 'If you really want to try that, I don't mind having a go to see if I can put up with it.' Men! First he gives me a phobia about being smelly, then he offers to do it in such a way that he turns me off before we start! I just said, 'Don't bother, it was only a little fantasy. I don't suppose I'd like it much anyway.' Since then I've not bothered making any moves, and left to his own devices he only seems to need it every few months or so. What do I care? I've bought myself a vibrator and three or four times a week I have a wonderful session with that, imagining that some young hunk really loves having oral sex with me. It beats my non-events with Tim any day ... and the batteries don't run out after three minutes!

Women's fantasies in the nineties

Twenty years on, and with the publication last year of her follow-up investigative volume, *Women on Top: How Real Life Has Changed Women's Sexual Fantasies* (Hutchinson), Nancy Friday reports via a recent article in *Cosmopolitan* magazine that, while sexual guilt and the rape fantasy certainly haven't disappeared, most of the women in her new book, if they feel guilt at all, 'take it as given'. 'Guilt, they've learned, comes from without – from mother, from

Church,' says Friday. 'Sex comes from within and is their entitlement. If there is a rape fantasy, today's woman is just as likely to flip the scenario and rape the man. In these new fantasies the emotions that most often prevail are anger, the desire to control, and the determination on her part to reach total sexual release.'

Well, if it's true that women have more success than men when it comes to acting out their fantasies in real life, all I can say to any man reading this is: you have been warned. So if you're timid by nature, take cover, if you're not, gird your loins!

To be fair, Friday does point out that the majority of women who talk and write to her about sexual fantasies are still in their 20s. Therefore, only time will tell if age, marriage, career and motherhood will exert their usual inhibitory effects on these women's sexuality, dampening both their physical ardour and their dreams. Nevertheless, she also firmly believes that, because today's generation of young women grew up in a world 'wallpapered with sex', they naturally accept good sex as their basic right. Thus, she predicts, 'the female sexual pattern will run differently from that of earlier generations'.

According to Friday, women have switched from the more passive type of fantasy (rape, submission, coercion, and the kind of passionate love that sweeps a woman along in its wake rendering her powerless to resist her lover's advances) to more dominant themes out of a sense of frustration in their real lives. And one of the theories she puts forward for this is the 'glass ceiling' factor, i.e., being able to see the top rung of the corporate ladder, but being prevented by men from attaining it. 'More women,' says Friday, 'are grinding their teeth these days because of the glass ceiling. And women are terrified of rebuttals from other women so they turn their anger on to an easier target – men.' Not necessarily in real life, you understand (although current trends do show some evidence of this), but certainly in the one area they do still retain complete control: their imaginations.

Certainly as far as *Cosmo* women are concerned, 22 per cent reported that they enjoyed 'pretending to fight physically' with their partners, while 17 per cent enjoy pinching, biting and slapping their partner. On the other hand there's still a great deal of evidence to suggest that today's women are, on the whole, still a fairly submissive lot. For example, out of the 12 per cent of *Cosmo* women who admitted to participating in anal sex (the figure could be much higher, but as this practice is illegal some may be reluctant to admit to it), only eight per cent of them said they actually enjoyed it. Moreover, 32 per cent of this audience confessed to enjoying 'being held down', though only 20 per cent were actively participating in this form of sex play. Interestingly, there was no discrepancy at all between those who expressed a liking for flagellation or other forms of sado-masochistic behaviour, and those who were putting it into practice (two per cent).

By far the most popular forms of sexual practice, at least so far as the *Mail On Sunday*'s poll was concerned, appears to be sharing fantasies with a partner (men and women were virtually level-pegging here with 13 per cent of men and 14 per cent of women saying they regularly did this), and the wearing of sexy underwear (40 per cent of women wear it 'always or mostly' compared to 20 per cent of men). Unfortunately, as far as the latter is concerned, it wasn't clear whether it was the men who wore the sexy underwear themselves, or their wives. Which is a shame, because as it's generally accepted that women are less likely to be turned on by the visual, it would have been useful to know a) whether this still applies today and b) if it doesn't, what type of sexy underwear is currently being worn by men to turn their women on. That men like women to wear sexy underwear is indisputable, but that women equally enjoy dressing up for their own sakes is evidenced by a comparison between the number of *Cosmo* readers who said they enjoyed it (67 per cent) and those who actually do it (53 per cent).

Pornography versus erotica

Generally speaking, pornography does nothing for women. On the other hand, erotic literature can send their temperature soaring. Again this is partly because women have better imaginative abilities than men, and partly because they relate better to sex when some form of emotion is involved. That's why women are more likely to get turned on by films such as 9½ *Weeks* or *The Postman Always Rings Twice* than something like, say, *Caligula* or the kind of home videos that no self-respecting cinema dare screen publicly.

This is something 56-year-old Matthew has only recently discovered for himself:

> I've always liked blue movies, even the really tacky ones with badly dubbed dialogue. But my wife, Cynthia, thinks they're distasteful. For years I'd persuade her to watch them with me in the hope of one day turning her on. But she'd either walk out of the room in disgust, or she'd find them hilariously funny. Believe me, it's not easy to get turned on when your woman is rolling around with tears of hysterical laughter running down her face. To be honest, I'd more or less given up on this as a hobby. For one thing the old libido's started to flag a bit, and for another there didn't seem much point when she'd often refuse to make love to me after I'd watched one, saying she didn't like the idea of me being turned on by someone other than her.
>
> Then a couple of months ago, a friend told me about 9½ *Weeks*. He said it was really good and that it had even got his wife going. So I hired it from the video shop. Cynth wasn't too keen at first, but after about half an hour or so, she really began to get involved with the story. Well, it certainly did the trick for her. She was rampant by the time it finished. In fact, I'm almost embarrassed

to say it, but we ended up making love on the living-room floor, which is something we haven't done for about 30 years. It was brilliant! I felt like a 20-year-old again. Cynth hasn't changed her ideas about the blue films, but she has admitted that if I hear about any more of what she calls *real* films with a sexy love story, she'll be all for it.

For Matthew, the knowledge that women can get turned on by a romantic tale in which explicit sex follows as a natural part of the storyline was a revelation, to say the least. If only more men were to pay heed to this gentler, more romance-oriented side of a woman's sexual nature, they would soon discover that the dividends can be enormous – not to mention enormously pleasurable!

Women don't like seeing sex debased by photographs of models in explicit legs-apart poses. And as for porno magazines with page after impersonal page of carefully staged photographs featuring a largely unidentifiable welter of tangled limbs, exposed genitals and tongues protruding from pouting lips in a travesty of sexual ecstasy, quite frankly, it leaves them cold. It also leaves them highly embarrassed and more than a little wary.

Pornography does not make women feel relaxed. On the contrary, it makes them feel decidedly uncomfortable because it reminds them of all their youthful neuroses about the brutally animalistic side of men's natures and that they *only* want women for sex. 'What I hate about pornography,' said Coral, a 29-year-old nurse who's been living with her boyfriend for three years, 'is that people don't make love in it, they fuck. There's no feeling, no tenderness, no caring or concern involved. In fact, for all the interest the copulating couple show in each other, they might just as well be screwing machines. Porn is a four-letter word, just like lust, and fuck, and all the other horrible swear words you can think of that turn nice natural things into nasty, cold, crude, offensive objects.'

Erotica, on the other hand, is different. And the reason

why it is different, according to Margaret Reynolds, an English lecturer at Birmingham University and author of the book *Erotica – An Anthology of Women's Writing* (Pandora Press), is largely due to another four-letter word, 'love'. 'I had to make my own definition of the word,' said Reynolds in a recent interview with *New Woman* magazine. 'It comes from Eros, god of love, son of Aphrodite (goddess of love) and Hermes (the winged messenger). I imagine he inherited the best of both qualities from his parents and was the god who communicated love – hence the meaning of erotica for me. Pornography, however, is created for the specific purpose of causing sexual arousal.'

So great has women's interest in well-written, erotic literature become in recent years that even dyed-in-the-wool traditional romance publishers like Mills & Boon have seen the light (and a considerable rise in their profits), and launched a whole new series of sexually explicit novels under their *Temptation* imprint. And very raunchy they are too. But if you were to tear out the pages concerning the sex scenes and hand them in turn to several women to read, the chances are that women wouldn't become quite so aroused by the words as they could if given an opportunity to read them in their proper context as part of the entire book. And that's because women have longer fuses than men. Men can switch on to sex in seconds. Unfortunately, women can't. Men can become aroused by almost anything, a sultry voice singing on the car radio, the sight of a long-legged girl in a mini-dress, bare breasts or genitals in *Penthouse* magazine, or even by something totally unconnected with sex itself. And they never seem able to understand why the wife they leap on the moment they walk through the front door is both totally unmoved by the sight of a throbbing erection she had no part in raising, and downright reluctant to assist in relieving him of it, too!

'Men want to be aroused *now*, not on page 16,' said clinical psychologist Dr David Nias, commenting on this conflict in *New Woman* magazine. 'And since they don't need a slow, steady build-up to sex, they're often at a loss to understand why women do.'

Perhaps men would be able to relate to this problem far more easily if one were to couch it in terms they can understand. So to use an analogy: it's a darn sight easier to apply the brakes to a runaway motor than it is to force speed out of an engine that has no fuel. If men could be persuaded to think of their women in the same manner they often regard their cars, they might find that after they'd studied the manual a little bit harder, polished the bodywork a little bit longer, and spent as much time tinkering lovingly with their engines in order to improve and increase their performance, I'd be willing to bet that, just like their cars, their women would always be raring to go. And if just occasionally they could bring themselves to hold back a bit on the throttle, they might well find themselves enjoying the most thrilling, exciting and rewarding experience of their lives.

Oh, and in case you're wondering how and why I've chosen to draw an analogy between a woman and a car, hopefully the next chapter will enlighten you.

10

Men: Why Can't a Woman Be More Like a Car?

YES, I'M AFRAID the title of this chapter really was inspired by one man's recent comment to me.

So, what do men *really* want from their women *out* of bed? Would they prefer their wives and girlfriends to be beautiful, reliable but *silent* accessories? And if so, why? Is it because, as many women believe, men, generally, are afraid of emotions, preferring to have relationships that neither challenge them nor require more than a minimum of effort on their part? And why do men feel so uncomfortable with women's emotional displays? Why *can't* they talk openly about their own feelings? And why do they squirm when women discuss theirs?

Is it true that what all men really want is 'a quiet life', as one man recently confessed to me? And how widespread amongst men is this view?

Women complain that men are so wrapped up in their careers and traditional male pursuits that they neither have the time nor the inclination to become as deeply involved in their relationships as their partners are, or need them to be. How much truth is there in the poet Byron's famous proclamation that, 'man's love is of man's life a thing apart – 'tis woman's whole existence'?

Why *do* some men still cling so doggedly to their chauvinistic attitudes and beliefs? Could it be that, deep down, they are enormously fearful of what the female sex could be capable of? And, finally, how do women feel about – and cope with – the myriad baffling, and ultimately exasperating, contradictory aspects of men's natures?

Men are more susceptible to love

Throughout the preceding chapters we've seen quite a bit of evidence to support the accusation women are so fond of making: that men are, indeed, afraid of emotions. But, in defence of men, we ought by now to have realized that there are also some very good reasons why this might *appear* to be so. Through examining some of the genetically and biologically determined differences between males and females we have, hopefully, at least begun to comprehend why men and women, from conception onward, cannot help but think, feel and behave in different ways. And perhaps we've also gleaned a small measure of understanding from looking at the different cultural experiences that reinforce each sex's patterns of behaviour; patterns which, by the time we reach adulthood, have become so deeply ingrained in us they are immensely difficult – in some cases virtually impossible – to change.

If we have learned nothing else from the foregoing, the one thing that should have become glaringly obvious is that while men may indeed be afraid of emotions, that fear does *not* negate them. On the contrary, its very existence is a measure of how very deeply they run.

'All men are children,' Coco Chanel once said. 'If a woman understands that, she understands everything.' To which my reply would be, not quite everything. But it's a start, because women should never underestimate the power of the child within each man.

Before I go any further, let me make it clear that that is not meant to be regarded as a sexist or derogatory remark; the fact is, we *all*, men and women alike, for ever retain within us a part of the child we once were. We might rationalize it away into the depths of our unconscious and batten down the hatches of adulthood and maturity over it, but we cannot prevent it from clamouring for attention, and sooner or later its little voice, and its even larger insecurities, will be heard and felt. We cannot prevent ourselves from unconsciously responding to them.

'Men,' said Dr Joyce Brothers, 'are almost heartbreakingly susceptible to love. Much more so than women. A man seldom contracts a mild case. He falls head over heels into raging romance.'

There are two experiences of love: men's and women's. And when men and women are experiencing love, they will act, feel and think completely differently about it. But what is love? And how do we know when we're in it? Let's take a look at how men and women describe it differently, and also at what they expect from love.

Jamie, a 25-year-old bank clerk, thinks he has been in love twice in his life:

> Both times it was that eyes across a crowded room thing. The moment our eyes met something passed between us, and when I danced with them I got a sort of tingling feeling from touching them. Both were very physical relationships. We couldn't keep our hands off each other, all we ever wanted to do was make love. I wanted to spend all my time with them and when I wasn't actually with them I had to be talking to them on the phone. There's a certain amount of jealousy involved because you can't bear the thought of them not wanting you, but you feel that so long as you've got them in your life you're invincible.
>
> I think love must be something that comes from an instinct inside you. Your body recognizes the other person as someone special, even if your head doesn't agree. Your mind could be saying, 'No, you're wrong, this person doesn't have x, y or z, so you can't be in love', but some gut instinct is drawing them to you regardless.

I'd like to get married some day. What I want is a woman who will love me, be kind and thoughtful, a good mother, and very keen on sex, because that's important to me. But I do need to be the boss, so although I don't want a woman who has no mind of her own, I think she'd have to respect my opinion and not be too argumentative just for the sake of it. I certainly don't want a women's libber.

Sheila, who is also 25, says she's been in love so many times she's lost count. So how does she know when 'this is it', and if each one was 'it', why didn't it last?

For me it normally happens very quickly, like within the first week or two. I find myself thinking about them all the time. I feel softer somehow when I'm in love. There has to be a strong physical attraction, and I like my men to be fairly dominant; not to push me around but to be strong, authoritative and determined.

The kind of man I want to marry will be a professional man, someone other people look up to, and someone I can respect. He's got to be tolerant, attentive, considerate, and he must have a good sense of humour.

Why haven't any of my relationships worked so far? Most of them said they weren't ready to settle down. I didn't mind waiting a while, I wasn't asking for instant marriage, but some form of commitment would have been nice. But men don't seem to understand that we need to know that they're serious about us, that they're not just out for what they can get for as long as it's going.

At 44 Geoffrey wants to settle down again. He's been married once, but that ended in divorce 11 years ago. Since then he's slept with 'over one hundred women'. Some of his relationships have lasted several months, others only weeks or days:

We all have a checklist of what we're looking for, or at least hoping to find. Sometimes you overlook the fact that some element you think you require is missing, simply because the girl might have other qualities that compensate. But it's hard to put a name to what you feel. I can have the most wonderful time in bed with someone, and though it makes me like them more and warm to them more, I know I'm not in love with them. Other times the sex can be good, but not great, but still you think you're crazy about the person.

When you meet someone and there is an immediate spark of attraction, then you find you really like their intellect, and then you find yourself really liking their personality, that's when you know you've got the basis of something good between you. If I can spend eight hours just talking to a woman without even touching her and still want to be with her the next day and the next because I just love being in her company, that's pretty close to what love is for me.

As for what I want from a relationship? I want a woman I can trust. Someone I can relax with and feel secure with, who'll love me despite my faults and failings. I don't like women who push and nag or demand. I like my women to be tolerant, kind, understanding and sympathetic. Above all, I want someone who's prepared to work at understanding me.

Sophie, a 42-year-old public relations consultant with two marriages behind her, firmly believes that marrying for love is the worst thing two people can do:

I get accused of being a cynic. But you know what the definition of cynic is? It's a disappointed romantic. When I was young I passionately believed in love. Love transcended everything and it could surmount any obstacle put in its way. That's how I've loved in the past. I've been tolerant, forgiving, understanding, and put my men's welfare before my own. And what does it earn you? A kick in the teeth. I think there's a lot of truth in the 'treat 'em mean and keep 'em keen' maxim. Men only seem to want two types of women; either those who treat them badly, because they're a constant challenge to a man's ego, or those who hang on their arms adoringly and act like the sun shines out of their backsides. I'm not the type to do either. I'll love him madly, and he'll have no doubt that I do, but I won't play clinging, helpless little wifey in order to make him feel like a giant of a man, and I'm far too honest to treat men badly or play games. Love is about commitment, respect, tolerance and sharing.

I've confused chemistry, passion and sex with love in the past. I've also confused kindness with it. Perhaps I want too much, but I'd like to have all those things as well as the certainty of knowing beyond a shadow of a doubt *who* the man is, and what he stands for. I don't want a weak, clinging man or an obsessive one. He must be secure enough within himself to accept my need to be independent from time to time, to accept me as a person in my own right and not see me simply as an extension of him. He must be fairly dynamic career-wise, because I am, and he'll have to earn at least as much as me because I hate the idea of keeping a man. I know that sounds sexist, but women are brought up to believe that providing is the man's job.

I think there's infatuation – when you're in love with the ideal of love, and with how a person can make *you* feel – and then there is real love, which is much calmer, more durable, less selfish, and totally unconditional. And real love doesn't happen overnight, it's something that grows gradually.

Clearly one man's love is another man's infatuation. Or, to put it another way, there is love, and then there is love. But then again, there's also sex, and chemistry, and neurosis, and all sorts of other emotions that can so easily be mistaken for the real thing.

Love as we think of it today is a 20th-century phenomenon. Romantic love was a myth first created during the medieval period when knights swanned around the country rescuing beautiful damsels in distress and slaying every dragon who got in their way. It was an era when men were honourable and brave, maidens were modest and virtuous, wars were fought on ideals, and nobody had to worry about paying the mortgage at the end of the month. In short, life was too wonderful for words and love was too illusory to be real. But still we can't quite stop ourselves from believing that some day, somewhere, and with someone really special, we'll discover that 'happy ever after' really does exist. And men cling on to this ideal of love far more tenaciously than women generally will.

In 1959 a survey was carried out amongst American male students asking whether they would be prepared to marry a woman they did not love providing that she was perfect for them in every other respect. 60 per cent of them said no. 20 years later that question was put to another generation of male students; this time a staggering 86 per cent of them said no.

Men, it has been found, experience the heightened emotion of what the experts term 'first stage love' (i.e., the heart pangs, the adrenalin high, the strong sexual attraction, and the desire to be with the lover all the time, etc) far earlier in a relationship than women are likely to. This was borne out by the results of another survey conducted in America in which 250 young men and 429 women of a similar age (all of whom were either 'in love' or recovering from love) were asked how long it had taken them to fall in love. Over a quarter of the men said they had fallen seriously in love before their fourth date, but only 15 per cent of the women had. Moreover, half the women actually said that they hadn't felt they were in love until well after their 20th date, and even then there was still some lingering uncertainty about their feelings.

What do men want?

So what do men want?

'In a nutshell, we want it all,' said Robin, a 44-year-old salesman who, after one four-year affair, and two very long live-in relationships, is now living alone. 'I know it's unfair and it's certainly unrealistic, but what every man really wants is his 'mother', with the added bonus of sex thrown in. We want to be loved, wanted, looked after, cared for, pampered and made to feel as if everything we do out there in the big wide world is admired and appreciated because we're doing it for the woman we love. What we get instead is a woman who starts off loving us for all our good qualities, and ends up criticizing us for all our shortcomings.'

'Why can't a woman be more like a car?' asked Michael, a 38-year-old divorced marketing consultant. 'What men need is a disposable woman: someone we can get pleasure from when we need it, who'll look good, be faithful, reliable, attractive, a bit of an attention-getter, but whom we can stow away, like a car in a garage, when we don't need her.'

Presumably, as with their cars, men like Michael will part-exchange their women when their interest has gone, which is precisely what women are afraid of. But then we mustn't judge all men as harshly as we might be tempted to judge Michael.

Take Ben, for example. His 15-year marriage has recently been under strain because his wife feels he doesn't give her enough attention:

> Sometimes women expect too much from us. They seem to think we should do nothing but worry constantly about their needs. How often do they study ours? They have no idea of the kind of pressure we have to put up with, or the crap we have to take at work. They can give up work, stay at home, look after the kids, and generally have a

very nice life indeed. But we can't. If we hate our
jobs we can't leave, because the mortgage has to be
paid and the kids must be fed and clothed. It's
tough out there in the big world, and women don't
have a clue what it does to a man. Is it any wonder
we don't have much time or energy left to think
about emotions?

Women think marriage should always be like
courting. That's fine when you're young and you
don't have the pressures of a family, but it's
unrealistic to expect that marriage should always
be like love's young dream.

Many men complained to me that women are too
demanding and too needy. 'But that's only because they
don't give us enough attention,' retaliated Sonia, a
34-year-old housewife. 'They've always got the energy to
go out for a drink with their mates, or to play a round of
golf at the weekend. Yet when we want a little time and
attention spent on us they say they're too tired, or we're
nagging.'

Clearly, men and women have different expectations
from relationships. Once a man has committed himself to
a relationship or marriage he appears to see the future in
terms of being able to relax, secure in the knowledge that
his home and his comfort are assured, so now he can turn
his attention to other equally important parts of his life
such as his career. For a woman, the relationship *is* the
most important thing. Therefore her vision of their future
consists of one central picture of her, him, and probably
one or two little thems, and anything else is just a mere
shadow around the edge of the frame. But expectations, as
we all know, can so often be the prelude to disappointment and disillusionment.

Men are less discriminating about love

In addition to falling in love earlier, men also appear to be
far less discriminating about love. Experts agree that men

weigh women up in a remarkably short period of time. In fact seven seconds is the average amount of time a man will spend on deciding whether he wants to get to know a woman better. He will see a girl he likes the look of and the attraction can be immediate, and often all it takes for a man to find a woman attractive is for her to possess some resemblance to his conditional ideal.

When a man thinks of love, he thinks about heady romance, gloriously passionate sex, comfort, tenderness and maybe even the security of once more feeling omnipotent in a woman's arms. But he wants what he wants in the here and now, and that's why he rarely thinks about marriage or tomorrow.

And when a man is *in* love, he will be intensely aware of his emotions and feelings on a deep visceral level. But ask him to describe or discuss them and the embarrassment and discomfort he'll feel will be so great, he'll very likely switch the conversational gear to safer and far more comfortable ground.

A man's emotions and feelings, even when they have *everything* to do with you, have *nothing* to do with you. They're his, and he feels them more keenly and more deeply than any woman is ever likely to know. But his instinctive reaction is to keep them locked away. Besides, he daren't dredge them up to the surface because once he's acknowledged them on an intellectual level he also has to face their darker side: need. Men don't want to need women, because to them need is an emotion which equates with weakness. And as for subjecting their emotions to the cold unromantic light of analysis or discussion, well, even if a man wanted to, which believe me he doesn't, he'd find it virtually impossible to achieve because he genuinely *doesn't* know how.

'Men have less patience with emotions,' said Paul, a 44-year-old divorced engineer. 'Emotions – especially women's emotions – are foreign territory, and men simply do not know how to cope. Women aren't straightforward like us. They get angry but they won't say why, and yet they expect you to automatically understand what's upset them.'

The problem is, as we've already learned, women are far better at detecting subtle nuances of behaviour than men are. Moreover, because women are also innately interested in people and emotions, and have greater intuitive ability, it's not an effort for them to identify what their man wants and needs. But where women fail is in assuming that simply because *they* intuitively know when something is wrong, and sometimes even identify *what* is wrong, they assume that men can, or at the very least should try to, do the same – but they can't. Therefore, when a man says he doesn't know what he has done to upset you, he is not being difficult or obstructive, neither is he being obtuse; he is simply speaking the truth. The more you berate him for not knowing, or for being insensitive to your needs, the more miserable, confused, and guilt-ridden he will become.

Though his conscious mind may not acknowledge the fact, when a woman accuses a man of doing something wrong, or of not doing something right, she is criticizing him. And the one thing a man cannot bear is criticism. The other thing he cannot cope with is guilt; criticism and guilt are two very powerful and excruciatingly painful reminders of *failure*.

Remember the baby boy, secure, content and omnipotent in mother's loving arms? And then recall how bereft, abandoned, and unloved he felt the first time mother failed to bestow the dazzling warmth of her approval on him. What had he done wrong? Why had mother withdrawn her love? How had he failed?

He didn't know then, and he certainly doesn't know now. Why? Because, to put it very simply, men are nowhere near as complicated as women. When men want something, they'll tell you. When they're angry, they'll let you know about it. They won't sulk for days or throw a leftover of last year's argument in your face, and they certainly won't switch tactics in order that tears can win where tantrums have failed.

'You can't win with women,' said Derrick, 23. 'First they sulk, then they won't tell you what they're sulking about because 'we ought to know'. And by the time we've spent an hour convincing them we're not mind readers, they've convinced themselves that we don't love them enough because *they* wouldn't need to be told if they'd upset *us*. Is it any wonder we get so frustrated and we end up losing our patience and our tempers? And *that's* when they really get irrational; aiming missiles at us, or worse, they turn on tears. Why can't they simply tell us what's wrong at the start? It's senseless wasting all that energy and emotion on hostilities when it could be put to better use dealing with the problem that caused it in the first place.'

Of all the weapons a woman has tucked away in her not inconsiderable armoury of defence tactics, men regard the one she usually saves till last as the deadliest and most offensive weapon of all: tears.

'When all else fails,' said Jerry, a 53-year-old double glazing contractor, 'women resort to tears. And that's when we know we've been defeated, because there is nothing we can do to defend ourselves from a woman who is crying. We've only got two choices. Either we must walk away and work off our anger and frustration in another way, or we have to wave the white flag. Only a beast could fail to be defeated by a woman with tears in her eyes.'

Peter, a 33-year-old computer programmer who has only recently got divorced, admits to being totally perplexed by women:

> They're so changeable. You never can gauge their moods. One moment they're all sweetness and light, the next they're at your throat. One minute they're telling you they love you just the way you are, and before you know it they're trying to change you. If you're too tired to be loving and attentive, they get offended, seeing insult where none was intended. And when you're loving and

thoughtful they start talking you to death. Why are they so inconsistent? And why are they for ever theorizing, analysing and worrying about all the things they imagine are wrong? Why can't they just be happy and enjoy all the things that are right?

Why? 'Because we're afraid,' said Hazel, who at 45 is terrified that her second marriage might fail. 'We need to be reminded of how much they love us. To know that all the little things that meant so much in the beginning haven't been forgotten. And besides, it's only through sharing our emotions, and theirs, that we can feel really close and secure. I know what he feels, but I need to hear him tell me now and then.'

Woman: *the inveterate reformer*

When I asked several young men what they feared most about women and relationships, one fear that came close to the top of their list was the fear of having to change.

'They do it gradually,' said Louis, a 20-year-old sociology student. 'They wheedle and they flatter, they manipulate you in the name of love, but all the time they're working towards one end. They want to change you. They have this need to make you over in the image of what they consider to be the perfect man. Although, more often than not, it's what their girlfriends tell them the perfect man ought to be.'

'I don't want to be perfect,' interjected Chris, 19. 'I'm happy with the way I am. I like me, I like what I do and the friends I have. But my last girlfriend was always trying to make me into something I wasn't.'

'My ex-girlfriend told me I was totally different from her usual type of man,' said Danny, 19. 'She goes for men who are the opposite of me in every way. And yet she fell in love with me. Then her friends started applying the pressure, and soon we were arguing all the time. I can't change my looks, my height or my colouring to suit her. And I certainly wasn't going to change anything else. So we broke up. But now she's on the phone to me all the time, telling me that even though she's now going out with a guy who's all the things she likes and wants, it's me she loves and misses. If she loves me so much, why was she always trying to reform me? And why should *I* feel guilty for not being what *she* wants me to be?'

In fact one of the biggest mistakes a woman can make with a man is to attempt to remould or reform him. For implicit in this tactic is the disquieting accusation that he is *not* perfectly wonderful and lovable as he is. Take away a man's dreams of being perfect, or at the very least a hero, and you devastate him with the knowledge of his own failure.

Romantic love does not exist

The biggest problem men and women have to cope with in relationships today is the idealized vision we all have of a love that does not exist. Perfect love is an illusion. Yet we all pursue it as if it were the Holy Grail. Perfect love, we imagine, will transform us from being an ordinary person into an extraordinary one. The woman who believes she is secretly a goddess, or at the very least a princess in disguise, and the man who knows that beneath his business suit beats the heart and soul of a hero both long for confirmation of this knowledge, and both yearn desperately for the one truly perfect being who will recognize them for who and what they really are.

The vision of love we all crave is doomed to elude us for ever for there are only three situations in which idealized 'love' can continue to exist, and not one of them resides on the plane of reality in which we all must live.

The first version of idealized love is generally referred to as 'star-crossed' – this means that a 'hopelessly insurmountable obstacle' must exist to prevent the couple from being together, in which case an imperfectly ordinary love can be catapulted straight into the 'star-crossed lovers against the world' stratosphere where tragedy reigns supreme à la *Romeo et Juliette*.

The second is termed 'unrequited'. This allows the disappointed lover to cast himself in some form of purgatorial role, such as the tormented pre-Raphaelite artist burning with unfulfilled passion alone in his garret, pouring out his yearnings onto canvasses that repeatedly fail to capture the poetic essence of his muse's eyes.

And then there's the third one – which also happens to be the very best one of all, simply because the possibilities are infinite – the 'tragically doomed' love, in which one lover has the misfortune to die before the reality of life has had a chance to erode the romance. Which means, of course, that the remaining lover gets the good fortune to play the martyr by elevating his or her departed love to such saintly heights that all future opportunities are rejected because there is no way they ever can compare with 'what might have been'.

The latter is the one that appeals most to women, while the other two, especially the first, are enormously attractive to men. Why especially the first? Because it offers a man the one opportunity to fulfil all his dreams; he can become the hero he has always longed to be. And *that* is the very first, the very last, and the most important thing of all that women must learn to understand about men. Because inside every man there is a hero just waiting to burst free. Men love the idea of donning their armour, leaping astride their white chargers and galloping off into the sunset to tilt at windmills, save the world, or at the very least commit an act of such derring-do that princesses will swoon at their feet and dragons will die of fright.

Men want to worship their women, and, likewise, they need to be worshipped in return. But as Irma Kurtz once said, 'He doesn't want to do great things *with* her, he wants to do them *for* her.'

Unfortunately, somewhere deep inside each man there

resides a dreadful and primeval fear, generated by his strong sense of self-preservation and fed by a deeply ingrained (and not entirely without foundation, either) suspicion; a voice is warning him, 'Beware! What if, in slaying the dragon, you should discover that it wasn't the dragon who died but your own heroic dream?'

'Men are always doomed to be duped, not so much by the arts of the (other) sex as by their own imaginations. They are always wooing goddesses and marrying mere mortals.' So wrote Washington Irving in 1822. And that is what every man fears. You see, men intuitively know that women can prove to be far more dangerous foes than dragons. And the moment they surrender their heart and life to the service of a princess, the chances are she'll immediately start finding fault with his own particular brand of heroism and then commence her subtle campaign to reform, restrict, and slowly but surely transform him into a totally different, bigger, better kind of hero – one who has stepped straight out of *her* dream.

Because the one thing you can be certain of is that her description of a hero bears no relation to his, as the next chapter will reveal.

11

Women: Where Have All The Heroes Gone?

'WHERE HAVE ALL the heroes gone?' cried Alan, a 41-year-old twice-divorced, many times disappointed misogynistic solicitor who was so outraged on hearing the title of this chapter, he could hardly hold his anger in check. 'I'm sick to death of the flak we men continually have to take from women. Well, what we men would like to know is, "Where have all the virtuous damsels worth saving gone?" There is a distinct difference between what women say they want and need and their deep prime-evil (sic) subconscious desires. Women are born knowing how to lure and trap men. They're devious, manipulative, conniving and dishonest, and what's more, they plan their strategies like a military campaign so when one ploy fails to work, they have always got an alternative tactic tucked up their sleeves. Women don't seek heroes, they seek victims, and we men are the unfortunate, unwitting spoils in their nasty little game of war.'

'The trouble with men,' pronounced Maureen, 41, a divorced company director and mother, 'is that they only ever view women in terms of love and hate. They loved their mother, but they can never forget or forgive the fact that she once held total power over them. And they spend the rest of their lives making every other female they meet pay for it.'

Ouch! With comments like these, it's not surprising that relationships between men and women have been described as a *battle* of the sexes. It rather makes one wonder, if men and women always have hated, feared and despised each other so very much, why do we all continue to seek the one person in all the world of whom such damning indictments might not be true?

If goddesses have feet of clay and heroes do not exist except in our imaginations, and *every* love affair is destined to end in disillusionment and disappointment on both sides, why can't men and women simply accept the *status quo* and lower their sights to a more realistic level? Why do women still hanker after heroes when all their experience teaches them that heroes simply do *not* exist? Is biological programming so powerful that, despite all the progress women have made since that long ago time when they were reliant solely on the protection of men, the female species still cannot dispense with her inbuilt, inherently primeval need to search out and strive towards capturing and keeping a hero for her very own self? After all, women do have opportunities of their own now, so none of us need be financially or in any other way dependent upon a man. Unless, of course, we want to, and therein lies the rub.

Given that we have seen enough scientific and sociological evidence by now to be convinced that women are by nature both more emotional and intuitive, and yet at the same time far more pragmatic and rational in love than men, one might have thought that they would have reached the conclusion (if only on a biological level) that 'holding out for a hero' is a waste of their very precious procreative time, and found a better and more practical method of selecting a mate with whom to parent the next generation. After all, as Anne Moir and David Jessel ponted out in their book *Brain Sex*, 'Women are not the ones blinded by testosterone-fuelled desire.' Moreover, if it's true that women are less susceptible to the kind of swift romantic impulses that catapult men into being 'in love', and more inclined to evaluate a man's worth in terms of practicalities, wouldn't it better suit their pragmatic natures to dispense altogether with such foolhardy notions of 'romance' and 'heroes'?

Or could it simply be that the word 'hero' has an entirely different connotation for a woman than it does for a man? Therefore, when men complain bitterly that women expect and want too much from them, what they're really railing against is *their* failure to attain *their* own potential to be a hero according to *their* definition of the word.

All men have the potential to be heroes in a woman's eyes

Every woman has a slightly different definition of what a man must be or do to be considered heroic in her eyes. Some do, indeed, seem to require a man more godlike than mortal, while others are far more realistic in their requirements, as well as far more forgiving than many men would believe. But the one particular attribute which every woman I spoke to agreed was a vital component was a willingness to *truly share his life with her.*

'All I want,' said Rona, a single beautician aged 29, 'is a man who will be honest, open and sincere with me. Men tell you they want an honest relationship when what they really mean is, they demand honesty from you but they don't want to be totally honest in return.'

'I want a man who will be my friend,' said Natalie, a single secretary aged 25. 'I want someone I can relax with, someone I can feel safe and secure with, who knows me in all my different moods and loves me regardless. I can't stand the sort of men who're all over you when they want something but back off and call you demanding when you need a cuddle or want to talk a problem through. It's an old-fashioned word, but I guess what I'd really like to have is companionship with the man I love.'

'Men are emotionally illiterate,' said June, a 33-year-old single journalist. 'The older I get, the more men I meet, the more I realize how impossible they find it to discuss their emotions. Each man I've fallen in love with has made a point of letting me know in one way or another what he expects from a woman. He doesn't come right out and say so, of course, he just tells you over a period of time all the things he didn't like about his previous girlfriends. But what I've noticed is they never say, "When she did such and such it made me *feel* like x", they simply criticize the things she did, or say, "She had a nasty habit of doing such and such". They talk to you in code.'

Elizabeth and Charles have been married for 45 years. Until they retired Elizabeth had a responsible, high-pressured job as the principal of a private girls' school and Charles was a carpenter. Elizabeth earned a great deal of money, Charles' salary was meagre. And yet, not once in all the 48 years that Elizabeth has known Charles, has she ever seen him as anything less than her hero:

> I know people think I'm the dominant partner, Charles the passive one. They probably think I rule the roost at home while he does as he is bid. Certainly in the past I've known people to speculate about what I see in a man whom they regard as my intellectual, physical, and temperamental inferior. Likewise, many men have suggested to Charles that he must hate being under the thumb of a bossy, domineering woman who earns more than him. Either that, or they dismiss him as a mouse.
>
> They are all wrong. We have a wonderful relationship. What other people regard as a weakness, I see as a measure of Charles' strength. He loves me, and he's never been too proud to tell me how much he needs me. But we have something else that I so often see missing in younger people's marriages: Charles listens to me. Not in the sense of taking orders from me, but

when I need to talk, to feel weak, to show my emotions, or need him to discuss his, he cares enough to give me what I need. He's protective, yet regards me as an intelligent, independent person who can make her own decisions. If I need his advice, he'll give it to me, if I don't, he'll respect my opinions and decisions. We have what I've always wanted in a relationship with a man: total trust, total commitment, total sharing, and, above all, total caring. And that means far more to me than having a man who appears to be other people's definition of a perfect man. When I say I worship Charles, I'm not saying it lightly. My husband is my hero in every sense of the word.

Women don't want men, they want supermen. At least that's what many men I spoke to believe. In fact, they're wrong. When a woman loves a man her capacity for patience and tolerance can be infinite, providing the man is giving her what she needs.

Ask a man what a woman's definition of a hero is and he'd probably describe some godlike adonis who will leap out of bed in the morning, still strong and virile after having made mad, passionate, but tender love to his goddess. He'll wear Giorgio Armani business suits and drive a Ferrari Testarossa to his high-tech HQ where he'll slay a few office dragons before lunch, as well as a handful of corporate jungle cats after. And in between he'll find the time to brighten up her afternoon by arranging for the delivery of a few dozen roses accompanied by the romantically cryptic message 'Just because ...'; or interrupt a crucial board meeting to arrange for a chartered plane to whisk them off to Paris for dinner followed by a romantic moonlit trip along the Seine in a *baton mouche*; then, unable to stop himself from drowning in a sea of sensual passion inspired solely by her beauty, he'll dazzle her with his ability to instantly compose a charming sonnet or two before bedtime and have yet another bout of the kind of mad, passionate but tender lovemaking which makes her truly aware of what it means to be 'a woman fulfilled'.

Well, yes, I'm certain every woman will see the merits in that little daydream, too. On the other hand, most women are also practical enough to know that while daydreams of this nature provide great fantasy material, there are other scenarios which are equally likely to turn them on. Such as the one in which he demonstrates his love for her by being interested enough to spend an hour listening to what she has to say, and sharing with her the news about his own day over a takeaway, followed by an offer to share a few mundane chores (such as the washing, the ironing and cleaning the kitchen floor), before snuggling down under the duvet for a session of comfortable and not necessarily all that torrid sex.

Victorian maidens who had nothing to do all day but lounge around looking beautiful and fragile may have spent their time spinning fantasies and swooning at the thought of being rescued from a life of apathy by super-men, but times have changed and women have long since leapt (unaided) from the *chaise-longue*.

Today's women want far more from their lives than merely playing passive maiden to some man's own version of a superhero. And as for fulfilment, well, not only has she learned to stop looking to a man to fulfil all her needs, she's just as likely to be actively engaged in providing more than 50 per cent of that for herself, if not from the satisfaction of pursuing a full-time career, then from being free to do what *she* wants to do, whether it is combining motherhood with a part-time job, further education, or even a private hobby or interest that stretches her mind.

Men, it seems, aren't in the least bit pleased at being let off the hook. Take Rick, for example. When he married Claire six years ago he knew she wanted to defer having children until she'd achieved her aim of becoming a barrister and then practising for a few years afterwards. A successful commodities broker himself, Rick is now beginning to get a little peeved at the amount of time Claire devotes to her career:

We're both 30 this year, and I think it's time Claire started easing off. I know she works hard, and it can't be easy having a home to run as well. We have a cleaning lady and I help out as much as I can, but I'm beginning to feel uncomfortable. Intellectually I know Claire has every right to fulfil her ambitions and do whatever it is she feels she needs to do. But I get quite a few days off and sometimes I'd like her to spend the day with me. However she can't because she might have a case to work on. I try not to get irritated because it isn't fair to her, but there's this little voice that keeps saying to me, 'A woman's place is in the home, and a woman's role is to please her man.'

It makes me sound really sexist, and I'm not. At least I like to think I'm not. But I want a wife, and I'd like to start thinking about children soon, and part of me can't quite get to grips with the idea that a woman can get all the fulfilment she needs from a career and not need anything from me.

On the contrary, women do need something from their men, particularly working wives and mothers. Unfortunately the very thing they're most in need of is the one thing many of them say their husbands appear to be incapable of giving: practical help and emotional support. Joanna, aged 37, said:

I used to think I could have it all. When Nigel and I married we agreed I'd give up work when the children came along. But after five years at home I was climbing the walls. I love my children, and I believe I'm a good mother, but it's not enough for me. When I was offered the opportunity to return to my former job as a marketing director on a part-time basis, I jumped at it. Unfortunately, Nigel wasn't convinced it would work out at all well. 'You'll be too tired to have energy left for the kids and me,' he'd say. I almost found myself begging him, making every kind of concession in order to convince him that we'd all benefit, not suffer. He gave in, of course. Well, he had to, didn't he? I love my work, I like feeling dynamic again, and having power and responsibility. But I'm constantly having to juggle all the balls in the air to keep things running smoothly at home and at work. And sometimes I wonder how long it will be before one slips through my fingers. I daren't ask Nigel for any help, I just know he'll give me that, 'I told you so' look. Sometimes I wonder whether he's cleverly manipulated the situation so that I'm constantly having to try extra hard to prove to him and myself that I can handle the extra burden. If I thought that was the case I'd be furiously resentful … in fact, I already am. If I can be supportive of his needs and the things he wants to do, why can't he do the same for me?

Guilt – part of the job when Mum goes back to work

As I said before, women don't want or need supermen, they want the kind of man who respects them as an individual and who is not afraid of sharing and caring. Working women who combine full- or even part-time careers with bringing up a family face the kind of conflicts men rarely ever have to experience. When they're at work, they worry about whether the children are missing them, or likely to develop psychological problems because, 'Mummy was never there'. And when they're at home, they worry about the things that still need to be done at work. They worry about how to fit into their evening all the little household chores that are being neglected during the day, and then how they're going to find the energy to devote to their husbands in bed. And it doesn't matter how much they worry, or how well they organize their lives, their guilt just goes on and on amassing and gaining in strength.

As TV producer and presenter, Esther Rantzen, admitted during a recent TV interview, working mothers are simply 'riven with guilt. I just pray that in the long run my children are going to think that I did balance my life properly. But I can't pretend I'm confident.'

And yet, if men only realized how much they would be contributing to their own happiness by helping to contribute to their wives', they'd soon discover the benefits that true sharing can bring to a relationship. According to a recent survey conducted by Dr Jacqueline Olds at Harvard University, when husbands share child-rearing responsibilities with their part-time working wives, there's a far better chance of the marriage being happier and lasting longer. Whereas those marriages in which wives are banned from working are more likely to end up in the divorce courts the moment the children leave home.

Women who are denied the opportunity to fulfil other needs are, according to Dr Olds, more likely to feel some confusion and resentment, on the one hand hating to be tied down but on the other becoming too protective of their roles as child-rearing experts. 'We found that full-time homemakers often unconsciusly discouraged their husbands from participating in bringing up the children,' said Dr Olds. 'The combination of feeling stuck with the kids and insisting no one else could do an adequate job of looking after them led to estrangement from their partners.'

This is a syndrome Sally, a 42-year-old single parent, knows only too well:

> I had a career before the children, but my husband wanted me to give it up. I loved him so much I did what he wanted. Unfortunately I found myself becoming resentful at having to sacrifice my career and yet still being expected to be vibrant, lively, and sexy for him when he came home. I enjoyed being a wife and mother, but it simply wasn't enough for me. I became starved of stimulation, my mind was going to seed, but instead of helping

me by understanding my need for intelligent conversation, he simply refused to discuss or debate
any topic with me, saying all he wanted when he
came home was to relax. All hopes and illusions I'd
had about him as a person, and marriage as a
partnership, soon died. And so eventually did my
love.

I never said what you think you heard

In the same way each sex has a different perspective on
and experience of love, so too are their perceptions and
experiences of marriage equally different. But neither sex
is totally to blame for failing to meet the other's
expectations.

A man and a woman could live, love, and share an
entire lifetime together, most times happily, sometimes
miserably, but always making assumptions about each
other based on what each partner thinks he heard the
other one say. Meanwhile, neither of them ever stops to
consider that there might be two meanings to each piece
of information or communication that is being exchanged,
as well as two entirely different interpretations that are
being placed upon what each thinks they are communicating to the other.

When women ask questions, men misinterpret their
interest as probing and prying. When men pass comment
or offer advice, women misinterpret their behaviour as
domination or bossiness. When women offer men
reminders, men become defensive because they feel they
are being criticized or nagged. When men offer reminders,
women perceive themselves as being patronized, trivia-
lized or diminished in some fundamental way.

The same is true for every single form of relationship
that could possibly exist between a woman and a man,
from the first date scenario outlined in chapter 1,
right through to a marriage that has survived 60-plus
years.

As a simple example, let's take a look at the totally different ways in which a man and a woman relate to and interpret the same shared experience.

'Why is it that the moment you sleep with a woman she starts moving in on your entire life?' groaned 29-year-old Gary, who owns his own car sales business. 'Charlotte is great in bed and I really like her, but it makes me nervous when she starts acting like she's taking over the whole of my life.'

'Once I'd slept with Gary,' said Charlotte, 27, 'I felt as if I had shared with him a little private piece of myself. Sex may represent nothing more than scratching an itch to him, but I don't see it that way. I naturally felt warmer and closer to him, and I don't have a problem showing that. But that doesn't mean I'm threatening his independence in any way. For me, it's purely another stage in the process of the relationship, regardless of where it's going to lead.'

When viewed from *both* perspectives, however, it's not difficult to see how our behaviour and actions can be – and, in fact, usually are – misconstrued by the opposite sex.

Nothing annoys a man more than to have a woman hang all sorts of 'meanings' on a sexual encounter that, for him, meant nothing more nor less than that. But then again, nothing hurts – and angers – a woman more than to have a man misinterpret her spontaneous expressions of warmth and caring as a sign that she's about to start behaving like a woman obsessed.

For most women, when they share their body with a man, they're sharing a little bit of their inner 'self' and their emotions in an atmosphere of intimacy. Once that step's been taken, they naturally feel a bit more connected to him. They've passed the 'let's keep things at a distance barrier' and they can let their emotional guard down a fraction and feel that little bit freer to express their very natural need to give and share affection. What it most certainly does *not* mean is what he *thinks* it means: that either she's already started planning her trousseau, or that she's mentally calculating how she's going to fit the entire contents of her wardrobe into his.

Men misinterpret a woman's natural inclination to *share* and to show real concern as the kind of unhealthy curiosity that killed the proverbial cat. 'Why do they want to know every little detail about what you did at work or who said what when you went out for a drink with your mates?' said Paul, 27, who works in a bank. In fact, far from being turned off by a woman's natural curiosity or inquisitiveness, men really ought to be flattered. Because when women ask questions it's not because they're being nosy, but simply because they're *interested* in what make's people – or to be more specific, men – tick.

Women, remember, are far more concerned with establishing *intimacy*, and one of their methods for achieving this is to ask all sorts of questions designed to give them a handle on why a man is the way he is, what's currently happening in his life, why he responds the way he does, and also what pleases him and what doesn't. The reason they do so is because they want to achieve a real understanding of a man's *emotions*. Apart from which, *nothing* is guaranteed to make a woman feel more loved and valued by a man than his sharing the little details of his daily life with her. It doesn't matter how insignificant or inconsequential his doings might be, it's the *choosing to share them* that's important, because that in itself signifies his willingness to involve and include her in *all of his life*.

Men, on the other hand, are far less interested in the details of their women's lives, or even in the *whys* of women's behaviour, because, at heart, they're far less concerned with the things they regard as trivia.

Tell a man something important (which usually means either a) something *he's* interested in, b) something he doesn't already know, but which it would be to his advantage to know, or c) something that directly affects *him*) and he'll be all ears. But try passing the time with chit-chat about nothing in particular, telling the juicy details about your colleague's disastrous affair with the managing director, or starting any conversation that involves the minutiae of your life, and before you know it he'll probably be asleep.

That's not intended to be taken as a disparaging comment, it's merely the way men are. You see, not only are men genuinely *un*interested in all the little details that round out stories, they're also far less inclined to psychoanalyse people or to seek hidden meanings behind specific statements or actions.

That's why, when men's relationships go wrong, you'll rarely find them talking to all and sundry in an attempt to work out what went wrong or why it went wrong. That's alien to their more private natures. Granted, they'll spend hours and hours on a post-mortem of a lost football match, or a deal that didn't quite come off, but that's because those things are not *personal* to them, and therefore they can remain detached. But when it comes to delving into intensely private matters such as their emotions, men can't help experiencing a distinct feeling of discomfort simply because this is unfamiliar territory to them.

In every fundamental way men and women are different. The ways in which our brains are biologically programmed are different. Our individual cultures are different. The conditioning processes that apply to us are different. And when it comes to communicating and relating to what is being communicated, we are separated by a huge cross-cultural divide. In other words we each place entirely the wrong meaning, not only upon what the other sex does and says, but also upon their motivation for doing so.

For instance, the issue of *status* has a great deal to do with the way men relate to women *and* how they interpret the things women say and do. For example, being told what to do implies being relegated to an inferior position to the one occupied by the person who is telling you what to do. Consequently, since much of male society is concerned with the jostling for or establishment of hierarchical status, men will tend to view repeated requests from women in a defensively negative light, whilst at the same time seeing their own dominant behaviour as a positive, manly, *protective* thing to do. Make no mistake, the word 'protective' is an important one in the male vocabulary, for not only does it cover a multitude of sins (of the 'but I didn't want to hurt you variety'), but the very action itself immediately places him in the *superior* position.

Women seeking love

As we discovered in the previous chapter, men have a facility for instant attraction, a fact which has certainly been underscored for me in the past by the number of men I've personally known who told me the moment they set eyes on their wife they *knew* she was the girl they were going to marry. This is something I've never heard from a woman. But then that's hardly surprising as, on the whole, women do prefer to take their time, and they're also less likely to be influenced by the way a man looks and more interested in what kind of person he is.

A woman's shopping list of essential ingredients for a life-long mate is never far from the forefront of her mind. Not because she's desperate, but because her subconscious mind always has one eye fixed on that inner biological clock which is reminding her with each passing tick that she only has so much time left in which to build, furnish and populate her little family nest.

A woman will want to know what values a man holds, what he does for a living, what prospects he might have, and even, maybe, how much money he earns, because this is the kind of knowledge she needs to help her assess his potential as a permanent partner. If a man doesn't meet a woman's criteria for good partner material, but she's attracted to him anyway, she may well follow her heart into an affair, and sometimes even into marriage, but she's far more likely to keep the brake firmly pressed down on the pedal of her emotions until such time as her instincts tell her it's safe to let go.

But there's another reason why women are more realistic about romance than men. And that's because they are more in touch with their feelings. They learn very early on in their lives to differentiate between infatuation and real love, and while they can indulge themselves in the former, there's far too much at stake for them to confuse it with the latter. But once a woman has made up her mind about a man, she'll revel in every euphorically giddy moment of being 'in love'. Every emotion she is capable of feeling will be unleashed and displayed, because, once aroused and ignited, a woman's emotions, which are never far from the surface anyway, will be allowed total free rein. When he loves her she'll visibly float on an overwhelming metaphorical cloud of happiness. And when he hurts her, tears will never be far away.

A woman needs to share her feelings, to take them out and inspect them often. She also needs to discuss them with her man, and to hear him talk about the way she makes him feel. Sharing her emotions, and having him share his with her, is a woman's security blanket, which is something men very rarely understand.

When a woman contemplates marriage she anticipates a relationship that will involve companionship, emotional sensitivity, interaction (both in and out of bed), mutual support, sharing and communication, and emotional intimacy in sex. Conversely, when a woman does not feel emotionally intimate with her partner, sex will be the very *first* thing to suffer.

Men, on the other hand, are both far less emotionally demanding and more independent than women. For him, marriage and home will provide something of a back-up system. His role, as he sees it, is to provide financial security, to be a decision maker (not necessarily arbitrarily, because many men are quite prepared to consult their wives over major decisions), and to be the lynchpin on which the family's welfare depends. And he'll undoubtedly want, nay even expect, a very good sex life. And because a man's temperament is not susceptible to or governed by the same kind of hormonal fluctuations, it never occurs to him that women can often be influenced by or at the mercy of their own emotions. Which is a shame, because so far as most women are concerned, *that* is the one area in the marital garden where the seed of discord is most likely to take root and flower.

Shere Hite, author of *The Hite Report on Female Sexuality* discovered the same after questioning 4500 American women about the problems within their relationships. A staggering 98 per cent of women complained that the most frustrating thing about their relationship was the lack of 'verbal closeness'. In fact, emotional closeness (which, as we all know can only be achieved through communication) is so high on every woman's shopping list for a hero that when women feel they can't or don't have it, they will very often seriously question whether the relationship is viable at all.

'Women will forgive many failings in a man they love,' said my female psychologist friend, 'but the one thing they find really hard to tolerate is a man who is emotionally cold or uncommunicative.'

'I forgave my husband's adultery because I knew we had been going through a bad patch,' said Shirley, 35, 'but what hurt me more than the adultery itself was the way he shut his emotions away from me while it was going on. I understand he couldn't share with me whatever it was he was feeling for the other woman, but that he didn't even attempt to discuss the fact that he was feeling neglected and unappreciated *before* he sought diversion with somebody else ... well, that was the most painful and the most unforgivable thing of all.'

Carol, a 25-year-old secretary who's engaged to be married: 'I can't bear it when he shuts me out. Men have a habit of squirrelling their emotions away. If he's got a problem, even one that has nothing to do with me, my first inclination is to want to help him. But if he won't share it with me, how can I know when something's wrong?'

Anna, a 19-year-old actress: 'My boyfriend says when he doesn't tell me things it's not because he doesn't care, but because he wants to protect me. He can't understand that I don't need his protection, I need his confidence and trust.'

Belinda, a-31-year-old working mother: 'I feel so insignificant when Mark withdraws into himself. It's as if he doesn't think I'm intelligent enough to understand. When I have a problem I always share it with him, and even if there's nothing he can actually do to help me solve it, just knowing that he's willing to listen is enough for me. Why can't men do the same with us?'

Many a man has been heard to level the accusation that women are calculating and mercenary by nature; that they are more willing to compromise their dream of love and romance in exchange for security and a family. And perhaps now that we know a little more about the subtle influence a woman's biological programming has on her emotional make-up, they might at last begin to understand why.

Another accusation men are fond of making is that women *say* they want nice men but then they ditch them for charmers and 'bastards'. To be fair there is a modicum of truth in this claim, but what most men fail to recognize is that charmers and 'bastards' are usually supremely adept at disguising their true natures and intentions behind the personas of nice men.

On the other hand, a comment that often crops up in women's conversations is: scratch the surface of a self-professed non-sexist, sympathetic, caring 'new man' and you'll very likely find there's a domineering, chauvinist lurking beneath.

At the age of 38, Jillie has achieved all the goals she set for herself at the beginning of her career. But in order to do so she's been forced to sacrifice her dream of combining a career with marriage and motherhood:

I've lived with three men, but I'll never do it again. They all said they were happy for me to pursue a career, but the moment my success outstripped theirs, their egos couldn't handle it. The more successful I became, the more they tried to dominate me. It's as if they needed to prove something to themselves. They certainly didn't need to prove anything to me other than that their original words were sincere, which of course they weren't. I've finally reached the conclusion that successful women intimidate men. They feel threatened by them, and that really is a big disappointment to me. I suppose if I'm really honest, I haven't quite given up all hope of finding the kind of man who doesn't see my career as being competitive with his. But I don't rate my chances very highly.

And Jillie is not alone in her experience, for many men, it appears, are indeed intimidated by today's breed of self-sufficient female. But it's not so much the successful career women they fear, so much as how they themselves will be perceived for behaving in the only way they know how.

Recently I came across an article in the London *Evening Standard* written by 28-year-old Toby Young, in which he claimed that, thanks to feminism, an entire generation of men have grown up believing it's insulting to ask a girl out. 'Why risk being accused of treating women as objects, or having a one-track mind, or only being interested in one thing?' he opined, when, 'As far as most men my age are concerned, you're better off watching a game of football.'

'Sexism, like racism, is the ultimate sin,' wrote Toby. 'To view women as sex objects rather than people, as the saying goes, is on a par with regarding black people as slaves. These days, if a man makes an improper suggestion he's more likely to end up in court than in bed.'

Moreover, Toby reckons it's not just because his generation is wary of censure that it's reluctant to play the field, but that it actually does recognize that women have every cause to complain that men have behaved badly towards them in the past. But, he argues, if the only means of achieving a new kind of relationship – one that's free from all deception or guile – is for men to discover a new source of masculinity, then the very fact that this would require an 'almost impossibly large' amount of re-education on their part could result in many of them electing to opt out of the game altogether.

Women want it all

'Women are no longer content simply to be wives and mothers,' lamented Jim, 56, who makes no secret of the fact that he absolutely hated it when his wife returned to work after 30 years. 'Why can't they be satisfied with being women? Why must they continually strive to become more and more like men?'

Well, can you blame women? After all, if men spent less time banging the drum of their own self-confessed superiority, or ramming down women's throats how wonderful it is to be a male, and more time communicating their appreciation of all the many different skills and qualities women do have, as opposed to continually devaluing them, who knows, perhaps women might indeed have been content with the way things once were?

Furthermore, I don't believe I'm the first writer to have made the observation that, if Freud was correct when he said all women suffer from penis envy, how come it never occurred to him to deduce that our envy could only ever have been created by man's continual insistence that a penis is the only possession worth prizing?

Who and what do we really want to be?

In their book *Brain Sex*, Anne Moir and David Jessel

reported the results of a number of interesting studies conducted over recent years to identify the qualities, characteristics and personality traits each sex would most like to have, and also how each evaluates *happiness* in relationships.

Men, apparently, would most like to be 'practical, shrewd, assertive, dominating, competitive, critical and self-controlled', whereas women most want to be considered 'loving, affectionate, impulsive, sympathetic and generous'. When it comes to values, women assess social, aesthetic and religious values highest, while men rate economic, political and theoretical values the most. Where women value 'interesting experiences' and 'being of service to society', men value 'power, profit and independence'.

Furthermore, men place 'prestige, competition, scientific toys and principles, power, dominance and freedom' highest on their list of priorities, whereas women rate 'personal relationships and security' as being more important to them.

Insofar as married couples are concerned, the surveys showed that, while the men appeared to equate marital happiness with a wife's performance of 'services', i.e., looking good, cooking, shopping, housewifery, etc (and also, presumably, sex), the women's ratings of marital happiness seemed to be connected to how much affection their husbands had shown on the day they were asked to complete the questionnaire.

Men, it seems, express love through action; they'll buy you a box of chcolates or flowers on impulse on the way home, they'll wash your car, decorate your house, or even take you to watch their favourite team play in the Cup Final, all of which are their own uniquely male methods for showing you how much you are loved – and, incidentally, which are infinitely more preferable to being asked or forced to articulate what they know they *feel* for you but don't quite know how to say. Men are not unperceptive, but their perception is limited by the fact that their brains are designed and wired for 'physical action and problem solving', whereas women's brains are better equipped to deal with emotions – women 'notice', they 'feel' and they 'care'.

What more evidence do we need that, while men and women *are* vastly different creatures in *every* sense of the word, the one thing we have in common is our need to love and share? And given that there isn't any alternative to loving and sharing with each other, the only question that remains to be asked is: Where *do* we go from here?

12

Where Do We Go From Here?

A<small>T THE BEGINNING</small> I said that relationships between the sexes are founded upon three things: sex, lies and love.

Throughout the preceding chapters we've heard a great deal about how and why each sex relates differently to sex and love, and, hopefully, we've gained some insight into how and why these differences create so much confusion and dissent between us. And though we haven't overtly discussed lies, I hope by now you've realized that the worst kind of deception that goes on between the sexes is *self-deception*.

Few men and women, particularly those who sincerely do want to form a relationship with and understand the opposite sex, deliberately lie with any malice aforethought or serious intent to deceive. But whenever someone makes it clear that a piece of information is incorrect, or we perceive a conflict between what someone *says* to us and what their behaviour demonstrates, we always assume they are lying. It rarely occurs to us, of course, that we might be lying to ourselves!

However that's precisely what we do when we form an assumption based on our *own interpretation* of the hidden meaning behind what other people say and do. And when it transpires that they didn't actually *say* what *we* thought they *said*, or *mean* what *we* thought they meant, we naturally assume that they deliberately intended to deceive us, when, in reality, it's very often we who have deceived ourselves by misunderstanding and misinterpreting the meaning of their attitudes, their words and their behaviour.

If relationships between men and women are in crisis today, then it's a crisis of our own making. In part we are hampered by our own natural biological patterns whose programmes were designed, orchestrated and set in a prehistoric time when mankind had vastly different priorities and needs to the ones we have now. The fact that these fundamental biological patterns which still govern our emotions and instincts have now come into conflict with an intellect that has long since evolved, outgrown and dispensed with the need for them is, in one sense, unfortunate, because anything which threatens to upset nature's delicate balance can only work to our detriment. And when the paths of men and women diverge to the point where we all become so mistrustful, cynical and at odds with each other that our relationships start to flounder in the ensuing sea of confusion, believe me it will be to our detriment indeed.

Today, as never before in our history, the needs of men and women appear to be more diametrically opposed than they ever have been. Today's men blame all their problems on feminism, while today's women blame all their problems on chauvinism. But how we got here is not nearly so important or crucial an issue as where we go from here.

While no woman can fail to admire those brave women who launched the first feminist offensive which undoubtedly did much to eradicate many of the inequalities that existed in the past, I can't help but wonder, at the risk of upsetting some of the more radical and strident members of the feminist brigade, how many of today's single (and married) women are asking themselves whether the price they're now being asked to pay in their relationships is worth it? No one can deny that women should have every right to choose a career if that is what they want, or that they deserve to be given every opportunity and equal encouragement to climb the corporate ladder if they so desire. Equally, however, we cannot deny that, sooner or later, the very natural urge to mate and nest is likely to exert its powerful primeval influence on their hormones and emotions.

Over and over again the same questions keep being asked, and the same age-old battles go on and on being fought. Surely, by now, the answer ought to be crystal clear: men and women, thank goodness, are *different*. We each have different strengths, different weaknesses, different needs, and different desires. Neither sex is superior or inferior in any sense other than the purely biological one we have already discussed.

Time was when we gloried in our differences and, by and large, relationships between the sexes were all the better for it. Yes, men *controlled*, and therefore their power *was* deemed to be greater than any female's ever could be. But women have always intuitively known that power can take many vastly different forms. A man held dominion in society, but a woman held dominion in the home and over her family. Although her power was far more subtly expressed and wielded, few women doubted the fact of its existence. And while I'm not suggesting that women might have done better had they remained content to be the power behind the proverbial (male) throne, neither am I convinced that they're all that much better off, or happier, or more fulfilled, or even more content, for having fought so hard for the right to acquire a throne of their very own.

As writer Rosie Boycott, former editor of the feminist magazine *Spare Rib*, said in a recent interview published in the *Sunday Express*:

> Feminism was immensely straightforward and simple at the beginning because there was a belief that if you could change the laws there would be

an automatic change in women, and that women would become MPs and captains of industry. It was a naïve expectation that you could fix something that had been in existence for a very long time.

Quite a lot of people are now questioning whether it was worth it because we haven't got the things that traditionally make women happy. Our generation is paying a very high price for trying to do it differently.

Nature did not design men and women to *compete* with each other. She designed us to *complement* one another. Moreover, if only one thing has emerged from the stories, complaints, comments and many laments contained within these pages, surely it must be that men and women both experience and relate to love in different ways. And yet, in spite of all our many differences, at our best and at our worst, we're all past masters at the art of self-deception. For though we each profess to be seeking that special someone to fall in love and share our lives happily ever after with, what we're *really* seeking is someone who will make *us* feel loved.

When our chosen partner no longer makes *us* feel loved, we retreat behind our walls of hurt and disappointment and arm ourselves against further pain and disillusionment by withholding our own love. Rarely do we ever pause to consider that our selfishly based need to be and feel loved applies equally to those whom we profess to love. Or, more importantly, that the specific actions or behavioural demonstrations which make *us* truly *feel* that we are indeed being loved almost certainly will not have the same meaning to our partner. That is one of the major reasons why relationships between the sexes are fraught with misunderstanding. But still we cling on doggedly to the hope and the belief that love can and will transcend all. And so it can. But not without understanding, and not without tolerance. And certainly not without some willingness *on both sides* for a cessation in the hostilities that have kept the Battle for the Supremacy of the Sexes raging for so long.

Clearly we have the hope. Hopefully we have the will. All we need now is to accept, first that relating subjectively to each other can be every bit as damaging as not relating to each other at all, and second that we all need to be more tolerant and to put more effort into increasing our understanding of *why* each sex cannot help but be other than the *way they are*. And if, instead of wasting our individual energies and efforts on battling for supremacy or contriving ways of blaming each other for our own failures and disappointments, we put as much effort into understanding, accepting, and celebrating the differences that exist between us as we have into *criticizing, blaming and deploring* these in the past, perhaps we finally will recognize that true fulfilment can never be attained in a relationship until 'I' becomes 'WE' and 'ME' becomes 'US'.

Are You a Possessive Lover?

Are you a possessive lover? Do you feel such overwhelming and intense passion for your lover that you simply cannot control your emotions – or the actions that result from them? Can jealousy make you hurt physically as well as mentally? Or are you the one that feels suffocated and restricted, but unable to escape from the endless emotional hoops your lover makes you jump through in order to prove, time and again, your real love for them?

Possessiveness and jealousy are two emotions that can create havoc and destruction, and even transform love into hatred. Contrary to popular theory, it's not only women who suffer from these uncontrollable emotions. Indeed, in extreme cases many men are serving prison sentences for murder resulting from a 'sudden fit of jealousy' of the woman they love.

Sex differences

Although men and women are both affected by jealousy, their jealousy takes different forms. Research shows that men are especially likely to be jealous when they are made to feel inadequate. Women, on the other hand, are most prone to jealousy when they are dependent upon a relationship and can see no alternative possibilities open to them at the time.

For men, jealousy focuses around the issue of sexual penetration, presumably because of the instinctual fear of 'wasting' resources on raising offspring that carry the genes of another man. Platonic relationships, if credible, do not present much of a threat to most men. The jealousy of women, however, is more often centred upon the question of affection and rival relationships. An occasional lusty diversion on the part of the male partner may be reasonably well tolerated, but indications that he is becoming romantically involved with another woman will be taken much more seriously.

There are also sex differences in the way jealousy is handled. Men are more likely to respond with anger, perhaps extending to violence, such as bar-room brawling or wife-beating. And while women obviously may get angry too, they're more likely to become depressed. For every woman who either poisons her rival or the lover that betrays her, there are many more who poison themselves.

Deception

'Betrayal' can never be defined in terms of the act itself. It is always a question of the extent to which an understanding or 'contract' has been breached. While some relationships involve an explicit or unspoken commitment to sexual fidelity, others are relatively open and permissive, with each partner condoning the other's need for variety. At one end of the scale there are couples who wouldn't be able to forgive even one little furtive kiss; at the other end there are the swingers who get turned on by watching their partner make love to someone else. Happily, most of us are somewhere between these extremes, but generally speaking it is the deception involved that often hurts rather more than the actual act itself.

Envy

There is another component of jealousy that does not involve betrayal, and that is envy – the adult equivalent of the child who is upset by seeing another child eating an ice-cream. Most of us can recall a twinge of jealousy when we see a person whom we find highly attractive going out with somebody else, even though our only claims upon them are in our hopes or fantasies. When we experience jealousy of this kind, it's often the first sign that we are becoming involved, or falling in love, with another person.

Intrusion

We expect our partners to meet other people socially at certain times. We cannot expect to have them entirely to ourselves. What hurts us is the feeling that we are being displaced by other people to the extent that our attachment is threatened. When this happens, the degree of hurt that we feel depends upon how central a role our partners play in our lives. If the relationship is peripheral to our lives we will not be greatly affected, but if our partner controls access to other facilities and rewards such as money, children, accommodation, friends, occupational advancement, transport or leisure pursuits, then the extent of anticipated disruption may be considerable. In other words, the stress that we feel when a relationship is unsettled has its ramifications in other areas of our lives, as well as invoking the fear of losing the relationship itself.

When the person we fear losing is a fiancé/e or spouse, there is usually a complex social and economic network surrounding the relationship. Consequently, the prospect of disruption cuts deep into our sense of identity.

Insecurity

There are, then, many good reasons why one might feel jealous concerning a partner. However, there are also some less attractive, 'immature' reasons. After all, jealousy is not just a situational thing, it is also a personality trait. There are some people who feel jealous nearly all of the time, regardless of who their partner is or how they behave.

Such people are prone to jealousy because they are possessive – they feel as though they own their partner. Other relationships therefore will be perceived as a violation of their 'property rights' to which they will feel entitled to respond with anger. Engagement and marriage are a kind of social endorsement to warn others off. Nevertheless, the individual who emphasizes this aspect of a relationship is generally a person who is insecure and lacking in self-esteem. Their behaviour is not only unattractive but also counter-productive, since ultimately it is likely to destroy what is most valuable in that relationship – true love.

Answer the questions below to discover whether you are a secure or 'clinging' lover. Select one answer to each question.

1) Your partner/lover is offered a fantastic job which would mean them being away from you for several days a month.
You:

a   Urge them to accept and say how delighted you are for them.

b   Think they should accept, but that they ought to arrange for you to go along some of the time.

c   Cry and beg them not to go and leave you.

2) On holiday, your partner/lover insists on finding an out-of-the-way nude beach. You:

a   Enjoy getting an all-over tan.

b   Feel slightly uncomfortable with all that nudity.

c   Watch every move they make.

3) Your partner enjoys going out with same-sex friends. You:

a   Arrange to do the same a couple of times a week.

b   Occasionally go along to check their alibi.

c   Get angry if they ever suggest going without you.

4) Suppose you fall in love with someone who has a 'ready-made' family with a couple of kids.
Would you:

a   Do everything you can to make them all happy.

b   Plan to have one of your own with your partner as soon as possible.

c   Insist they get a nanny and send them to boarding school.

5) Your partner has a long-standing friendship with a much older person of the opposite sex to whom they turn when in trouble.
You:

a   Like to think a more experienced person than yourself can help your partner.

b   Would prefer your partner to rely on you more.

c   Tell your partner they must only come to you from now on.

6) Despite a passionate affair, your lover or partner wants you both to maintain separate living accommodation.
You:

a   Are glad of the 'space'.

b   Consider it a bad financial arrangement.

c   Want marriage or an end to the affair.

7) How would you react if your partner/lover confessed to having made love to someone of their own sex while they were involved with you?

    a   Be prepared to discuss what urges had driven them.

    b   Be shocked and very upset.

    c   Feel betrayed and totally unforgiving.

8) If your partner muttered someone else's name in their sleep, you would:

    a   Tease them about it in the morning.

    b   Shake them awake and demand an explanation.

    c   Search their belongings for incriminating evidence.

9) At a disco your partner gets into a clinch with some-one on the floor.
    You:

    a   Don't regard it as significant.

    b   Pretend it's an 'excuse me' and push in.

    c   Throw your drink in their face when they get back to you.

10) Your partner arrives 45 minutes late for a date with you in a pub.
    You:

    a   Get chatting to a friendly group of people to fill in the time.

    b   Get a bit tipsy and 'paw' your lover when they arrive.

c Make a dreadful scene and sulk for the rest of the evening.

11) Your lover still wears a ring given to them by their last love.
You:

a Can't see how jewellery could upset your love affair.

b Buy them another ring to wear on the other hand.

c Throw it in the rubbish bin and pretend it's gone missing.

12) You smell perfume on your partner's hair.
You:

a Compliment them on the attractive new fragrance they are wearing.

b Check for a matching scent on the dressing table.

c Demand to know what they have been up to.

13) Someone hangs up the phone when you answer it. The next time it rings, you:

a Suggest your lover picks it up.

b Lift the receiver and say nothing.

c Torture yourself, thinking it is a rival.

14) You discover two used theatre tickets in your lover's coat pocket.
You assume:

a They took a business colleague and forgot to tell you.

b   They have been in their pocket for ages.

c   They are dating someone else.

15) After a series of lonely nights when your partner/lover claims to be working late you decide to:

a   Join an evening class to keep yourself occupied.

b   Insist they take you out for an expensive meal.

c   Phone them every hour at the office to confirm they are really working.

16) Your partner's mother is suddenly widowed and they suggest she comes to live with you both.
You:

a   Welcome her and insist she is not a burden.

b   Give her a space of her own within your home so you are independent from her.

c   Refuse, knowing how close they are and the potential risk to your relationship.

17) In your opinion, most women get married in order to:

a   Avoid being left 'on the shelf'.

b   Create a stable atmosphere in which to rear children.

c   Show the world their man belongs to them exclusively.

18) You and your partner are invited to a party but you have a previous commitment. You expect your partner to:

a   Go without you and enjoy themselves.

b Ask if you would mind them going alone.

c Stay home solo and pine for you.

19) Old friends of your partner come round to dinner and spend the evening reminiscing about the 'good old days'.
You:

a Enter into the spirit of things, pleased for your partner's sake.

b Attempt to steer the conversation round to include your interests.

c Go to bed early in a huff and leave them to it.

20) During passionate lovemaking your lover fantasizes aloud about a sexy friend.
You:

a Encourage them and elaborate on their story.

b Tick them off gently and remind them who they are with.

c Freeze instantly and find it impossible to continue lovemaking.

21) An anonymous Valentine's card arrives for your partner.
You say:

a 'It must be from your mother.'

b 'Who have you been chatting up?'

c 'How could you do this to me?'

22) Some of your best times spent with your partner are when:

a   You are with good friends sharing mutual interests and affections.

b   You go out to a romantic restaurant and only have eyes for each other.

c   You can have your partner all to yourself for an evening.

23) Your partner is very popular with the opposite sex and is constantly surrounded by admirers.
     You are:

a   Proud of them and flattered that they chose you as a partner.

b   Somewhat irritated and annoyed that you are not the centre of attention.

c   Extremely miffed and eager to make it plain that they belong to you.

24) Do you consider jealousy to be:

a   An ugly emotion, best kept under control.

b   A healthy sign of a flourishing, caring relationship.

c   The only way for someone to prove they really love you.

25) Your partner seems to be uninterested in sex.
     You would:

a   Try to think up new ways to excite them.

b   Plan a weekend away together.

c   Accuse them of having an affair.

26) Your lover is very complimentary to your best friend.

You:

a   Thank them for being so nice to your friend.

b   Complain that they don't say how good you look.

c   Determine to see less of your best friend.

27)   Going for a picnic in the park with your partner, you bump into their 'ex'.
You:

a   Invite them to join you.

b   Have a brief chat, then excuse yourselves.

c   Ignore them and tell your partner how ghastly they look.

28)   At a party, your sexy host makes a beeline for your partner.
You:

a   Look on, mildly amused.

b   Greet the host effusively and introduce your partner.

c   Glare at the host and cling to your lover's arm.

29)   A handwritten letter marked 'personal' arrives for your partner.
Do you:

a   Give it to them and leave it up to them whether they want to discuss the contents.

b   Hand it over and expect them to tell you what it contains.

c   Watch them open it and read it with them.

Sex, Lies & Love

30) Your partner's mother wants you both to spend Christmas with her.
You:

a   Compromise and divide your time between both sets of parents.

b   Have Christmas dinner with them and go to a party with friends in the evening.

c   Book a Caribbean cruise so you have your partner all to yourself.

31) You discover some pornographic books hidden in a drawer by your partner.
You:

a   Express disappointment that they did not think you game enough to enjoy them too.

b   Lay them out on the bed that night and see what happens.

c   Dispose of them and berate your partner for keeping secrets from you.

32) Going through an old photograph album you discover pictures of your partner's first love.
You:

a   Show them to your partner and say you wish you could have met them.

b   Hide them away so as not to revive memories.

c   Destroy them, together with the past.

33) Your partner takes to early morning jogging in the park.
You:

a   Run a bath for their return and prepare breakfast.

b   Buy some running shoes and get fit with them.

c   Tell them running is bad for their heart.

34) Your lover has particularly stunning eyes – noticed by the opposite sex.
You:

a   Love the attention they get.

b   Get the occasional pang of envy.

c   Buy them dark glasses.

35) The local massage parlour rings to confirm an appointment for your partner.
You:

a   Make a date for yourself as well.

b   Tell your partner they could save money if you gave them a massage.

c   Cancel the appointment saying they have left town.

36) Your partner hires an extremely sexy new assistant at work and praises their efficiency.
You:

a   Think the assistant will give business a boost.

b   Invite the person round for a meal to see your domestic bliss at first hand.

c   Continually phone your partner at work and pop in unexpectedly.

37) A mutual friend has one spare ticket for a concert you both want to see.

You:

a   Insist your partner goes.

b   Don't tell your partner and go yourself.

c   Decline the ticket and don't tell your partner.

38) Your partner is made redundant, leaving you as sole breadwinner.
     You:

a   Help them find a new job and their self-respect.

b   Pay them a 'salary' to run the home.

c   Like them to be dependent on you.

39) When you go to a cocktail party with your partner, you have an unspoken agreement that you will both:

a   Separate to meet and mingle with new people.

b   Talk to everyone and meet up to compare notes.

c   Stick together for the entire evening.

40) Which quality do you value most in a person you would have a permanent relationship with?

a   Spirit of adventure.

b   Eternal optimism.

c   Undying love.

Possessiveness quiz – scoring and interpretation

Give yourself two points for every 'c' answer that you endorsed, one point for each 'b' and zero for each 'a'. Total up your points to arrive at a possessiveness score which may be anything between 0 and 80.

0–20   This means that you are a very liberal and permissive lover. You are happy to let your partner have their space, and in all probability you're the kind of person who is understanding, patient, tolerant and fun to be with.

However, there is a less flattering possibility that should be considered: people do feel jealous when they care – so could it be that your lack of jealousy and possessiveness simply means that you do not care enough? It is important to distinguish between the *feeling* of jealousy and the immature, undignified or vindictive *acts* that may stem from it. It is quite normal to feel a twinge of jealousy when someone we love shows an interest in another person, but it is usually unjustified and sometimes even neurotic to react with great hurt and indignation, or to make a public display of bad temper or vengeance. The absence of childish tantrums and violence is a good thing, but the absence of any emotion suggests a rather cold detachment and lack of involvement. Ideal as it may sound, it is not in the character of most people to want their loved partner to find enjoyment and fulfilment in the arms of another person.

If your score is less than 20 you should ask yourself whether you are being over-generous with your partner – to the extent that you are being naïve and treated like a doormat. Hopefully this is not the case, but remember that it is quite in order to express emotion in a reasonable and civilized way. Of course this is a delicate balance to strike and maintain, but there is no point in giving *carte blanche* to your partner if you are 'eating your heart out' inside. If you are really hurting, it would be best to tell your partner in a non-accusatory way rather than bottle it up until explosion point is reached.

20–50   This puts you in the range of most normal people. You are reasonably tolerant, considerate and flexible, but occasionally catch yourself behaving in a jealous and possessive way. Which isn't surprising if your relationship means a lot to you. However, you should try to remember that selfish and demanding expressions of jealousy will not endear you to your partner. In fact they're more likely to be counter-productive inasmuch as they could make your partner feel trapped and resentful. Perhaps it would help if you ask yourself whether your own conduct is totally blameless if, as is most likely the case, you are less than a model of virtue and fidelity, the realization of this may help you to moderate your expectations concerning your partner.

50+   This may reflect a very passionate and expressive nature. You probably think of yourself as very much in love and you may well be an exciting person to deal with. However, you should be warned that not many people can stand living with a partner who behaves in this way for any length of time. Your behaviour suggests a degree of possessiveness that threatens to be destructive to your relationship, so if this is important to you, you might consider what can be done about it.

Dealing with the green-eyed monster

The first step, surprisingly, is to recognize that your behaviour stems from jealousy and over-possessiveness. Many people are good at rationalizing their behaviour (inventing desirable motives for it), or projecting the blame for their unreasonable behaviour so that external circumstances, and especially other people, are seen as the cause. Seeing beyond these defences, and acknowledging the power of your own emotions, are prerequisites to coping with jealousy.

Having acknowledged your jealousy, you can minimize your guilt by reminding yourself that it is a perfectly natural instinct that's experienced by all normal people who fear that attention due to them is being directed elsewhere.

Work on your own self-confidence by reminding yourself of your good points and think through the many little things your partner does that suggest he or she really loves you. Build your self-esteem positively by attending to your own grooming and making yourself pleasant to be with. Rather than remonstrate with your partner, determine to smile more, pay them compliments, and tell them that you love them. This is much more useful than extracting from them under duress a statement that they will love you exclusively and for ever.

If you do feel a need to express your jealousy, do so in an open, straightforward way – without righteousness, indignation or hostility. If possible, use it to spice up your love play by acknowledging it as evidence of your love and sharing the scenario you most fear as a voyeuristic/vicarious fantasy with your lover – paradoxically encouraging them in their lust and exploration. This does not come easily to everybody, but if it can be achieved it will probably enhance your lover's feelings for you.

Use your own behaviour and feelings as a model for understanding your partner's behaviour. Think of occasions when you've had social contact with other people that parallels the behaviour which is upsetting you now, and try to reflect upon their meaning to you at the time. Ask yourself whether your partner would be entitled to be upset at these incidents and how you would view jealous outbursts on their part in similar circumstances. This process might help you to realize that you are being petty and childish.

How Well Are You Communicating?

Surveys on marital happiness repeatedly reveal the importance of communication within a relationship. Many couples, when questioned about the breakdown of their marriage, cite reasons such as adultery, cruelty, neglect or sexual incompatibility, but these are frequently recognized as symptoms of a lack of communication between the couple.

But what, precisely, do we mean by communication? Difficulties in agreeing about the meaning of the word arise from the fact that it has at least two aspects. The first is your ability to express your true feelings to your partner, whether directly through words or indirectly through body language. True communication depends upon your capacity to 'relay' clear messages rather than signals that can be misinterpreted because they're either irrelevant, ambiguous, misdirected or otherwise confused. For example, venting anger on your partner when another person is really responsible for upsetting you is not only unfair and confusing for them, but also likely to cause more harm than good. Similarly, there is nothing to be gained from kicking the cat, smacking the children, or being rude to salesgirls in shops when it's really your spouse you're annoyed with. And bottling up your emotions doesn't help either. Not only is this virtually impossible to achieve, but suppressing emotions like anger and anxiety can also induce all sorts of physical and mental symptoms like ulcers, asthma, high blood pressure, heart disease, alcoholism, depression, and possibly even cancer.

We may smirk at the curious manner in which our American cousins articulate their emotions, or at what our discreet British ears interpret as the unacceptably direct, confrontational approach of such cringe-making phrases as, 'Your refusal to help with the household chores makes me feel angry and resentful,' or, 'I feel anxious and jealous when you go away on weekend business trips.' But many experts are now suggesting that the remarkable reduction in stress-related diseases in America recently (compared with rising levels in Britain) may well be attributable to their new-found ability to openly and honestly express their emotions.

A second aspect of communication is the amount of understanding shown by the partner; for no matter how effectively we express our thoughts and feelings, we won't succeed in getting through to our partner's if he or she is completely indifferent to our well-being or actively resistant to the message we are trying to put across. For example, you'd get little result from communicating your distress at your partners' continual lateness in arriving home from work if he or she were involved in a joyously illicit affair with someone else and had no intention of changing the *status quo*. They simply would not want to listen. Communication in a partnership therefore involves being in tune with each other – and that means understanding as well as expressing.

According to Glenn Wilson, the importance of communication in marriage was highlighted in a survey conducted by Dr R J Burke and colleagues at York University, in which almost 200 couples were asked how likely they were to disclose unpleasant and distressing feelings to their spouse. The survey results revealed that wives were more likely to disclose their feelings than husbands, and couples with happy marriages were more likely to discuss their problems than unhappy couples.

Husbands and wives gave similar reasons for disclosing problems to their spouses, most commonly 'unburdening' or 'catharsis', the seeking of solutions, advice, clarification, new perspectives, emotional support or enhancement of mutual understanding. Those wives who withheld their feelings reported that the reasons they did so were either because they did not want to worry their husband (who had enough on his mind already) or because they thought it would be a waste of time (i.e., he'd most likely be unresponsive to their problems anyway). Husbands who withheld their feelings either did so out of a preference for separating work from home, or because they felt that their wife lacked the knowledge necessary to appreciate their difficulties.

In response to the question of how they would like their spouse to change, the wives said they'd like their husbands to be more responsive and receptive to their problems, while the husbands said they wished their wives would react to their problems less hysterically, because hysteria only increased their stress.

Obviously there are both individual differences in the methods of communication between men and women and some average differences, and these could well be at the root of a great deal of marital stress. Most of us need to share our inner feelings with someone and ideally we ought to feel free to do this with the person we love and live with. Research has also revealed that, apparently, wives are not only more expressive than husbands but also *more sensitive to the emotional states of their husband* – thus confirming the stereotype of the wife who is intuitive and supportive. However, this wifely empathy was found to decline markedly if the wife was working or with the appearance of children (presumably because both factors compete for a woman's energy and attention).

Clearly, the ability to communicate effectively within a partnership is of vital importance. Partners who lack either the will or the ability to understand each other's points of view emotionally, intellectually, sexually, or even in general, could, in time, find their relationship degenerating to the point of divorce.

To find out how well you are communicating with your partner answer the 40 questions below, choosing one answer to each question.

1) You want to make love. How do you indicate this to your partner?

    a   By touching and speaking low to them in a seductive way.

    b   Tell them in a straightforward manner.

    c   Complain that you hardly ever have sex.

2) At a dinner party, you want to leave early.
    You:

    a   Remind your partner of an imaginary early start in the morning.

    b   Drum your fingers on the table and direct knowing looks at your partner.

    c   Yawn loudly and pull a sulky face.

3) You get sore during love making – how do you tell your partner?

    a   Talk it over in a less heated moment of passion in the hope of finding a solution.

    b   Blurt it out as soon as they have finished.

    c   Yell out when they touch you.

4) What gesture do you use to show affection to your partner?

a   A special little signal that you share only with
     each other.

b   A hearty squeeze.

c   A pat on the head that you otherwise reserve for
     the family pet.

5) You are woken from sleep by your partner urgently
    pressing up against your body.
    You:

a   Succumb to their caress and dreamily make
     love.

b   Mumble grumpily that they can go ahead as
     long as you are not disturbed.

c   Protest angrily and drag off the duvet to sleep
     on the sofa.

6) Your partner asks your opinion of the meal they have
    prepared for you.
    You:

a   Say it is delicious and praise their efforts.

b   Tell the truth at all costs.

c   Say it would probably have been cheaper to eat
     out.

7) You are somewhat distressed that your partner climbs
    into bed without bathing first.
    You:

a   Make a sexy ritual out of bathing them late at
     night.

b   Point out that natural body odours are not
     always the greatest turn-on.

c   Pointedly spray air freshener in the bedroom last thing at night.

8) A bad day makes you snappy with your lover.
You would:

    a   Apologize quickly and explain your ill-humour.

    b   Tell a joke to relieve the tension.

    c   Leave them to suffer since they do the same to you.

9) Your partner continually just misses touching the spot which gives you most pleasure during sex.
You:

    a   Invent a fantasy in which you describe the pleasure the characters receive when touched in a certain way.

    b   Impatiently grab their hand and slap it on the place.

    c   Get frustrated and irritable with them.

10) You say something really hurtful to your lover just as they are leaving for work.
You would:

    a   Ring them and apologize for being so horrid.

    b   Leave a 'sorry' note for their return home.

    c   Dismiss them as being over-sensitive.

11) What would you do if your partner was repeatedly failing to give you satisfaction during lovemaking?

    a   Tell them how to satisfy you.

    b   Buy a vibrator or masturbate to top up afterwards.

    c   Avoid sex as much as possible.

12) A good time to discuss an important issue with your lover is:

    a   In bed at night.

    b   Over the kitchen table at breakfast.

    c   The minute they walk through the door after work.

13) Your partner suffers from a lot of flatulence. You:

    a   Attempt to modify their diet.

    b   Leave a bottle of charcoal pills in a prominent place.

    c   Sleep in another room.

14) You most often greet your partner with:

    a   A kiss and a smile.

    b   A few words of greeting.

    c   A list of chores that need doing.

15) When you are making love you:

    a   Often whisper little fantasies to your lover.

    b   'Talk dirty' if they require it.

    c   Always do it in complete silence.

16) You influence your partner by:

    a   Gentle persuasion.

    b   Stubborn determination.

c   Shouting the loudest.

17) Your partner will usually do as you ask because:

a   They adore you.

b   They are a bit frightened of you.

c   You have the strongest will.

18) You can heal aches and pains in your partner by:

a   Lovingly applied massage with warm oils.

b   An effective analgesic.

c   Telling them their favourite film is on at the local cinema.

19) When your partner faces a disappointment they know you will respond with:

a   A big hug and a shoulder to cry on.

b   Embarrassment.

c   Remonstrations concerning their failure.

20) How often do you express your feelings for your partner?

a   There are literally dozens of ways, in words and actions, that you show your love for them.

b   You try to remember to be nice.

c   You cannot express emotion easily.

21) Discussing your relationship with your partner you:

a   Constructively deal with any problems you may have together.

b   Discover you can't always get through to them.

c   Want to bang their head to make them see reason.

22) You suspect your lover of being unfaithful to you. You:

a   Enquire in a gentle, teasing way whether it is true.

b   Come straight out with your suspicions and demand an answer.

c   Keep nagging and taxing them until they clam up completely.

23) When you do something stupid, like locking yourself out of the house, what do you do?

a   Tell your lover what an idiot you've been.

b   Swear, bang the door and lose your temper generally.

c   Blame your lover for distracting your attention and causing you to forget your keys.

24) What do you talk about mostly when you are alone with your lover?

a   Anything and everything.

b   The way your relationship is heading.

c   Domestic matters and monetary problems.

25) If you have been watching a play or documentary together, what happens afterwards:

a   You both voice your opinions even if you don't agree.

b   You try to avoid a discussion since you already
        know their viewpoint.

c   You seldom enjoy watching the same type of
        programme.

26) Your partner has a habit – like smoking – which you
     loathe.
     You would:

a   Tell them how happy it would make you if they
        could give it up.

b   Threaten them with dire consequences if they
        continue.

c   Flush their cigarettes down the toilet.

27) Most of your disagreements occur over:

a   Small matters easily resolved.

b   Money.

c   Basic misunderstandings.

28) Your partner reveals a rather personal quirk of yours
     at a party.
     You:

a   Laugh it off, knowing it was not meant
        maliciously.

b   Tell them off soundly.

c   'Spill the beans' about all their funny little
        habits.

29) When you are in a different room and your lover calls
     you.
     Do you:

a   Go to see what they want.

b   Call back 'just a minute'.

c   Pretend you have not heard.

30) Do you criticize your lover's sexual performance?

a   No, you would not dream of destroying their confidence.

b   If you can back up your criticism with a useful comment.

c   Only when you seek revenge for their criticism of you.

31) What do you do when your lovemaking is so predictable it becomes boring?

a   You would never let things get to that stage.

b   Ask your lover to tell you if it is your fault.

c   Say something icy when they attempt to touch you.

32) Your partner tells you they don't like the way you are dressed just before you are going out together.
     You:

a   Would take it as a constructive remark and change.

b   Get flustered and upset.

c   Make a sarcastic remark back.

33) Navigating new territory, your partner, who is driving, takes a wrong turn.
     You:

a   Get out the map and trace a new route.

b   Pretend not to notice you are going the wrong way.

c   Sit back smugly and tell them what a fool they are.

34) On your birthday, your partner buys you something you don't like.
You:

a   Thank them for the gift and comment on their general kindness.

b   Tell them honestly the damaging truth.

c   Say it's about time they knew what you wanted.

35) In an intimate moment, your lover confesses that they are very unsure of themselves.
You:

a   Build their self-confidence in every possible way.

b   Use it against them when you are next having a row.

c   Cannot bear weakness in other people.

36) Your partner is more experienced than you sexually.
You are:

a   A willing and eager pupil.

b   Too proud to admit there are aspects of sex you are not very knowledgeable about.

c   Reluctant to have them 'experiment' on you.

37) A candlelit dinner in a restaurant with your partner is a time when:

a   You can relax and get sexy with each other.

b   You unload all your problems on to them.

c   You find you have nothing to talk about.

38)   You stay with your partner because:

a   You make each other extremely happy.

b   You've grown used to each other; it's a habit.

c   You are 'trapped' in a situation from which you can't escape.

39)   Your partner is away and an urgent decision needs to be made which affects both of you.
You would:

a   Be pretty sure that they would agree with your decision.

b   Worry about what to do.

c   Decide on what suits you best and too bad if they don't like it.

40)   Your partner tries to tell you their troubles.
You:

a   Listen attentively and try to help.

b   Get a glazed look in your eyes and pick up a newspaper to read.

c   Think they have a nerve, what with all that you have to cope with.

Communication quiz – scoring and interpretation

Give yourself three points for each 'a' answer, two points for each 'b', and one point for each 'c'. This will give you a total score varying from 40 to 120.

100–120 *Excellent*. You appear to have a very warm and

effective level of communication with your partner, so it's odds on your relationship is a very happy and comfortable one. You give the right social and emotional strokes, yet at the same time you know when it is best to withhold your advice and information because it might be intrusive.

80–99 *Reasonable*. Yours is a fairly typical relationship. For the most part you understand and empathize with each other but there are occasional lapses (probably on both sides) and these lead to slight misunderstandings. You may not necessarily need to talk more – it could just be a matter of choosing the right moment to say things and the right tone of voice. Remember that sometimes a degree of warmth and subtlety is necessary to make an idea palatable to others. Honesty may be a virtue but bluntness can sometimes be hurtful.

60–79 *Less than satisfactory*. Your communication is slightly deficient and you should consider how your relationship might be rebuilt by injecting more consideration into it. Basically the skill you need to learn is how to express your thoughts and feelings in such a way as not to antagonize your partner. Telling a person directly and explicitly why you are upset by them can put them on the defensive, thus reducing the likelihood that they will respond constructively.

40–59 *Disastrous*. It appears that your relationship may already have broken down beyond repair – unless, of course, it's the mutual hostility and distaste for one another which keeps you entertained and motivates you to continue. Probably this will come as no surprise to you – you've been aware of the cold war for a long time and this quiz has only served to confirm and quantify it. But if not, and you really would like things to improve, then you'd be well advised to seek the help of a marriage guidance counsellor.

Assuming your performance was less than perfect you may find it instructive to go back over the quiz questions to see where you 'went wrong' and how your behaviour might be modified so as to enhance your relationship.

At this point it must be conceded that the 'ideal' answers are inevitably a matter of opinion to some extent. Sometimes the author's choices could be backed up by scientific studies but in other instances the scoring is based on intuition. The reader is therefore free to disagree with the scoring values, though it may help if the criteria used are explained.

'a' answers usually reflect a communication pattern that is considerate as well as expressive. People responding in this way are usually effective in informing and persuading their partners because they adopt an approach that is subtle, gentle, warm and loving. They recognize that there are times when it is best not to confront their partner with truths that are certain to be hurtful and unlikely to be helpful.

Surprisingly, direct expressions of thoughts and feelings do *not always* rate highly in the scoring. One example is the item concerning reactions to a meal your partner has cooked which you did not enjoy (question 6). In this case, notifying your partner of your tastes and preferences should take second place to *your* appreciation of *their* efforts to please you. It is not so much a matter of telling white lies as focusing praise on what is good in the situation. Put another way: feelings may be just as true as facts.

'b' answers usually imply a willingness to communicate but an inability to do it right. Sometimes there is disclosure which is too direct, too explicit, too aggressive. For example, the person who announces that they want to make love immediately (question 1) may catch their partner ill-prepared and, therefore, unsure of their ability to respond with full warmth. The intention may be admirable but the execution slightly clumsy.

In other cases, the 'b' answer may be slightly oblique or even irrelevant to what is really called for in the situation. For example, upon realizing that you have misdirected your anger to your partner when they were not deserving of it (question 8), the correct thing to do would be to apologize directly, not attempt to redress the balance by subsequently being nicer than you otherwise might have been. Thus, while 'b' answers are not particularly damaging, they can often fall short of optimal in various ways.

'c' answers are characteristically cold, hostile, selfish and destructive and there is little more that can be said about them. They are almost invariably symptomatic of a relationship that is heading for, or already on, the rocks and, therefore, their only effect is likely to be one of smashing the wreckage around even more. They are counterproductive rather than constructive and the bitter, resentful, vengeful element to many of these responses suggests retaliation for similar treatment from the partner. Who fired the first icicle in the cold war may be as difficult to determine as whether the chicken or the egg has priority.

How Good A Lover Are You?

Why are some people considered great lovers and others disastrous flops? How important is it to have a high SQ (seduction quotient) like Casanova or Warren Beatty in his pre-fatherhood heyday? How far does passion figure in the equation? Or is being a 'good lover' wholly dependent upon the courtly medieval romantic ideal of being prepared to 'sacrifice all' for the sake of love? As Edward VIII demonstrated when he chose to abdicate for the love of Wallis Simpson.

Whilst we all like to think there's more than a trace inside us of the Juliet or Tristan just waiting to be released by the love of our very own Romeo and Isolde, the love that inspired such grandiose gestures and self-destructive behaviour was, in reality, founded more on fantasy than any real knowledge of the object of their affections.

Idyllic relationships are all very well in the pages of romantic literature, but expose them to the realities of the daily grind of domestic existence and, doubtless, Romeo would soon be suing for divorce and custody of the castle. As for poor old Isolde, how long would it be before she got fed up waiting for Tristan to mend the leaking turrets of her bedchamber so she could get a decent night's kip? The love of ordinary people may be more difficult to sustain, but at least it's based on reality.

Successful seducers, such as Casanova and Don Juan, knew how to make a woman feel so good she'd melt into their arms and their beds. But to be a good lover you have to know how to sustain a woman's interest and ardour.

And that's where thoughtfulness – like surprising your partner with an inexpensive little gift, cooking their favourite meal, or even taking on a hated chore such as washing their car for them – attentiveness – noticing and complimenting them when they're looking good, as well as offering sympathy and support when they're feeling down – and being sensitive to their needs, both in bed and out – are all vital components of 'skilled loving'. Equally important are respect (for their wishes, and their need for personal space and/or privacy) and acceptance of their right to retain their individuality. Skilled lovers don't settle for simply telling their partners they are loved, needed and appreciated; they make a point of knowing what specific actions or behavioural expressions their partner needs to see or have displayed in order to make him or her *truly* feel they are *being* valued and loved.

An essential part of being a good lover is being aware that your partner's needs are not necessarily identical to your own, and, therefore, the things that have meaning for you may well be meaningless to them.

Select one answer only from each group of alternative answers to the questions below, and find out how skilled a lover you *really* are.

1) What is a good lover?
   A person who:

   a   Sacrifices their own personality and feelings for their lover.

   b   Will lay down their life for love.

   c   Makes the world a happy and beautiful place for their lover.

2) How often must you have sex to be a good lover?

   a   Twice a week.

   b   When your lover wants it.

c   When you desire each other.

3) You know your lover appreciates you when:

a   They accept expensive presents from you.

b   They are prepared to kill to protect your honour.

c   They love you despite your faults.

4) Your partner fancies someone of the opposite sex.
    You:

a   Beg them not to be unfaithful.

b   Vow to destroy your rival.

c   Would find it strange if they fancied no one but
       you.

5) The words 'I love you' should be told to you:

a   When you ask your lover.

b   Every time you speak to each other.

c   When they are spontaneous and genuine.

6) After living together you find there are some things
    you can't stand about your lover.
    You:

a   Are determined to bring them round to your
       way of thinking.

b   Hate imperfections in people and would prefer
       to end your relationship.

c   Accept that we are all different and concentrate
       on enjoying their good points.

7) What gift would you buy a lover, given a large budget?

a   A new car.

b   A priceless jewel.

c   Something small that was of particular and exclusive value to them.

8) What is the best recipe for long-term success in a relationship?

a   Secure financial ties.

b   Devoted, undying love.

c   Friendship, trust and deep affection.

9) Introducing your lover to a social set they are unfamiliar with, the first thing you do is:

a   Register with everyone to whom they 'belong'.

b   Find a secluded corner you can rush off to when they have met a few people.

c   Effect an introduction to the most interesting and amusing people in the group.

10) What effect would children have on you and your lover?

a   Children would hold your relationship together.

b   Children would interfere with your idyllic state.

c   Children would be facsimiles of you and your lover and a constant reminder of each other.

11) The way to satisfy your lover is to:

a   Perform like a sexual athlete.

b   Consume them with passion.

c   Discover precisely what thrills them.

12)   How often do you titivate yourself with cream and fragrances?

a   When time or the 'occasion' permits.

b   When you are meeting your lover.

c   You take care of your body with a regular grooming routine.

13)   Would you dress up specially for your lover?

a   You don't have to impress them any more.

b   You dress exclusively for your lover.

c   You especially enjoy turning them on by wearing something exciting when you make love.

14)   Are you fastidious about personal hygiene?

a   Only 'dirty' people need to bathe daily.

b   You will only bathe with your lover.

c   Hygiene is an essential part of lovemaking.

15)   Which statement do you agree with:

a   It's up to a man to 'call the tune' sexually.

b   A man would be robbed of his masculinity if the woman is aggressive.

c   Most men adore being 'taken' by an adventurous and sexually assertive woman.

16)   Could you tell better than most people what your lover is thinking?

    a   How can you possibly know if they don't tell you.

    b   You share some mystical telepathy with your lover.

    c   You are so completely in tune you know instinctively what they desire.

17) Are you complimentary to your lover on their achievements?

    a   You always flatter them falsely to hold their attention.

    b   Everything your lover does is 'God-like' and you praise them lavishly.

    c   You respond with warmth and admiration when they achieve something deserving.

18) If your lover has a problem they would:

    a   Sort it out for themselves.

    b   Not want to bother you with it.

    c   Discuss it at length with you.

19) Your lover enjoys a particular kind of food that you don't.
You:

    a   Suggest that they buy it if they want it.

    b   Force yourself to enjoy it too.

    c   Keep a constant supply in the fridge for them.

20) Could you remember the last conversation you had with your partner?

a   You forget – they were prattling on about something or other.

b   You cling to their every syllable.

c   Your conversations are always of interest to you both.

21) You are ready to go out on a date and your lover arrives to collect you – weary from overwork.
You:

a   Get angry and suggest you go without them.

b   Stay home to appease their every need.

c   Offer them a hot bath and massage to relax them before you go out.

22) How much do you have to learn about your lover?

a   You know all there is to know about the opposite sex.

b   You await their every move with baited breath.

c   You discover new facets of their personality every day.

23) Does your lover trust you completely in sex?

a   They get pretty sensitive for fear you might handle their genitals roughly.

b   Their faith in you is blinding and implicit.

c   They willingly abandon themselves to your exploring fingers.

24) What is your ultimate 'goal' when you make love?

a   To obtain maximum satisfaction for yourself.

b   To enter into a spiritual orbit together.

c   To make each time fantastic and memorable for your lover.

25) Your lover is bedridden but feeling sexy.
     You:

a   Put something in their tea to kill the desire.

b   Can't bear to see them incapacitated and prefer to go away until they recover.

c   Look for new ways to give them sexual fulfilment.

26) Do you have any major disagreements on what you do in bed?

a   You can't pluck up enough courage to tell them you don't like a lot of things they do.

b   You never discuss it – lovemaking is an aesthetic, ethereal experience.

c   Nothing you do to them sexually has ever caused dissension between you.

27) Do you go out of your way to create imaginitive scenarios for your lover?

a   Sounds like a pretty infantile way to behave – straight sex is fine for you.

b   You only see them in exotic faraway places.

c   Yes, the mind is probably the most powerful aphrodisiac of all.

28) Have you ever whispered to your lover when you are out together that you are not wearing any underwear to excite them?

a   You wouldn't dare – supposing you got run over by a bus ...?

b   No – you are usually wearing nothing prior to lovemaking.

c   Yes – you adore to slowly tease them.

29)   A candlelit dinner together would be:

a   A good way to hide physical imperfections.

b   The only way to dine.

c   An opportunity for sexy talk and a prelude to lovemaking.

30)   After a night of passionate lovemaking, the first thing you do in the morning is:

a   Tell your lover to fetch breakfast since you gave them such a good time.

b   Draw the curtains and drift back to sleep in their arms.

c   Get your lover some coffee and slip back into bed with them.

31)   Your lover complains of a headache.
You:

a   Tell them where to find the aspirin.

b   Could not conceive of them suffering in your company.

c   Ease the pain with deft finger-work on their forehead and nape of neck.

32)   Circumstances force you apart for several weeks.
You:

a   Are pleased to have a break to sort out your life.

b   Pine away and cannot eat.

c   Keep in touch with funny anecdotes and sexy stories.

33)   Top of your list of priorities after a long separation is:

a   Sorting out domestic problems.

b   Re-affirmation of your lover's devotion to you.

c   An urgent desire to make love.

34)   A long holiday together would result in an overall feeling of:

a   Boredom and loneliness.

b   Sublime togetherness.

c   Lust and sexual fulfilment.

35)   Your lover starts filling the house with erotic paintings and statues.
      You:

a   Refuse to put them on show in case the neighbours see them.

b   Are impressed by anything they do or say.

c   Take delight in finding new objects to add to your collection.

36)   Naked in bed beside your lover, you would:

a   Pull up the bedclothes so you don't freeze.

b   Lie cradled in their arms and drift off to heaven.

c   Stroke and caress them all over with your hands, lips and body.

37) Your lover asks you to relate a fantasy to them whilst you are lovemaking.
You:

a   Are not very inventive and prefer to concentrate on what you are doing.

b   Do not need fantasy to interrupt your perfect love.

c   Willingly oblige, knowing what a stimulating effect it has on them.

38) Do you use special terms of endearment when you want to be nice to each other?

a   You call each other by your given names, or else nothing.

b   You have a special mystical name for each other.

c   You address your lover by a number of pet names that are very affectionate.

39) How long can a sexual relationship realistically last?

a   Once you have exhausted all the physical possibilities, familiarity and boredom set in.

b   As long as you have each other.

c   The more you find out about a lover, the easier it becomes to excite them.

40) Do you genuinely enjoy lovemaking?

a   Only occasionally, you mostly do it because it is expected of you.

b   The act itself serves to engulf you and your lover and you become one.

   c   Making love is one of life's greatest pleasures.

How good a lover are you? – scoring and interpretation

Each question had three possible answers, labelled 'a', 'b' and 'c'. Add up the numbers of 'a', 'b' and 'c' responses that you gave separately, to arrive at three scores out of 40. Note which category you scored highest on and interpret your performances as follows.

Mostly 'a's
It seems that you are somewhat lacking in skill as a lover. Either that, or the particular relationship you're in at the moment is so stale and unrewarding you're not motivated sufficiently to turn in your best performance. One way or another, it is hard to imagine that you or your partner are getting much genuine satisfaction out of being together.

Then again, perhaps you do not have a partner at the moment, or find it generally difficult to attract the opposite sex. If that is the case, then it has to be said that this is not entirely surprising, for your approach and attitude to lovemaking is not one that would endear you to many people in the long term.

The main problem is that you seem excessively wrapped up in yourself, your own security and satisfaction. You are so intent on receiving what you think is due to you that you lack the capacity to give of yourself – warmth and affection being more important than material contribution.

You also appear rather inhibited and worried about what other people might think – you're more concerned about impressing the world at large than those closest to you. Often you seem to take the attitude that you can coast along in your relationship on a basis of some kind of imagined credit that you have built up in the past, or take your lover for granted because they are committed to you by bonds of social pressure, habit, economic necessity or suchlike. If so, you might one day receive a nasty shock, perhaps returning to an empty house and a farewell note.

If you have a relationship that you wish to preserve, think well about your behaviour and how rewarding you would be to live with. Put yourself in your partner's position for a moment and ask yourself how you would feel. If you are anxious about your lack of success in the mating game, ask yourself the equivalent question – how would you react to a lover who behaved like yourself?

Mostly 'b's
To all intents and purposes you would appear to be the perfect lover, approaching lovemaking with unswerving dedication and devotion. Unfortunately your rather extreme behaviour is based on a somewhat naïve perception of human beings.

Perhaps you've only just fallen in love and, therefore, are more concerned with the *idea* of love than the reality of the person you're loving. Or perhaps your rather melodramatic idealism is a result of reading too many romantic novels. You appear to have lost sight of the fact that even the great lovers of history had 'off days'.

Your desire for an exclusive 'life or death' relationship with your lover will eventually become stifling and oppressive to them – and your romantic dream could become a nightmare from which they will want to escape. It does not seem likely that anyone could bear the demands you would make on them, so could it be that you do not have a current lover and are fantasizing about your concept of a perfect love?

In fact, you have many attributes which are admirable, including unselfishness and a generous heart. If you can adjust your perspective and tone down some of your ideals, you could make your lover a very happy person. Try to come to terms with human frailties and prepare to accept others' faults. Nobody can take being elevated on a pedestal for the rest of their life – and if they don't come crashing down in your eyes at some point in time, they are bound to take a suicidal leap. With your passionate nature and so much to give, all you need to do is learn to love more honestly and realistically. Then you and your lover will be set to enjoy a very fulfilling relationship.

Mostly 'c's

Your lover, if you have one, is a very fortunate person. Your love is realistic and practical besides being warm and supportive. You have the skill and willingness to provide them with sexual stimulation and companionship based on a wholly realistic perception of their personality and needs rather than looking past them as people to some ideal concept that has no reality beyond your imagination. Your rose-coloured spectacles may have been shattered at some time, or been deliberately discarded by you, but still you manage to give warmth, affection and friendship to your partner.

If you are currently without a partner, I would be surprised, but it can hardly be put down to your deficiency in social skills. You have a great deal to offer and it is only a matter of time before somebody will want to enjoy a relationship with you. Perhaps you think you are better off without any attachment or commitment, but I doubt it. You are a born lover and will find your deepest fulfilment in exercising your skill.

Mixture of 'a's, 'b's and 'c's

Of course few people will have consistently opted for one scoring category. Probably, the comments made above all apply to you to some extent. The balance of the three scores will help you to discover the extent to which the advice in that category applies to you personally. But do feel free to reject that advice if, without ego-defensiveness, you genuinely disagree with it. Other people can call things the way they see them, or offer suggestions, but ultimately your relationship with another person is your own responsibility and nobody's business but your own.

How Good Is Your Lover?

Now that you have found out how good you are as a lover, you may like to make a similar assessment of your partner.

Obviously it's impossible to determine how good he or she might be with other lovers, only with yourself. But then I imagine that's all that really concerns you. Again, select one answer from each question.

1) You have to leave your lover to go abroad on business. You spend your time:

   a   Preoccupied with worrying whether they are being faithful to you.

   b   Looking out for someone to have a fling with, pretty sure that your lover will be doing likewise.

   c   Getting on with the job in hand whilst looking forward to their telephone call every evening.

2) Would you describe your lover as having sex appeal?

   a   Not really, more like a nice person.

   b   A bit too much for your liking.

   c   It was their 'animal' sexuality which attracted you in the first place.

3) How well do you communicate with your lover?

a   You like to be 'one jump ahead' of them since they can be a pretty tricky customer.

b   They never tell you anything important; only seem interested in going to bed.

c   You are totally in tune to the point where they can anticipate your next move.

4) Your favourite TV programme is on at the same time each week as a 'soap' your lover wants to watch on another channel.
They:

a   Arbitrarily switch the TV over to their favourite programme.

b   Retire to another room and watch another TV set.

c   Are prepared to watch the programme you like.

5) You are not in the mood for sex. Your lover:

a   Tells you that you are frigid/impotent.

b   Threatens to run off with a sexier person.

c   Is prepared to wait until you feel like it too.

6) When you go out together, your partner makes you feel:

a   Like an expensive 'appendage'.

b   Like last year's 'model'.

c   Like the most desirable person in the room.

7) Alone with your lover, what do you tend to do?

a   Your own 'things'.

b   Make love.

c   Share your secrets in bed.

8)   Friends who know you as a couple would say your
     lover was:

a   Uninterested in you.

b   Likely to run off at any time.

c   Exclusively devoted to you.

9)   Introducing your partner to your parents, you want
     them to look good.
     You would:

a   Pretend they were dressed badly because they
        had just been gardening.

b   Go out and buy them a new outfit to wear.

c   Feel confident they would make a good
        impression.

10) If you have a row, who makes the first move to make
     up?

a   You have to, they are very stubborn.

b   You can both go for days without speaking.

c   Usually the one who started the row.

11) You both want to see a show with a 'big name' star.
     Your lover:

a   Expects you to queue in the rain for several
        hours to get tickets.

b   Bumps into you in the foyer with another date.

c   'Magically' produces two tickets as a treat for
        you.

12) Your lover writes you a letter from abroad. It is:

    a   Typed on a word-processor.

    b   On an airletter to keep the cost down.

    c   Sealed with a loving kiss (SWALK).

13) A play you had free tickets for turns out to be a monumental bore. Your lover:

    a   Passes loud, rude remarks which make you cringe.

    b   Is too busy touching you up to notice.

    c   Quietly slips off to the pub with you in the interval.

14) When you are feeling unwell, your lover:

    a   Tells you to stop being a hypochondriac.

    b   Suggests you go to bed and then goes out.

    c   Makes a fuss of you and tries to make you feel better.

15) You give up your weekend to watch your lover enjoy their hobby.
They:

    a   Are too busy eliciting your praise to notice your sacrifices.

    b   Make you jealous by flirting constantly with other people.

    c   Are appreciative of your efforts and proudly show you off to their other friends.

16) When people are talking about your lover you are:

a Afraid to listen because it's not likely to be complimentary.

b Suspicious and eager to know if they have been having an affair with anyone else.

c Pleased and grateful to know such a popular person.

17) What would your lover list as most important?

a Their career success.

b Their success with the opposite sex.

c Making you happy.

18) In bed, does your lover take trouble over the way they present themselves?

a They expect you to be grateful they are with you at all.

b They like sex that is raw and natural and don't bother much with grooming.

c They always make themselves clean and sweet-smelling for you.

19) Does your lover usually keep promises they make to you?

a No, they constantly disappoint you.

b Only if their own pleasure is also involved.

c You trust their word completely – they never let you down.

20) At a party, how does your lover behave towards you?

a They make critical comments about the way you conduct yourself.

b   They pursue other attractive guests and expect you to fend for yourself.

c   They ensure you are having a good time, paying special attention whenever you are looking left out.

21)   When you go on holiday, who chooses the place?

a   You always leave those decisions to your partner.

b   You both want to go where there are plenty of opportunities to meet the opposite sex.

c   You enjoy the process of looking at brochures and choosing the destination together.

22)   What is your lover like when it comes to giving?

a   Rather selfish, they only give you something if they know it is to their advantage.

b   If they really needed something you would ask for, and possibly get it.

c   They are spontaneously generous by nature.

23)   Do you laugh a lot together?

a   Their humour is not to your taste.

b   You can usually enjoy a sexy joke with them.

c   Even in the most serious situation you can share a laugh.

24)   If you are 'having a moan' to your lover, how do they respond?

a   You don't dare complain in case they get bored with you.

b   They say you are a dreadful nag and usually go out.

c   They listen attentively and try to put things right.

25) You fly into a temper because you're feeling tired. How does your lover react?

a   They threaten to leave you if you behave irrationally.

b   They rant and rage back at you.

c   With good-natured patience and sympathy.

26) If you had a big problem you would:

a   Keep it to yourself for fear of an angry rebuke from your lover.

b   Know it would not interest your lover.

c   Try to solve it by discussing it at length with your lover.

27) Does your lover pay attention when you talk to them?

a   Practically everything you say goes 'in one ear and out the other'.

b   If you shout loud enough they will listen.

c   You are their favourite person for conversation.

28) You are in the bathroom with the door closed. Your lover would:

a   Barge in without knocking.

b   Bang on the door and demand to know what you are doing.

c   Respect your privacy and leave you alone.

29) Do you sometimes feel your sex life is so stale you would both be better off with someone else?

    a   There are times when your lover makes you feel like an object.

    b   Whatever else goes wrong, your sex life is pretty good with your lover.

    c   Of course sex, like anything else, cannot always be perfect, but you can't think of anyone other than your lover with whom you would like to be.

30) A picnic in the country with your lover usually means:

    a   Hard work for you.

    b   Driving around to find a heavily populated spot.

    c   A time to enjoy each other.

31) Are you disappointed with the way things have worked out between you and your lover?

    a   If only they could be the way they were when you first met – they used to be so charming.

    b   If they could keep control of their 'roving eye' you could be good pals.

    c   You can't think how they could endear themselves more to you.

32) Which attributes do you value most in your lover?

    a   Kindness to dumb animals.

    b   Good looks and figure.

    c   A warm heart and generous spirit.

33) A letter arrives for you from a foreign country. Your lover would:

    a   Rip it open and read it without your permission.

    b   Stand over you while you tried to read it.

    c   Leave you in peace to open it and let you decide whether you wish to discuss the contents.

34) When your lover is sexually satisfied, do they:

    a   Turn over and fall asleep.

    b   Suggest you go elsewhere if you haven't had enough.

    c   Ensure your satisfaction too.

35) Under what circumstances would your lover give you a massage?

    a   Never, they prefer being on the receiving end of a massage.

    b   If they thought it was turning on someone watching whom they fancied.

    c   Often as a prelude to lovemaking, or just to give you relaxing pleasure.

36) On your birthday or anniversary, your lover would:

    a   Forget the date and have to be reminded by you.

    b   Take you to a restaurant where they knew they could be the centre of attention.

    c   Always surprise you with an imaginative gift or outing.

37) Arriving very late for a date with you in a restaurant, your lover would:

a   Demand to know why you have not ordered.

b   Probably find you chatting up the waiter/waitress.

c   Apologize profusely and do their best to make amends.

38) On a long plane journey a very attractive traveller occupies the seat next to your partner. Your partner would:

a   Pretend to be someone very important.

b   Spend the entire journey chatting up the stranger.

c   Be friendly to the stranger and introduce you as their partner.

39) You have had an extremely busy week at work. Your lover:

a   Arrives home with a crowd of people, expecting you to whip up a meal.

b   Gets petulant if you are not inclined to go to a party.

c   Shows you every consideration and has a delicious meal ready for you.

40) Does your lover go to great lengths to seduce you?

a   Hardly, they think you are there for the taking – as and when they want.

b   They have a pretty polished seduction routine.

c   There is no need – their wanting you is sufficient turn-on.

How good is your lover? – scoring and interpretation

Each question allowed you to give one of three answers, marked 'a', 'b' and 'c'. Add up the number of 'a', 'b' and 'c' responses you gave separately – this will give you three scores out of 40. Look at the relative size of these three scores and interpret as follows:

Mostly 'a's

You are very insecure in your relationship and unsure about the character of your partner, which isn't surprising since it appears, from an outside, objective point of view, that they treat you very badly indeed. It's possible that you do not realize this and regard their behaviour as quite normal for a long-term partner – but hardly likely, as the pattern of your replies suggests you have a pretty good idea that your partner behaves in a way that is selfish, inconsiderate and unloving.

So why do you still tolerate this person? Is it that you are about to break up and the results of this quiz are no more than confirmation of the need to go ahead and do so? Or could it be that you feel trapped in the relationship in some way? Perhaps you lack confidence in yourself and, rightly or wrongly, believe that you will not be able to attract anyone else – let alone somebody who would treat you with greater love and respect. No one knows for sure whether you would be able to do better than your current partner but you certainly couldn't do any worse. Perhaps you should consider the possibility that you might be happier living alone, rather than devoting yourself to another person who cares so little for you and treats you so badly.

On the other hand, perhaps you are married to this person already and caught up in all the peripheral commitments that marriage entails: children, shared property, relatives, etc. If there are sound practical reasons for your reluctance to disband the relationship you could perhaps try some marriage guidance counselling – first alone, then, hopefully, accompanied by your partner. Sometimes an outsider's point of view can provide new insights which would help your partner to love you better. Failing that, you could at least leave your answers to this quiz lying around where they are likely to find them.

Mostly 'b's

You and your lover certainly have a passionate and volatile relationship. The fact that it's based on sex isn't necessarily a bad thing – so long as you do not decide you would like to settle down to a more comfortable, conventional lifestyle. Life is just a big sexual play-pen to your lover, who seems to be constantly seeking new exciting outlets for his or her high libido.

Could it be that your partner is extremely young and wants to play the field before finally making a nest? There's nothing wrong with this, of course, but you should consider that, with all the variety around, *you* may not be the bird who eventually gets to help feather their nest! On the other hand they may be going through some kind of mid-life crisis and are in need of reassurance as to their attractiveness and sexual potency. Your inability to trust them out of your sight may well be justified, but while they are going through this 'phase' it is doubtful that you can do much to change them. Acting on the defensive all the time will not help; you need to make it clear how hurt you are by your lover's behaviour.

Alternatively, perhaps you're something of a fun-loving 'swinger' yourself, in which case there is no real problem. If, however, your flirtatious behaviour is motivated mainly by a need to retaliate and give your partner a 'taste of their own medicine', then there is a danger that mutual jealousies could spiral out of control. In any case, it is improper to use the affections of other people as pawns in some game of political chess you are playing against your lover.

Mostly 'c's

Yours seems to be a healthy, complete relationship in which your partner treats you with great love and consideration. Your mutual intimacy, trust and communication is something that most people can only envy and try to emulate. No doubt your lover is a beautiful person but I suspect your own behaviour towards them is a major factor in this equation. The whole world loves a lover – long may your mutual happiness continue!

The chemistry of scores

If you have previously completed and scored the quiz to assess how good a lover *you* are, you might find it interesting to compare your own scores with those of your lover.

If, for example, you both came out with mostly 'a's, then it could be said that you deserve each other. Alternatively, you are both perfectly nice people but your relationship has spiralled downwards so that you no longer give each other sufficient physical or emotional 'stroking'. Whether you treat your partner badly because of the way they treat you, or vice versa, is a chicken and egg conundrum that has no easy solution.

If you are a dreamy, romantic 'b' scorer and your partner is anything other than 'c', then you are probably surviving on your fantasy. That's fine for now – but some day your bubble is bound to burst. If both of you are 'c's, this is the ideal and you may be assured of a long and happy future. If your partner is a 'c' and you are something else, think hard about what you stand to lose, as well as how likely you are to do so, should you carry on with your current mode of behaviour.

What Type of Lover Are You?

The words 'I love you' can express a multitude of emotions and feelings ranging from warmth, caring and consideration right through to the deeply passionate possessiveness of obsessive love. But whichever emotion is at the root of the words, the one thing we never can be sure of is whether our own perception and experience of 'love' corresponds with that of someone else.

According to Canadian sociologist, Dr John A Lee, there are three primary types of love. Lee's analysis, described in his book *The Colours of Love* published in 1975, was based on answers to an exhaustive questionnaire which covered virtually every aspect of people's relationships, from how they began, how soon they became intimate and whether jealousy was strongly felt, right through to the nature and frequency of arguments, break-ups and reunions. These are:

1 *Eros or Passionate* – This kind of love is both passionate and predominantly sex-based with a powerful sexual chemistry that can draw people together in an all-or-nothing relationship. Passionate love can be romantic, obsessional and intensely exclusive, and people in this type of highly charged relationship often tend to idealize each other a great deal. The physical attraction will often be immediate, the need for close contact and intimacy very strong. Such relationships can also be compulsive, elusive and transient affairs involving much emotional turmoil,

trauma and tears. Passionate lovers are tactile, open, sincere individuals who are inclined to be verbal and get a great deal of enjoyment from experiencing intense emotions and sex.

2 *Ludus or Playful* – *Ludus* is Latin for play or sport, and playfulness is what this type of love is all about. It's free of commitment, fun-based and hedonistic. And while sexual chemistry obviously does figure too, it's usually not as strong as the eros, or passionate kind, and the pair will tend to avoid becoming too involved or making any commitment to each other, preferring to keep their options open, to keep each other guessing and to be allowed to flirt and have affairs with others if they wish. The *Ludus*, or playful type of lover, prefers casual, mutually enjoyable relationships but would rather steer clear of intense emotions or intrusions upon their privacy.

3 *Storge or Practical* – Lee likens this type of love to a deep-caring friendship in which neither partner is totally preoccupied with the other, though they may well share many interests, hobbies and other pursuits. Couples with this type of love usually have a great deal of mutual trust and gain most of their pleasure from sharing things such as building a home and raising a family together. *Storge* types tend not to become too preoccupied with their partners, often don't feel or show strong emotions and can be fairly shy about sex. *Storge* relationships tend to be long-term and somewhat devoid of passion, although warm affection, understanding and loyalty may be present.

Of course we may experience all three different types of love with different people at different times in our life. And we may even experience all three types of love at different times in the same relationship. But there are also individual differences regarding the preferences and the frequency with which these types of love will occur for us.

Men, apparently, are more likely to seek playful relationships while women tend towards the practical. But, as far as passionate love is concerned, there's little, if any, differentiation between the sexes at all, and both are equally likely to perceive it as 'a bolt from the blue' and, therefore, beyond all rational control.

Generally, however, we will be happier with a partner who perceives the relationship in similar terms to ourselves. For when a couple have widely disparate approaches to love, misunderstanding is inevitable. For example, a *Ludus* (playful) lover could well become resentful of a *Storge* type (practical) partner, perceiving their attempts at 'sharing and building' as a ruse to entrap them. Meanwhile, the practical lover might construe *Ludus*'s playfulness as being lustful or lacking in respect.

Likewise, the passionate-type lover's need for instant intimacy could turn off the practical type, who believes that sex should be postponed until the relationship is more firmly founded.

Two 'practical' lovers probably have the best chance of a permanent relationship, while a 'playful' couple are more likely to go their separate ways after a brief encounter.

There are no right or wrong answers to the questions that follow, but by choosing one only (the one that best applies to you) you'll not only identify your own characteristic style of love, you'll also gain a better understanding of why and where you might be going wrong now. Don't worry even if you discover that you and your partner are mismatched. By gaining insight into the kind of lovers you both are you'll be better equipped to deal with any potentially problematical areas of your future relationship.

1) Which do you rate as most important?

    a   Love.

    b   Sex.

    c   Marriage.

2)   What sort of party most appeals to you?

    a   One with lots of influential guests.

    b   Soft lighting, music and gardens to roam in.

    c   A crazy group where anything goes.

3)   How many sex partners do you have?

    a   One at a time.

    b   Two or more at a time.

    c   Sometimes none, when there is no one special.

4)   Where would you seek to find a new partner?

    a   A computer dating agency or marriage bureau.

    b   An overseas holiday.

    c   Parties and discos.

5)   Whose opinion counts for the most with respect to your relationships?

    a   Your relatives and neighbours.

    b   Your friends and workmates.

    c   Your own and your partner's.

6)   Which birthday present would you most appreciate?

    a   Perfume or cologne.

    b   An erotic video tape.

    c   An attractive table-lamp.

7)   How long would you expect your love to last?

a   As long as you ignite a spark in each other.

b   As long as you can bear each other.

c   For ever.

8)   Which kind of quality do you find most appealing in the opposite sex?

a   Considerate and reliable.

b   Good-looking and charismatic.

c   Sexy and humorous.

9)   How would you address your lover?

a   By his or her first name.

b   A pet name such as 'Bunny' or 'Pussycat'.

c   A standard term of endearment such as 'darling' or 'dearest'.

10)   Where would you prefer to make love?

a   In front of a mirror.

b   In bed at night.

c   In a secluded forest.

11)   If you saw your lover embracing someone passionately, how would you feel?

a   Jealous and angry.

b   Intrigued and slightly titillated.

c   Concerned for your future.

12)   How do you deal with disagreements?

a   Discuss the matter sensibly and arrive at a compromise.

b   Lie low for a few days until the argument blows over.

c   Have a flaming row and make up in bed.

13) What would you do if your partner had to go abroad for a month without you?

a   Pine by the telephone.

b   Redecorate your home.

c   Contact old flames to find some action.

14) How do you view sexual intercourse?

a   Exciting and pleasurable.

b   The ultimate expression of love.

c   A means of procreation.

15) If you won a great deal of money in a lottery how would you spend it?

a   Take your lover to a paradise island.

b   Buy a penthouse flat with sauna, jacuzzi and pool.

c   Celebrate with the family and invest the rest.

16) Meeting someone to whom you are magnetically attracted, you:

a   Have a brief, sensational affair.

b   Dream about them every waking hour.

c   Vow to forget so you don't jeopardize your relationship.

17) If you were to prepare a special at-home supper for your lover, what would it be?

   a   A healthy, well-balanced meal.

   b   Camembert, grapes and red wine.

   c   Coq au vin by candlelight.

18) Where would you shop for underwear for yourself or your partner?

   a   Mail order through a sexy magazine.

   b   A good-value department store.

   c   A designer boutique.

19) What is the ideal bed for yourself and your lover?

   a   Twin beds with firm mattresses.

   b   A four-poster with lace canopy.

   c   A water-bed with stereo music controls.

20) How often, ideally, would you like to see your partner?

   a   Every available moment.

   b   Evenings and weekends.

   c   Holidays and social functions.

21) Where would you like to be married?

   a   In a remote, ancient, village chapel.

   b   On a yacht in the Mediterranean.

   c   In the church you always attend.

22) Your partner reveals a penchant for a slightly unorthodox sexual practice.

You:

   a   Are delighted to experiment.

   b   Make them promise not to hurt you.

   c   Tell them to seek professional help.

23) You are feeling unwell and your partner wants to make love.
    You:

   a   Go to bed before they do and feign sleep.

   b   Go through with making love and feel better for doing it.

   c   Give them a cuddle and ask them to wait till morning.

24) What would you do if your partner had an alcohol or drug problem?

   a   Be sympathetic and try to support them personally.

   b   Put them in touch with a 'helpline' and leave home.

   c   See your doctor for advice about the best professional help.

25) Which of the following do you think is the best way to keep a relationship from falling apart?

   a   Buying expensive presents.

   b   Having children.

   c   Showing consideration.

26) What is the most important day of the year for you to be with your partner?

a   Your birthday.

b   New Year's Eve.

c   Christmas Day.

27) Your idea of a 'good lover' is someone who:

a   Can be relied upon as a friend.

b   Is deeply in love with you.

c   Knows every sexual position.

28) If your lover confessed to a homosexual relationship before you met, how would you feel?

a   Fascinated.

b   Betrayed.

c   Disgusted.

29) If you have been dating your partner for over two years do you:

a   Feel it's time for a change.

b   Hope it will last.

c   Suggest that marriage is the obvious next step.

30) On discovering your partner is having an illicit affair, you:

a   Turn a blind eye and hope that it will be a passing fancy.

b   Invite them both to dinner for a civilized evening.

c   Stage a dramatic 'showdown'.

31) If your partner found you too demanding sexually you would:

    a   Coax them on to greater things.

    b   Take on another lover.

    c   Sublimate your desires.

32) Suppose you enjoy making love with your partner but are seldom completely satisfied. What would you do?

    a   Teach them precisely what gives you pleasure.

    b   Leave relevant literature lying around the house.

    c   See a marriage guidance counsellor together.

33) How often would you offer to massage your partner?

    a   On holidays when you are both relaxed.

    b   When you wanted to turn them on.

    c   Only if they needed massage therapeutically.,

34) When do you laugh together?

    a   When there is a good comedian on TV.

    b   When having a few drinks with friends.

    c   At unexpected moments, out of sheer delight.

35) How do you think you would cope if your partner died suddenly.
You would:

    a   Fall into deep despair, remembering all you had done together.

    b   Force yourself to form a new relationship quickly.

c   Immerse yourself in funeral arrangements and check your financial security.

36) What aspect of your relationship do you value most?

a   Good times and sexual frolics.

b   Companionship and shared responsibility.

c   The fusion of body and soul.

37) What are the main reasons for you quarrelling?

a   Money and the number of outings you go on together.

b   Your partner does not pay you sufficient attention.

c   Your partner hems you in and encroaches on your personal freedom.

38) How do you regard sex with your partner?

a   Joyful.

b   Orgiastic.

c   A duty.

39) As you spend more time together, you regard your partner with an increasing amount of:

a   Understanding and tolerance.

b   Intimacy and involvement.

c   Boredom and restlessness.

40) If an important looking letter arrived for your lover while they were out you would:

a   Try to contact them.

b   Open it and read the contents.

c   Place it in a prominent position where they
        would find it.

41) When you go out to a restaurant alone with your
     partner, what do you talk about?

a   Your plans to go places with them.

b   Domestic problems that require attention.

c   Any topic which is stimulating.

42) Who is the most influential figure in your partner's
     life?

a   You.

b   Their boss.

c   Their mother.

43) If your lover continually broke promises and let you
     down, you would:

a   Teach them a lesson they would not forget.

b   Get fed up and issue them with an ultimatum.

c   Always forgive them when you see them smile.

44) Which of these traits would you find most unaccepta-
     ble in your partner?

a   Bad manners.

b   Lack of honesty.

c   Reckless behaviour.

45) An 'old flame' telephones unexpectedly while your partner is in the room.
You:

   a   Tell the old flame you are spoken for now and don't wish to make your lover jealous.

   b   Ask your partner to excuse you and take the phone next door so you can flirt.

   c   Invite them to visit you one afternoon with their new partner.

46) Prolonged foreplay prior to lovemaking is:

   a   An unnecessary delay.

   b   An unusual occurrence.

   c   An essential component.

47) Do you fantasize when making love?

   a   Never – there is no need when you have the real thing.

   b   Seldom – you don't feel relaxed enough most of the time.

   c   Often – it adds spice to an already exciting occasion.

48) You know your partner really loves you when:

   a   They turn down a chance to do something they enjoy to spend an evening with you.

   b   You feel a grotty mess and they tell you you're beautiful.

   c   They offer to be your nubile slave and obey your every command.

49) In which historical era would you most like to have lived?

  a   Victorian times.

  b   The Renaissance.

  c   The Roman Empire.

50) Here are three ways songwriters have described love. Which line from a song applies to you?

  a   'Love is a many splendoured thing, in the morning mist, two lovers kiss, and the world goes zing.'

  b   'One must never deny it, but after you try it, you vary the diet.'

  c   'Love and marriage, go together like a horse and carriage.'

Type of lover – scoring

Question	Playful	Practical	Passionate
1	a	b	c
2	b	c	a
3	c	b	a
4	b	c	a
5	c	b	a
6	a	b	c
7	c	a	b
8	b	c	a
9	b	c	a
10	c	a	b
11	a	b	c
12	c	b	a
13	a	c	b
14	b	a	c

Question	Playful	Practical	Passionate
15	a	b	c
16	b	a	c
17	c	b	a
18	c	a	b
19	b	c	a
20	a	c	b
21	a	b	c
22	b	a	c
23	c	b	a
24	a	b	c
25	c	a	b
26	a	b	c
27	b	c	a
28	b	a	c
29	b	a	c
30	c	b	a
31	a	b	c
32	b	a	c
33	a	b	c
34	c	b	a
35	a	b	c
36	c	a	b
37	b	c	a
38	a	b	c
39	b	c	a
40	b	c	a
41	a	c	b
42	a	b	c
43	c	a	b
44	b	a	c
45	a	b	c
46	c	a	b
47	a	c	b
48	b	c	a
49	b	c	a
50	a	b	c

Total up the number of answers you have given that fall in each of the columns of the preceding table, giving yourself a score out of 50 on each love style. This will give you an idea of your personal balance among the three primary types of love. Few people are so extreme that they score 50 on one and nothing on the others, but a score of 25 or more on any scale may be considered high.

Most people get on best with others who have similar scores while gross discrepancies may help to explain tensions in your relationship. However, small differences of say seven or eight points are not important, and don't forget the characteristic differences between men and women.

Are You and Your Lover Compatible?

There are two opposing theories about what makes a good relationship. Some psychologists believe in the 'complementation' theory, i.e. that each partner's characteristics and attitudes oppose the other's (opposites attract), thus together they make a complete, or complementary, unit. Others subscribe to the 'similarity' theory (i.e. birds of a feather ... etc), and while both can work equally well, research has shown that couples who share similar interests, attitudes and backgrounds are more likely to stay together longer. This isn't surprising really when you consider that the fewer areas of conflict there are in your relationship, the greater the chance of you and your partner achieving lasting happiness.

This is one of the reasons why arranged marriages are often successful. For example, whilst it's tempting to believe in the first flush of passion that your love can transcend the barriers of religion, class, education or even social and political differences in attitude, in reality the reverse is more likely to be true. Just imagine, for instance, a match between someone as forceful, dynamic and aggressive as, say, Margaret Thatcher and a character as mild-mannered, peace-loving and non-militant as, say, 'Rodney' in the TV comedy series *Only Fools and Horses*.

Shared hobbies and interests can also help to keep a couple together. Not only because they provide opportunities to 'do' things together, but because they also give them something to talk about apart from routine domestic matters.

When it comes to personality, similarity is still preferable though it's far less crucial to the success of a relationship than other factors. And, according to Dr Glenn Wilson, with whose help these self-evaluation tests were compiled, personalities that are complementary are equally viable.

In fact there are some areas in which certain differences are considered optimal in a relationship. Take height, for example – men are on average around four inches taller than women. There is evidence to suggest that where factors are equal, partnerships in which the man is taller than the woman are likely to prove more stable and enduring. Obviously, there will always be some exceptions, such as Dudley Moore, Ronnie Corbett, and their respective wives, not to mention Prince Charles and the Princess of Wales, but, in the main, the general rule will more usually apply.

The same principle also applies to certain other attributes of typical sex-based differences such as dominance versus submissiveness, sex drive, emotionality and artistic versus scientific/technical interests.

Despite all the noises currently being made about the desirability of 'new men', the most satisfying relationships still appear to be those in which the male is traditionally 'masculine' and the women traditionally 'feminine' in relation to the man.

But there's one other and very major (though less easily definable or measurable) contribution to compatibility that shouldn't be ignored. And that, of course, is the one that can often make or break a relationship: chemistry. Not the chemistry of smells or pheromones (although these are highly relevant) but what Glenn Wilson describes as 'the chemistry of the relationship' itself. This includes all the clues that may have some particular emotional significance for us – a particular gesture, the shape of a face or nose, hairstyle, the timbre of a voice – they may remind us of someone we've personally known and loved in our own past, or they might evoke an image of a particular hero or heroine we admire from afar.

We cannot discount also the Freudian concept that we seek unconsciously to replace the opposite sex parent to whom we became attached in infancy. Or that we each strive subconsciously to re-create a familiar pattern learnt in our childhood which, while it may not be ideal, does provide an element of security in that it is one we can recognize and, in a bizarre way, feel comfortable with.

It is obviously more difficult to address in a questionnaire these more mysterious aspects which affect the chemistry of our relationships, but they nonetheless appear indirectly. Good feelings and irritations are seldom merely what they seem, but rather they're motivated in many complex ways, including the 'unconscious' dynamics outlined above.

To identify how compatible you and your partner really are, choose one answer only to each question in sections A, B, C, D and E. Try the quiz on your own first, and then (but only if you think you could stand to hear the worst!) compare your answers with your partner's.

Section A

1) Do you often think about ending your relationship?

   a   It would be very painful if you were to part.

   b   When you are fed up with your partner.

   c   It is almost a daily occurrence.

2) How often do you and your partner confide in each other?

   a   You tell each other all your most intimate fears and fantasies.

   b   There are some things in your lives you would prefer to keep private.

   c   The survival of your relationship depends on regular deception.

3) On your birthday, your partner would:

a   Instinctively know exactly what would please you.

b   Probably buy you something you have to exchange later.

c   Manage to waste money on a totally unsuitable gift.

4) Do you like to be alone together?

a   Your partner is the most stimulating person you know.

b   You feel that a break from each other enhances your appreciation.

c   You try to reduce the boredom by surrounding yourself with acquaintances.

5) What sort of arguments do you have?

a   Disagreements are openly aired and quickly resolved.

b   There are some topics which you had better avoid discussing.

c   You bicker constantly – on trivia as well as major issues.

6) Have you made a good choice in your partner?

a   You have never met anyone who made you feel quite so fulfilled.

b   You believe life is a compromise and you are both reasonably well-suited.

c   You are making the best of a bad job and biding

time in the hope that someone better will turn up.

7) You arrive home hot and tired from work. Your partner would:

a   Make allowances for your bad temper and do their best to put you in a good humour.

b   Pour you a stiff drink and stay out of your way for a while.

c   Regale you with problems of their own before you could sit down.

8) When you go to a party, you are always on the lookout for:

a   Stimulating conversation.

b   New friendships.

c   A replacement for your partner.

9) You find your partner in a passionate clinch with a very attractive person. Your concern is for:

a   Your apparent inability to satisfy them.

b   Your lost youth.

c   Losing your financial security.

10) Overall, how would you describe your relationship?

a   The perfect love-match.

b   Passionate, but with definite ups and downs.

c   Slightly better than complete loneliness.

Section B

11) How does your physical height compare with that of your partner?

   a   Man taller than woman.

   b   Both around the same height.

   c   Woman taller than man.

12) And your weight comparison (proportionately)?

   a   Man heavier than woman.

   b   Both about average for height.

   c   Woman heavier than man.

13) Is there a gap in your ages?

   a   There are only a couple of years between you.

   b   The man is considerably older than the woman.

   c   The woman is considerably older than the man.

14) How do people rate you and your lover in looks?

   a   You are both considered highly attractive.

   b   Your lover is better looking in a conventional way but you have stacks of admirers.

   c   You are pretty plain compared to your lover.

15) What occupations are you in?

   a   You both have interesting jobs with a lot in common to discuss.

   b   You both have rewarding but very different occupations.

c   You stay home while your partner has an exciting career.

16) Are you a healthy person?

a   Generally speaking, you enjoy excellent health.

b   You are fairly prone to colds but seldom get anything serious.

c   You catch everything that is going around.

17) If you measured your biorhythms, you and your partner would be:

a   In complete harmony.

b   Largely in tune with each other.

c   In direct opposition.

18) How do you compare with regard to social class?

a   Pretty much the same.

b   Some discrepancy, but you are little affected.

c   You are often aware of a gap in social background.

19) Is your educational background similar?

a   Attended similar institutions and achieved much the same level.

b   Different types of school, but similar level.

c   Like chalk and cheese.

20) Is there any discrepancy in your national background?

a   None.

b   Some, but you currently agree on where you want to live.

c   There is likely to be disagreement about where to locate.

Section C

21) Do you have similar views on pornography?

a   You are in absolute agreement.

b   Your partner is perhaps a little more (or less) liberal than you.

c   You are strongly opposed to your partner's viewpoint.

22) In bed with your lover you feel:

a   Stimulated.

b   Content.

c   Bored.

23) Does your lover know precisely how to give you sexual pleasure?

a   You feel totally satisfied after lovemaking.

b   You are shy of telling them what turns you on most.

c   You've lost count of the times they've gone off to sleep leaving you frustrated.

24) Your partner brings home a tape describing techniques of erotic massage.

You:

    a   Can't wait to try it out on each other.

    b   Take a bath and wait for a demonstration.

    c   Think it commercializes sex.

25) Are there any aspects of personal hygiene which concern you about your lover?

    a   None at all, they are very fastidious.

    b   They don't always wash themselves as thoroughly as you'd like.

    c   Some of their habits rather appal you.

26) Your lover prefers sex in a position that causes you some discomfort. Do you:

    a   Tell them and try new ways of giving them satisfaction.

    b   Suffer in silence because you're prepared to put up with a little pain to make them happy.

    c   Stop lovemaking and feign a headache when they suggest it.

27) How do you rate the importance of fidelity?

    a   You and your partner have similar views.

    b   It can be a matter of debate and disagreement.

    c   Your values on this issue are diametrically opposed.

28) What do you think about contraception?

    a   You and your lover are of like mind.

b   There is some dispute as regards method.

c   You cannot agree as to whether it should be used at all.

29)   How does your libido (sex drive) compare with that of your partner?

a   You enjoy sex equally.

b   You sometimes find your partner too demanding or uninterested sexually.

c   You never feel like making love at the same time.

30)   How far would you be prepared to go to please your partner sexually?

a   You would happily succumb to their desires, knowing that anything they enjoy would please you too.

b   You would go along with their wishes, as long as they are prepared to meet you 'half-way' on yours.

c   It is of greater concern to you that your partner finds ways to satisfy you.

Section D

31)   On an evening out, do you easily agree on where to eat?

a   You both like the same food and have favourite restaurants.

b   You have some preferences which are not shared by your partner.

    c   You dislike just about every restaurant your partner suggests.

32) To what extent do you share political views?

    a   You are often surprised at how close you are in ideology.

    b   There are certain political points on which you could not agree.

    c   As far as you're concerned your partner is a dreamer when it comes to politics.

33) Do cultural differences in your background impose a strain on your relationship?

    a   You both respect the other's cultural background and you delight in broadening your cultural horizons through your partner.

    b   Cultural differences occasionally make you feel a distinct lack of communication.

    c   You are certain your partner's background is to blame for their peculiar behaviour.

34) Can you agree on how to raise children?

    a   Your love for each other will easily extend to your joint offspring.

    b   You can each more or less tolerate the other's ideals.

    c   You think it best not to have any since you could see their upbringing would cause major rifts between you.

35) Is religion a problem in your relationship?

    a   Not at all, you both have the same religious beliefs.

b   There are some differences, but you 'agree to disagree'.

c   Your religious differences cause major upsets.

36)   Do you disagree on the handling of money?

a   You always concur on how to allocate your budget.

b   You have occasional tiffs on money matters.

c   You find your partner overly mean or extravagant.

37)   If your lover asked you to an art gallery or poetry reading, you would:

a   Eagerly anticipate the event.

b   Go with some reservations.

c   Suggest they go alone.

38)   What do you think about your partner's taste in clothes?

a   They dress with impeccable good taste and usually to please you.

b   Most of the time they are a credit to you.

c   You are sometimes so ashamed of the way they are turned out, you pretend to be with someone else.

39)   How do you feel about your partner's friends?

a   Great fun and 'your kind of people'.

b   Some of their friends leave you cold.

c   You prefer to see your own friends.

40) How do you think the male and female roles should be divided?

   a   You take life as it comes and find it unnecessary to allocate specific tasks according to your gender.

   b   You have an understanding between you as to who should take responsibility for what.

   c   Your partner appears to be living in the Middle Ages, so blinkered is their thinking in these matters.

Section E

41) How well are you suited temperamentally?

   a   You really enjoy your partner's personality.

   b   Although you have different temperaments, you tend to complement each other.

   c   You are poles apart in temperament.

42) Do you have a high regard for your partner's intellect?

   a   They never cease to amaze you with their wide knowledge and insight.

   b   Whilst their intelligence may not be on a par with your own, they compensate with other attributes.

   c   A 'great mind' is not a particular feature in your partner.

43) What irritates you most about your partner?

   a   You recognize faults in them which you have yourself.

b   Their quick temper.

c   Their disgusting habits.

44) Is a shared sense of humour an important basis of your friendship?

a   You always have a good laugh together.

b   There are times when your partner's sense of humour eludes you.

c   You seldom find the same things funny.

45) Do you like to travel?

a   Yes – you both enjoy new experiences.

b   You are both content with the home environment.

c   One of you is an intrepid voyager and the other a stick-at-home.

46) Is your relationship marred by temper outbursts?

a   No – you are both very easy-going.

b   You sometimes have to bottle up grievances.

c   Rows are both common and bitter.

47) Are you or your partner inclined to depressive episodes?

a   No – you're both generally cheerful and optimistic.

b   If one of you 'has the hump' the other can usually lift them out of it.

c   You have a depressing effect on each other.

48) Is there a clear 'pecking order' between you?

   a   Yes, but each recognizes the other's superiority in certain fields.

   b   One of you is dominant in every respect.

   c   There is a perpetual struggle for power between you.

49) How adventurous are you?

   a   About the same degree.

   b   The man is more exploratory than the woman.

   c   The woman is sensation-seeking while the man is inhibited.

50) Are you troubled by fears and anxieties?

   a   Not really – both of you are fairly stable.

   b   One of you is prone to worry about things but the other is a calming influence.

   c   Both of you are on the verge of nervous breakdowns.

Compatibility quiz – scoring and interpretation

This quiz deals with five different, though overlapping, areas of compatibility and incompatibility (Sections A to E). For each section separately, add up the number of 'a', 'b' and 'c' answers that you have given. Give yourself one point for each 'c', two points for each 'b' and three points for each 'a'.

You should now have five scores representing your totals for each section. Each will be somewhere in the range of 10 to 30.

Interpretation

Section A: Relationship General

This section concerns the quality of your interpersonal relationship with your partner – how much you like to be together, how much intimacy and caring there is, how you deal with disagreements, jealousies, etc – the whole process of give and take. In many ways this is the most sensitive indicator of compatibility since it affects, and is influenced by, all the other more specific areas.

A score of 25 plus indicates a very high level of compatibility and 20–24 is a very reasonable average. 15–19 suggests some degree of discontent, while 10–14 is indicative of a rather sorry state.

Section B: Demographic

This group of items concerns statistical matters like age, height, occupation, etc – the sorts of things that insurance companies use to base predictions of risk. Ideally these should not matter in a marriage or relationship, but research and experience tell us that they do. To a degree, differences may add spice to a relationship but too many, and too striking, lead to incompatibility in the long term.

The same scale applies as above: 25 plus highly compatible, 20–24 satisfactory, 15–19 cause for concern, 10–14 unstable.

Section C: Sexual Compatibility

These questions deal with various aspects of your sex life. It may be possible for you to have a good relationship with a very low level of sexual activity if this is what suits you both, but difficulties arise when there is a great gulf between you as regards sexual attitudes, appetite and preferences.

As above, you may assess your sexual compatibility according to the scale: 25 plus excellent, 20–24 satisfactory, 15–19 below average, 10–14 unsatisfactory. If sex is your only, or major, focus of incompatibility you might consider whether sex therapy might have something to offer you.

Section D: Attitudes and Interests
This factor deals with matters of ideology, taste, preferences and general philosophy of life, which are known to be important determinants of long-term compatibility. Again, people do not have to be identical in order to live happily together, but a certain amount of common ground is necessary and the more shared viewpoints the better. Use the same scale as above to assess your compatibility in this area.

Section E: Personality
The last section of the quiz focuses on personality predispositions and temperament. As noted previously, not all differences in personality are detrimental, some may even enhance a relationship by a process of complementation. Nevertheless, there are several ways in which two personalities may clash and produce unhappiness, and the questions here have been chosen to identify these potential sources of strain in your relationship. The same scoring key applies as for the previous sections.

Overall Compatibility
Now that you have looked at your compatibility rating in the five different areas, you may like to consider it overall by adding your five scores together. This will give you a total score of between 50 and 150, which may be understood as follows:

130–150   You are exceptionally lucky to have such a good relationship. Your future as a couple looks destined to be long and happy.

110–129   Your relationship is fairly able to maintain a long-term happy association. A little more tolerance and consideration on your own part could only benefit you both. Remember that true love consists of willingness to give with no expectation of direct return.

90–109   Your relationship is average enough but with definite signs of discontent. If you are not yet married, you should think long and hard before committing yourself further. If you are already married you might ask yourself whether your relationship could be improved with a little more effort and unselfishness. You might also consider marriage guidance, perhaps taking your answers to these questions along with you for discussion.

50–89   If you are not yet committed to this person you would be well advised not to become further involved. If already married, perhaps you are staying together for the sake of the children, economics, convenience or some other external constraint. Ask yourself seriously whether you might not be happier living apart and talk it over with a marriage counsellor.